THE HYMNS OF
THE UNITED METHODIST
HYMNAL

THE HYMNS OF
THE UNITED METHODIST
HYMNAL

Introduction to
the Hymns, Canticles,
and Acts of Worship

Diana Sanchez
Volume Editor

ABINGDON PRESS
NASHVILLE

THE HYMNS OF THE UNITED METHODIST HYMNAL

This book is printed on acid-free paper.

Library of Congress Cataloging-in-Publication Data

The hymns of the United Methodist hymnal; introduction to the hymns,
  canticles, and acts of worship / Diana Sanchez, volume editor.
     p.   cm.
Includes indexes.
ISBN 0-687-43149-2 (alk. paper)
  1. United Methodist hymnal. 2. United Methodist Church (U.S.)—
Hymns—History and criticism. 3. Methodist Church—Hymns—History
and criticism. 4. United Methodist Church (U.S.)—Liturgy.
5. Methodist Church—Liturgy. I. Sanchez, Diana.
BV415.A3   1989
264'.07602—dc20   89-15085
                                                                              CIP

MANUFACTURED IN THE UNITED STATES OF AMERICA

CONTENTS

CONTENTS

PREFACE

This is one of two books designed to help you understand and use *The United Methodist Hymnal*. The other book, *The Worship Resources of The United Methodist Hymnal*, deals with the worship resources; this book deals with hymns, canticles, and acts of worship.

In the hymns, canticles, and acts of worship you will find much that is familiar, easy to sing and use in your accustomed way. Some will not be familiar to you. In either instance this book will help you to introduce and use them more effectively in your local church.

This volume is the work of many persons. Carlton R. Young served as executive editor. Diana Sanchez served as volume editor/project director and as coauthor of chapter 2 and the appendixes. Hoyt L. Hickman wrote the preface and chapter 1 and assisted with the editing and the appendixes. Thomas A. Langford, III was coauthor of chapter 2. Mary Brooke Casad, Craig B. Gallaway, Stephen T. Kimbrough, Jr., Austin C. Lovelace, George Lockwood, William J. Reynolds, Richard Shadinger, William Farley Smith, Marjorie Beadles Tuell, and Robin Knowles Wallace wrote the hymn and canticle articles in chapter 3. Laurence Hull Stookey wrote the articles in chapter 3 on the acts of worship. Further information about these persons is found in appendix 4. Raymond Glover and Terry York served as readers. Timothy Edmonds and Katherine Thomas Paisley, Section on Worship interns, assisted with the project.

Note that items from chapter 3 may be reproduced in accordance with guidelines set forth on the copyright page of this book.

For further information about the content of *The United Methodist Hymnal*, write or phone the Section on Worship, P.O. Box 840, Nashville, Tennessee 37202-0840 (615/340-7070).

CHAPTER 1

THE STORY OF
THE UNITED METHODIST HYMNAL

A. THE GROWING NEED FOR A NEW HYMNAL

When The United Methodist Church was formed in 1968, it was
not feasible to begin work on a United Methodist hymnal because
replacing *The Methodist Hymnal* (1966) and *The Hymnal* (1957) of The
Evangelical United Brethren Church was out of the question. At
the time of the union, therefore, *The Book of Discipline* 1968 (Par.
1388) provided that "the hymnals of The United Methodist Church
are the hymnals of The Evangelical United Brethren Church and
The Methodist Hymnal." Beginning in 1970, however, new printings
of *The Methodist Hymnal* were retitled *The Book of Hymns* without
any change in the contents. *The Book of Discipline* 1968 also
established a Commission on Worship, one of whose functions
was "to make recommendations to the General Conference
concerning future editions of the United Methodist hymnal" (Par.
1385.5). In 1972 the functions of the Commission on Worship were
given to the new General Board of Discipleship.

It soon became evident that our existing hymnals needed to be
supplemented. For example, many congregations and groups
within congregations wanted to sing from the then flourishing
repertory of folk and contemporary Christian songs. Beginning

9

with its first meeting in 1968, the Commission on Worship collected information about what was being sung in local congregations and then sponsored the publication by Abingdon Press of the songbook *Ventures in Song*. After 1972, there was not only an increasing interest in new forms of music for worship and education but also a growing awareness of the musical treasures in our various ethnic minority heritages. Growing out of a national Consultation on the Black Church, sponsored by the General Board of Discipleship in 1973, was a recommendation that the Section on Worship develop a songbook from the black religious tradition to be made available to United Methodist churches.

The 1976 General Conference voted to make ethnic local church ministries one of the missional priorities for 1977-80. As a result, moneys became available to enable the Section on Worship to work with ethnic caucuses and to fund the task forces, consultations, and editors needed to produce ethnic hymn and songbooks. The work which followed produced *Songs of Zion* (Abingdon, 1981) in the black heritage; the two-part *Celebremos* (Discipleship Resources, 1979 and 1983), supplementing *Himnario Metodista* (1973) in the Hispanic heritage; and *Hymns from the Four Winds* (Abingdon, 1983) in the Asian-American heritage. Following a national Consultation on Native American Worship held in 1979, the Section on Worship has cooperated in the development of several Native American worship resources.

There was also a strong movement at the 1976 General Conference to mandate the preparation of a new official hymnal, countered by strong resistance from those who felt such an action would be premature. A compromise was reached, and two actions were voted (*Daily Christian Advocate*, pages 614, 630, 914-15, 933, 964):

1) A recommendation for "the Section on Worship of the Board of Discipleship in cooperation with the Publishing House to publish a supplemental contemporary Hymnal, possibly loose-leaf in form for additions and deletions, for local church use. It should reflect our contemporary religious climate, as well as the heritage of many diverse groups in The United Methodist Church (i.e., Black, Native American, Hispanic, and Asian-American)."

2) "All matters of changes in the Book of Worship and Hymnal" were "referred to the Board of Discipleship for study."

The Section on Worship and the Publishing House immediately set up a joint task force to carry out the first recommendation. Carlton R. Young, who had been editor of *The Methodist Hymnal (The Book of Hymns)*, was named editor. While the loose-leaf format proved far too expensive to be feasible, the rest of the recommendation was carried out with great care in a five-year process. The result was *Supplement to the Book of Hymns*, published in 1982.

In response to the second action, the General Board of Discipleship asked The United Methodist Publishing House to join it in setting up a joint task force for a four-year study. This was done; the resulting study found that (1) the need for a new hymnal was growing but not yet urgent enough to require immediate action, and (2) the existing psalter and service music sections of the hymnal were seriously deficient, and research and field testing were needed to determine what psalter and service music would be suitable for United Methodists.

On petition from the General Board of Discipleship, the 1980 General Conference (*Daily Christian Advocate*, pp. 476, 983-84) authorized the board

to do research, preparatory work, editing, and design, in cooperation with The United Methodist Publishing House, toward a new official United Methodist hymn and worshipbook and to make a report to the 1984 General Conference.

This preparatory work would include:

1. Research to determine: (a) What in *The Book of Hymns, The Hymnal* of the former Evangelical United Brethren Church, *Supplement to The Book of Hymns*, ethnic minority hymn and song books, and other hymnals is being used or not used by United Methodists, and how they are being used. (b) What United Methodists want in a new hymn and worshipbook—types of hymns, specific hymns, services of worship, aids to worship, etc. (c) What United Methodists want in terms of format, size, price, and other general specifications.

2. Development, trial publication, and field testing, with suitable research, of a version of the Psalter suitable for United Methodist use.

3. Development, trial publication, and testing, with suitable research, of a collection of service music suitable for general use among United Methodists.

4. Development of general design and specifications.

5. Prepare a report to the 1984 General Conference, which would contain the results of the above research and development, with interpretation. In addition, the report would outline the proposed contents of a hymn and worshipbook.

For the next four years this work was carried out. Surveys were taken, which yielded much specific information as to what United Methodists were and were not singing, and what they wanted. Study of needs relating to the psalter resulted in the commissioning of a new translation of the Psalms by Gary Chamberlain, which The Upper Room published in *The Psalms* (1984) and *Psalms for Singing* (1984). Study of needs relating to service music resulted in a Service Music Project, which commissioned and tested a variety of new service music.

Two findings emerged from this work:

1) The need for a new official United Methodist hymn and worshipbook had grown to the point where full-scale development of such a book should begin.

2) More time was needed for developing and testing a suitable psalter and service music, and for developing the specifications and outline of the book as a whole.

These findings resulted in a petition from the General Board of Discipleship, adopted by the 1984 General Conference (*Daily Christian Advocate*, pp. E-86, 402, and 567 ff.), which constituted and authorized a quadrennial Hymnal Revision Committee "to prepare a single volume hymn and worship book for congregational use in The United Methodist Church and to submit the contents of this book to the 1988 General Conference for adoption as the official hymnal of The United Methodist Church."

B. The Making of the New Hymnal

The Hymnal Revision Committee set up by the 1984 General Conference legislation carefully established the membership of the twenty-five-member Hymnal Revision Committee. They were chosen from local churches of every size and character and from each of the major ethnic groupings. Former Methodists and former Evangelical United Brethren, male and female clergy, male and female laity, musicians and nonmusicians, young adults and older adults, persons with handicapping conditions, and a wide variety of musical tastes and theological viewpoints were all represented. The committee and support staff are named in the hymnal at page vi.

The cost of the entire revision process was borne by The United Methodist Publishing House. A hymnal revision office was established in December 1984 at the publishing house headquarters in Nashville. After a careful search, Carlton R. Young, who had been editor of *The Methodist Hymnal (The Book of Hymns)* and *Supplement to The Book of Hymns,* was named editor. Other publishing house staff were also assigned to the project. More than fifty consultants were brought in to express viewpoints otherwise unrepresented or to supply needed expertise. The 1,144-page *Report of the Hymnal Revision Committee to the 1988 General Conference of The United Methodist Church* presents the proposed content and describes in detail who the consultants were and how they worked. It was mailed to the delegates of the 1988 General Conference. The libraries of each United Methodist college, university, and seminary were also provided a copy.

From January 1985 through October 1987, voting members and continuing consultants to the committee spent an average of 1,250 hours per person on the hymnal project; office staff members devoted an average of 4,675 hours per person to the project (not including time spent by additional part-time staff); and the editor spent an estimated 6,875 hours on the project through its editorial content phase. All this is in addition to the time spent later by editor and staff on production of the report and the hymnal itself.

The General Conference action also provided that "the Board of Discipleship shall 'provide editorial supervision of the contents' in accordance with [*The Book of Discipline*] Par. 1314.3 through its representatives on the Committee and by supplying staff support to the developmental process" (*Daily Christian Advocate,* p. E-86). Board representatives on the committee kept the board informed of the committee's work and brought board concerns and recommendations back to the committee. Staff support was supplied by the Section on Worship.

The committee's work began in January 1985 with a review of the mandates from the General Conference that they be sensitive to

(1) inclusion of hymns from the EUB tradition; (2) inclusion of hymns representing various ethnic groups; (3) inclusive and non-discriminatory language, yet respect for the language of traditional hymns; and (4) the needs of small-membership churches. Each concern was assigned to a separate subcommittee and integrated within the implicit mandates and guidelines which guide the task of a revision committee: (1) reviewing recent hymnals and prayer books; (2) identifying constituencies; and, (3) securing the services of expert consultants in designated areas of concern.

The committee formed a series of subcommittees, by which the detailed preliminary and follow-through work was done. In this way, all proposals and materials were prepared carefully before being considered by the full committee, and the decisions of the full committee could be implemented efficiently. In addition to twelve meetings of the full committee and the subcommittee meetings which took place during those meetings, there were more than eighty subcommittee and consultation meetings.

The Worship Resources Subcommittee and its subcommittees—Ritual, Service Music, Psalter, Psalms Text, and Music of the Psalter Consultation—screened and evaluated these materials before presenting them to the full committee. An introduction to this material is found in *The Worship Resources of The United Methodist Hymnal*. The canticles and the acts of worship interspersed among the hymns are discussed in this book.

The hymns, which are discussed in this book, were the responsibility of the Hymns Subcommittee and its subcommittees—Texts, Tunes, Language/Theology—and the Wesley and ethnic consultations. They screened, evaluated, and in some cases recommended changes in hymns to be presented to the full committee. The Hymns Subcommittee invited and heard presentations by representatives of several United Methodist organizations and constituencies with distinctive viewpoints and concerns. They also commissioned thirteen poets to create new texts and four composers to create new tunes. In all, they examined the texts and tunes of more then 3,500 hymns.

Additional subcommittees of the fuller revision committee took responsibility for editorial production, public relations, auxiliary products, marketing, art and production services, manufacturing, and special services.

Basic to all the work of the Hymnal Revision Committee was the gathering of information through a careful process of deliberation, evaluation, and research in two distinct areas, each of critical importance.

1) The broadest possible range of hymn materials was assembled from well over a hundred hymnals and songbooks, as well as from other sources.

2) The needs, concerns, and preferences of local congregations were identified and clearly defined, so that the new hymnal would meet the needs of the average person in the pew. A continuing opinion research sampling called the Reader Consultant Network, numbering over 800 lay persons, clergy, musicians, and teachers, was established by the hymnal revision project office. Nine surveys were conducted at intervals throughout the revision process. Hymnal Updates were sent twice a year to 85,000 United Methodist pastors and lay persons. Reporters from the media were invited to committee meetings, press releases were prepared, and every effort was made to see that United Methodists were fully informed as to the deliberations and decisions of the committee. In response, more then 20,000 letters were received by the committee. All this combined to provide an understanding of what United Methodists wanted, an understanding which was taken with the greatest seriousness by the committee.

Guidelines were set up to structure the work of examining and evaluating every proposed hymn and other act of worship. The basic principles that guided the committee are summarized in the preface to *The United Methodist Hymnal*. Prayer and hymn-singing were a vital part of every meeting, and committee members and consultants applied themselves in a spirit of cooperation and concern for the whole Church. They shared differing and often opposing points of view, some in vigorous debate but always showing due respect for each of the advocates and the constituencies represented. In the process the committee became a working community with very high levels of trust and support.

After the committee finished its work in October 1987, and its work was endorsed later that month by vote of the General Board of Discipleship, The United Methodist Publishing House produced the 1,144-page *Report of the Hymnal Revision Committee*. This was mailed in February 1988 to the delegates of the 1988 General Conference, which met in St. Louis April 26 to May 6.

At the conference the report went first to the Committee on Discipleship. It was evident that the committee members already had given much study to the report, and they discussed it at length, first in subcommittees and then in the full committee. One hymn was added: "Lord of the Dance." Several other amendments were adopted, which deal with the parts of the hymnal discussed in *The Worship Resources of The United Methodist Hymnal*. The report as amended was then adopted by the committee by a vote of 99 to 0.

The report as amended by the committee then went to the full General Conference, where on May 3 it was debated and passed by a vote of 893 to 69 accompanied by a sustained standing ovation.

An enormous amount of additional work was then necessary in order to prepare the material in the report for publication in the summer of 1989 as *The United Methodist Hymnal*. This was done by The United Methodist Publishing House and the staff assigned to the hymnal project.

The editor, Carlton R. Young, has provided the following information concerning the editorial and production process for the new hymnal, comparing it in some regards to that which produced the 1966 hymnal:

"Although the political context surrounding the process was very different from that in 1966 and the collaborative consultative attitude of the 1989 hymnal committee's work ethic was unique, the actual selection of contents was very similar to that which produced the earlier hymnal. Since the general services were already approved by the previous General Conferences, the committee limited its consideration chiefly to hymns. The clear exception was the creation of an entirely new approach to formatting the Psalms for congregational reading/singing, as well as the adaptation of a new Bible translation for use in United Methodist worship.

"Text and tune selection began with a review of the 1966 hymnal and its precursors, extending into all major hymnals and supplements produced since 1935, the review of hundreds of unsolicited poems and musical settings, and finally the commissioning of new texts and tunes. At the close of the two-and-one-half-year selection process, summer 1987, there were approximately 850 hymns, prayers, canticles, and acts of worship approved for inclusion in the main portion of the hymnal!

"A century ago, formatting that number of texts would have been relatively simple, since there was no music on the page and page turns were an acceptable practice. The committee knew it had to restrict the size of the finished product, yet there was no way to measure the length of the total content of the hymnal, because the majority of the pages were to be set to music and the number of pages to be allocated for each item could not be determined until the *Report of the Hymnal Revision Committee* had been approved by the General Conference. The report of course was amended and could have been amended dramatically, which would have further complicated estimating the number of pages. So it was decided to estimate the length of the proposed hymnal, allowing for 660 pages of hymns, canticles, and acts of worship, with the remaining 300 pages given over to worship resources, the psalter, and indexes.

"The committee's work ended in mid-October 1987, allowing only ninety days to prepare the manuscript, obtain the permissions to print, produce, index, and deliver it for printing just after the first of the year 1988! The 1,144-page report, containing the hymnal's contents and the documentation of the revision process, was mailed to the 1988 General Conference delegates on time, February 1, 1988.

"The Hymnal Revision Committee early on had approved the specifications and colors of the bindings, the page size, the style and size of the typeface, the musical styles and sizes. General Conference action remanded to the Editorial Production subcommittee of the Hymnal Revision Committee the responsibility to oversee production of the hymnal, including the possible cutting of content should the music-setting process lead to a book that would be beyond the desired length, which was 960 pages. When enough of the music had been set to make an estimate, the book was projected to contain 1,014 pages rather than the desired 960 pages. That meant that 54 pages, or 5 percent, had to be cut across the board—hymns, prayers, worship resources, and psalter. This was accomplished in unanimous action by the Editorial Production Committee in September 1988.

"The Hymnal Revision Committee had kept very good records of its deliberations and decisions, which were carried in a data base for ease of cross-referencing and verification. Other computer-based techniques supervised by Gary Alan Smith immensely aided in reducing a four-year process to thirty months. Another major breakthrough was the development of a computer program that allowed for each syllable of each word to be hyphenated without having to go to the dictionary for each division. This probably saved ninety days of manuscript preparation. The entire production schedule was monitored by computer.

"Each two-page spread of hymns was individually designed, the approved texts and harmonized tunes hand copied, and the material then sent on to the computer-based music setter with instructions as to the allowable number of pages. The pages of worship resources and the psalter from the report were reset and redesigned. Each page in the hymnal was proofed a minimum of four times by eight readers.

"Concurrent with the design and in some cases the redesign and proofing of each page was the task of determining the ownership of approximately 1,000 items, securing permission for their use, researching correct spelling and dates of each translator, composer, arranger, and source for about 3,000 different entries.

"Prior to the actual printing of the hymnal, the efforts of twenty-four staff plus four members of the Hymnal Revision Committee were involved in the editorial/production effort as follows:

Manuscript preparation:	5
Music setting:	3
Proofing:	10
Research, permission, credits:	6
Design, production:	5
Support staff:	2

"The result is a hymnal for the whole United Methodist Church. It is a *people's* hymnal. It goes with us into the next generation of our history."

CHAPTER 2

BECOMING A SINGING CONGREGATION: CONGREGATIONAL MUSIC IN WORSHIP

From the time of John and Charles Wesley, Methodist and Evangelical United Brethren hymnals have constituted the "worship book" of our corporate and private piety and praise. Hymn singing has been a vital and distinctive component of our worship of God. From our beginning we have been "a singing people."

Our hymnals also serve as instruments by which the spiritual heritage received from the past is celebrated in the present and transmitted to future generations. Next to the Bible, our hymnals have been our most formative resource.

—from the Preface to *The United Methodist Hymnal*

The Wesleys knew the importance of musical expression for the Christian, and they integrated hymn singing into every facet of their movement. United Methodists have demonstrated during the preparation of this hymnal that hymnody is no less important today. The responsibility of singing is on each of us and together we can continue the tradition of being "a singing church."

We sing hymns because as we sing, they teach us about the Bible, our world, and our neighbors. We learn about God's abundant grace and steadfast love, Jesus' life and teachings, and the early church. Our hymns express social concerns, past and present, with an emphasis on Christian action. Hymns from different cultures give us an insight to peoples from different experiences, different lands, and different struggles. Hymns can be a statement of faith shared by the whole congregation. Hymns are scripture, prayers, and sacred poetry, expressing feelings, ideas, and the nature of God's relationship to all creation. Hymn singing unifies a body of individuals into one community. We share in that community as we praise God—Creator, Sustainer, and Redeemer, and as we celebrate in hymns Christ's passion, death, and resurrection.

The basic pattern for worship found in the services of *The United Methodist Hymnal: Book of United Methodist Worship* is the call-and-response pattern. This pattern is discussed in chapter 3 of the companion volume to this book, *The Worship Resources of The United Methodist Hymnal*. The implications of this pattern and style of worship are very significant in that congregational song and choral and instrumental music are meant to serve as responses to God's Word throughout the whole of worship. The calls and their responses are heard in a variety of ways: through prayer, scripture, proclamation, special music, invitation to Christian discipleship, or other actions of worship. God calls us and we respond through a prayer of confession, through offering, through singing a Doxology, *Gloria Patri*, or "Amazing Grace." A response may take shape within the worship service and may continue beyond the service. God's call prompts our appropriate response. Congregational song is the Church's vital and historic response.

Through the singing of hymns, the congregation responds to God's call and expresses its faith in community with others. Too often congregational singing is taken for granted in worship; it is not well planned and prepared and often poorly led and supported by song leaders and choirs. Congregational singing should be a highlight as all unite in one voice worshiping and praising God.

This hymnal is the songbook and worship book of the community. Every United Methodist congregation can be a singing congregation. What will your plan of action be as you integrate this book into your congregation's worship experience? How will you introduce new music to the congregation? What can you do to help your congregation sing?

20

A. Planning for Congregational Singing

Good congregational singing does not just happen. While people love to sing, musicians and pastors must intentionally work together to strengthen congregational singing. Planning for vital singing requires evaluation by each local congregation, serious study, specific standards, and a clear course of action with concrete plans.

BEGIN WITH YOUR CONGREGATION. As you begin planning for congregational singing, start where your congregation is. What do your people love to sing? What do they know? What are they willing to learn? Never assume that you know the answers to these questions before you ask. Take a congregational hymn survey and do it as soon as possible before or after you begin to use *The United Methodist Hymnal* in your church.

First, observe your congregation and gather information. Go through the old bulletins (as many as you can find) of past worship services. Review a marked copy of your former hymnal(s). Remember the hymns people have requested. Recall which hymns you suspect everybody loves but which have not been sung. Write down which hymns are in the current repertory of your congregation.

Next, open a copy of *The United Methodist Hymnal*. Put a check beside each hymn you believe your congregation already knows. You will be pleasantly surprised by all the old favorites you will find. Also mark those hymns you believe are known by your congregation but never have appeared before in one of our hymnals (such as "In the Garden," 314).

Third, take a hymn survey. Ask a variety of persons within your membership to look at every hymn in the hymnal. Be certain to include longtime and new members, youth, young adults, and persons from different cultures. Involve members of the choir as well as people who do not like to sing.

The people participating in the survey may work individually or together as a Sunday School class, youth meeting, or Sunday evening program group. Since many people do not know hymns just by their title, work with an actual copy of the hymnal for each person rather than a list of hymns. Ask each one to mark the hymnal (in pencil) using a rating system: three stars for a favorite hymn; two stars for a familiar hymn that can be sung without further help; one star for a hymn not known but desirable to learn. Have as many people as possible rate the hymns. The more people that help, the better.

Finally, the musician and pastor together should collate the material, take averages of the ratings, and make pencil marks in a copy of *The United Methodist Hymnal*. Rate each hymn with one, two, or three stars. This one hymnal will become the most valuable resource for congregational singing. Use this hymnal every week. After every service of worship, return to it and write down beside each hymn sung the date on which it was sung. Be prepared to change the number of stars; your congregation's repertory will change, and your planning must change with your congregation. If a new pastor is appointed or a musician hired, this book should be passed on to the new person to aid him or her in worship planning. Nevertheless, it is a good idea to do a hymn survey every so often and begin fresh.

GAIN UNDERSTANDING. Once you have taken the hymn survey, evaluate your congregation's repertory asking these questions: Why do the people love what they do? Why do they not appreciate other hymns? What is the favorite style of music of the congregation: gospel, spiritual, contemporary, or classic? What style of singing does the congregation enjoy: full accompaniment, piano, or a cappella?

Be sensitive to your congregation's investment in their hymns. Based on your hymn survey, and your own insights, you should be able to anticipate which hymns your congregation wants to sing. For example, one congregation may be open to singing hymns from a wide variety of ethnic cultures; another congregation may want to emphasize contemporary and children's hymns; another may have a very limited expectation and repertory.

It is crucial that you become intimately familiar with the new hymnal as your primary worship resource. Open the book, turn every page, read or sing each hymn and scan each worship service. Next to your Bible it should be your closest companion in your worship and devotional life. Each day, read aloud one hymn and let it become your prayer. Try to learn by heart one new hymn every week, reflect on the history of each tune and text as found in this book.

The Hymns of The United Methodist Hymnal provides you with background information on every hymn, canticle, and act of worship. Reading the commentary on each hymn will be enlightening and fun. The companion book, *The Worship Resources of The United Methodist Hymnal,* describes each worship service and resource in the hymnal, including additional help on music in worship. Every musician, pastor, and church library should own a copy of both books and keep both on their desks.

DETERMINE STANDARDS. Now, having evaluated your congregation's hymn singing and begun to study the hymnal itself and the supplemental books, it is appropriate to set standards for you and your congregation. How will you choose hymns for congregational worship? How will your congregation use its voice in worship? How much should your congregation sing? Musicians, pastors, and worship committees must give serious attention to each of these questions.

While there are many standards that can be set by worship leaders of a local congregation, at least four standards and goals seem appropriate for most congregations.

1. *Provide more opportunities for congregational singing.* Look at the acts of worship within the services and make note of those which can be sung by the people. Look in the Index of Topics and Categories in the hymnal (pp. 934-54) under "Service Music" and discover all the ways the whole or parts of the service can be sung. Work intentionally to increase congregational singing.

2. *The Word of God in worship should be the nucleus and focus of all congregational singing.* The Word of God read, proclaimed, and heard should primarily determine what music, hymns, and psalms are chosen and sung in worship. For this to become a reality in worship, pastors and musicians will need to plan ahead. Invaluable in all this work will be the Index of Scripture (pp. 923-26) in the hymnal. Greatly expanded from previous hymnals, it is an essential planning tool as you coordinate hymns with scripture.

3. *Our music and hymnody must be inclusive.* In every congregation, women, men, and children come with a variety of needs and gifts. Our music should affirm that rich diversity of spirituality so

23

as to include those who enjoy highly structured worship as well as those who like charismatic and evangelical worship styles. Our selection of congregational song should encompass the multiplicity of races and cultures in our denomination. An obtainable goal for any congregation is to learn at least one new hymn a year from each of the cultures represented in the hymnal outside the congregation's dominant repertory: Afro-American, Hispanic, Asian-American, Native American, and Anglo-American. All ages are present in your congregation, which means hymns for older adults, children, and youth should be included. *The United Methodist Hymnal* opens for our Church the unique spiritual gifts of many peoples; encourage your congregation to share these gifts.

4. *Increase your congregation's repertory slowly and steadily.* Attempting to learn too many new hymns too quickly will frustrate you and your congregation. Carefully and wisely choose a variety of hymns, integrating them into your congregation's repertory over a period of time. Another goal for your congregation may include learning one new hymn for each major season of the Christian year. Over the life of *The United Methodist Hymnal*, your congregation should discover and learn to love a significant number of new hymns.

These four standards—encourage more congregational singing, focus on the Word of God, affirm diversity, and increase the congregation's repertory—may stimulate your work in setting standards for your congregation. You may add others or adjust these. Only you can set standards. Be realistic, and be bold!

CHART A COURSE. Prepare long-range plans. Knowing your congregation, understanding the new hymnal, and setting standards are the necessary steps prior to charting your course and implementing goals to strengthen congregational singing. As you make plans, three key elements are vital to any successful work.

The worship leaders, especially the musicians, pastors, worship chairs, and educators in your local congregation must be encouraged to learn all that they can about this new hymnal. Establish training opportunities for them in both informal and formal settings.

Evaluate your own work and commitment to congregational singing. Will a song leader help your congregation sing better?

How can you better support your congregation and choir? Have the resources needed for vocal and instrumental support of congregational singing been provided? With your leadership, congregational singing can and will improve.

Teach your congregation. Any new resource, and especially a new hymnal, creates a unique moment for learning. Such a time includes stress and tension as well as excitement and openness. Use every opportunity in your congregation's life to teach the new hymnal, including the Sunday School and other educational settings. Musicians and pastors working together with teachers can inform and bring excitement to the educational setting. This may be the time to reintroduce vital singing in your Sunday School.

Seek and gain congregational support. Musicians and pastors, along with teachers, can help you excite the whole congregation about a new emphasis on singing. Tell people they *can* sing! Describe hymns in your worship bulletins and newsletters. Create a hymn bulletin board that receives the contributions of all ages. Work with your Administrative Council or Administrative Board and Council on Ministries to gain their support. Worship and sing during church business meetings (possibly using one of the Orders of Daily Praise and Prayer, pp. 876-79, in the hymnal). Worship and sing during every congregational gathering, including fellowship dinners.

Now, with a better understanding of your congregation, having set standards and having prepared yourselves, begin making plans to strengthen congregational singing.

PLAN FOR A SEASON. Strong congregational singing requires the intentional and cooperative work of many persons. Musicians and pastors are foremost, but others, such as worship committee members and teachers, must participate as well. They must all plan ahead and plan together.

The following model of planning will work in a local congregation. There are other possible ways of planning, and you may develop your own model.

The first six steps are primarily the responsibility of the pastor and require a brief yet intentional time of commitment.

25

Step 1. Plan ahead. Set aside at least a half day to plan. Using a calendar, plan in advance for a whole season or cycle of the year at a time, at least two months before the season begins. For example, no later than October 1, plan for Advent and Christmas; no later than January 1, plan for Lent and Easter; no later than April 1, plan for June, July, and August.

Determine which services will be held during that season. Certainly include every Sunday and then add any special services such as Christmas Eve, Ash Wednesday, or a revival or preaching mission.

Make a worksheet for every service. Write in the day and date of the service. Make a file folder for each service to collect all the resources you discover as you plan this service of worship.

Step 2. Choose scripture lessons. Select the Bible passages which are the foundation of each service of worship. The Common Lectionary—a three-year cycle of selected Old Testament, psalm, epistle, and gospel readings—provides one method of choosing scripture. Or, scripture may be based on a theme or themes for a season. Or, one portion or book of the Bible may be used over several weeks.

Write down the lessons on the worksheet, selecting the primary lesson(s) that will be the foundation of the service.

Step 3. Choose the sermon focus. The sermon links the Word of God with the congregation. The sermon focus—the basic image, thrust, statement, or impact that guides the sermon—will give direction to the service. While preparing, ask: How does the Word affect me and this congregation? Where does the Word challenge? Where does the Word comfort? What responses does the Word call forth?

Now write the sermon focus—image, thrust, statement, impact—in a short, declarative sentence. Even though the sermon may not be prepared for several weeks, the sermon focus will prove invaluable to the preacher, musician(s), and worship planning team.

Step 4. Determine when there will be Communion. Will a Service of Word and Table be used? Will a Service of the Baptismal Covenant, installation of officers, or anything special or timely be included? Write everything down on the worksheet. When choosing a service found in the hymnal, write down the page number of the service.

Step 5. Schedule a planning meeting. Schedule a one- or two-hour meeting with the musician(s) and the worship planning team. Remember, schedule the meeting at least eight weeks before a season begins.

Step 6. Prepare for a planning meeting. Duplicate the worksheets for each service in the whole season—complete with date, day, scripture lessons, sermon focus, and special emphases. Distribute the sheets to all members of the worship planning team. The musician(s), pastor, and other worship planners should prepare suggestions concerning hymns, anthem(s) and other music, other worship leaders, and visuals.

Step 7. Select hymns. Together, the musician(s) and pastor choose hymns for the services. All the hymns should reflect and enhance the scripture of the day, the sermon focus, or the service emphasis. For example, the first hymn may be a hymn of praise, a second hymn related to the sermon, and a third hymn a response to the Word proclaimed.

One excellent way to choose hymns is to use the indexes in the back of the hymnal. As an example, for the Sundays of Advent, use the Index of Topics and Categories (pp. 934-54) to find the Advent hymns. Look at each hymn, read the commentary on each hymn in this book, and make your selection. Or, using the Index of Scripture (pp. 923-26) in the hymnal, compare the scripture lessons for the day related to particular hymns. Again, read the commentaries in this book and make your selection. As you choose hymns, even familiar ones, study them for changes that may have been made—for example, in "O Come, O Come Emmanuel" and "Good Christian Friends Rejoice." Unfamiliar texts and tunes need special study and preparation. As you choose hymns, be sensitive to the meaning in each stanza. In some hymns, stanzas may be omitted without damaging the whole text, but not in all hymns. Simply saying, "Let us sing the first and last stanza," without first reading the text, may rob the hymn of its full meaning. Pick the stanzas best suited for a particular service.

As you select hymns, choose both familiar and unfamiliar ones. While most hymns chosen for the services should be familiar to the congregation (based on your hymn survey), it is also important to choose unfamiliar hymns to expand and deepen the congregation's experience of worship. You may want to introduce a new text by using an alternate tune. At the bottom of some hymns there are suggestions for alternate tunes. And as you introduce new hymns, remember two rules: (1) Never use only new hymns in any worship service; and (2) Always teach a new hymn before using it.

Plan for the additional places the congregation may sing in worship. The basic pattern rejects the "slot theory" of congregational worship; that is, hymns, anthems, and music appear in the same place every week. Instead, leaders of worship should look at the flow and movement of each service and choose music accordingly. Ask what follows, what illumines, what carries out the theme, what interprets, and what fits best? For example, at the gathering the congregation may have a mini–hymn festival, sing some old favorites, or rehearse unfamiliar music and the psalm response. During the greeting, sing the opening stanza of "We Gather Together" (131) or "Morning Has Broken" (145). For Opening Prayer, sing "Just as I am" (357). The Act of Praise may be one of several *Glorias* (82, 83, 72). The Prayer for Illumination may be "Open My Eyes" (454). Following the gospel reading, sing one of the Alleluias (186, 486). Use the Index of Scripture and sing one of the lessons. A hymn may lead into a sung prayer, such as "Lead Me, Lord" (473). Explore the different Doxologies at the Offering (94, 95). The Sending Forth has many possible musical options, such as "Blest Be the Tie That Binds" (557). A choral Amen may conclude the service (897–904). In the Index of Topics and Categories, see the listings under "Service Music" for additional possibilities. Remember, the congregation could sing almost the entire service of worship. Write down the hymn titles and tune names.

Step 8. Choose anthem(s), service and communion music, and instrumental music based on the scripture lessons, sermon focus, or the service emphasis. The musician(s) and pastor need to work together to create an environment of sound that informs and enhances worship.

The anthem(s) may be a hymn from the hymnal, particularly if the hymn is unfamiliar. Let the choir(s) sing the hymn and invite the congregation to follow in their hymnal. The *Music Supplement* to the hymnal is one excellent resource for such hymns/anthems.

The psalm of the day has a musical response printed at the top of each psalm in the hymnal. Prepare the instrumentalists and choir members to teach each psalm response to the congregation. The best time to teach the response is before the service, during the gathering. Also see *The Worship Resources of The United Methodist Hymnal*, chapter 10, for help in teaching the musical psalm responses.

Both Services of Word and Table and Services of the Baptismal Covenant have musical responses (*see* pp. 17-31 and 53-54). Prepare your musicians and singers to introduce and lead your congregation in singing these responses. Again, *The Worship Resources of The United Methodist Hymnal*, chapter 4, describes ways of introducing the sacramental service music.

Do not forget the subliminal teaching power of the opening voluntary (prelude), offertory, and closing voluntary (postlude) to reinforce the recall of both old and new hymn tunes. Especially when teaching a new hymn, let the opening and closing music focus on the tune. Print the page number where the hymn can be found beside the name of the hymn arrangement so that the congregation can meditate on the text as they listen to the tune.

Choose singers and instrumentalists and contact them well in advance. All musicians need time to practice and rehearse. Choose persons who can prepare well and who can offer adequate leadership. And do not overlook new talent. For example, encourage a youth musician to introduce "Kum Ba Ya" (494) or a children's choir to lead "Jesus Loves Me" (191).

Now, write down your decisions.

You have planned for congregational singing. Beginning with your congregation's current singing experience you have gained understanding, set standards, charted a course, and planned for a season. We turn now to ways of improving your congregation's singing.

B.   Helping Your Congregation Sing

As you, the pastor or musician, continue to strengthen your congregational singing in the local church, there are three critical factors to consider: the quality of the vocal leadership, the strength of the instrumental support, and the pattern of introducing new hymns and music to your congregation. Vital congregational singing requires serious attention to all three.

PROVIDE FIRM VOCAL LEADERSHIP. Superior vocal leadership is critical for congregational singing. Several strategies will aid in providing such leadership.

Rehearse the choir(s) on all congregational music. The choir's primary role is to prompt and lead the congregation. The choir will not know every hymn. Even though hymns seem easier than anthems, they also require rehearsal. Familiarize the choir with the history of each hymn. Teach the choir correct phrasing. Ask the choir members to mark the places where they may breathe, and give other instructions such as places for unison and four-part singing and dynamics—loud and soft. The choir has the greatest responsibility in learning and leading service music such as the sung responses for Holy Communion and the Baptismal Covenant, Amens, Alleluias, Doxologies, and psalter responses. The choir is more than a select group who shares special music in worship; the choir is a *subset* of the congregation which provides musical support for the whole congregation.

Rehearse the congregation and Sunday School classes before worship. Many Sunday School classes share in hymn singing as part of their time together. Visit Sunday School classes for all ages and rehearse hymns for worship. The members will become leaders in among the rest of the congregation and with encouragement will be strong advocates for congregational participation. Teach new hymns and service music to the congregation during the gathering time before worship. If announcements are a part of the gathering time, introduce the new hymn following the last announcement. Immediately after the hymn is taught the opening music must begin.

A song leader or cantor may lead hymns. A song leader's presence at the chancel is helpful for many who need visual as well

30

as musical leadership. This person may be the choir director, pastor, or another person from the congregation. The leader should have a strong voice and a clear conducting style that invites active participation.

PROVIDE STRONG INSTRUMENTAL LEADERSHIP. Congregational singing is often dependent on the quality of the music played by the congregation's instrumentalists. The piano, organ, guitar, or other instrument played by a leader of worship with a strong sense of rhythm is a prerequisite to vital singing. Several suggestions will help improve this leadership.

Insure that the accompanist knows the music well in advance of the service. The accompanist should be given a list of all service music at least a week in advance. Discuss the tempos and registrations for different stanzas with the accompanist. Correct rhythms and tempos are crucial—hymns played too slowly may lead to lethargic singing, hymns played too fast may discourage singing. The organist or pianist should make an effort to reflect the hymn text through organ registration and pianistic color. The textures and moods of stanzas can be complemented with creative preparation.

Use other instruments to enhance a musical setting: a flute, violin, clarinet, or trumpet may highlight the melody. For example, *"Una Espiga"* ("Sheaves of Summer") (637) is best sung when accompanied with flute and rhythm instruments. Instead of organ, use piano or guitar. Or use rhythm instruments such as drums, maracas, finger cymbals, and triangle to add rhythmic interest. Handbells also provide wonderful accompaniment to hymns.

INTRODUCE NEW HYMNS TO THE CONGREGATION. *The United Methodist Hymnal* has a total of 624 hymns and canticles. Of those hymns and canticles your congregation may use less than 100 over the next several years. Most of those hymns will be current favorites, yet every congregation should have the opportunity, need, and desire to learn new hymns. How can this be accomplished? Teaching and introducing new hymns takes planning, constant reinforcing, and patience. The following method is one way to introduce new hymns to your congregation.

First, you as a musician or pastor must learn and know the hymn before you effectively teach it! Then, teach your worship leaders. Those involved in the leadership of worship should learn the hymn before the congregation is introduced to it. This includes the instrumentalists, director, choir, pastor, and everyone else in front of the congregation. If the hymn is worth introducing to the congregation then it is worth the worship leaders' time in learning it. The pastor must be willing to communicate the value of congregational singing and enthusiastically participate in the singing of all hymns, old and new. The choir, too, needs to take seriously its primary role of assisting congregational singing. Others who may learn new hymns before the gathered congregation are Sunday School classes, fellowship groups (United Methodist Women, Men, Youth), or prayer and Bible study groups.

Encourage a strong, energetic, positive person to lead the congregation in singing. In most cases the music leader will want to introduce new hymns, since the congregation is accustomed to this person's leadership in worship and respects his or her knowledge and authority. In many congregations, however, the music leader is both choir director and organist. In these cases, it is better not to introduce a new hymn or service music from behind the organ console or piano. Instead, a strong singer with a pleasant voice, clear enunciation, and strong sense of rhythm should be asked to introduce the new hymn. This leader should stand in front of the congregation and with a positive attitude motivate the congregation. Nothing diminishes a singer's enthusiasm for singing more quickly than feeling apprehensive about what and when they should sing. The best approach is one of gentle patience, constant encouragement, and a dash of humor. Rehearsal between the accompanist and music leader is necessary before rehearsing the congregation.

Sharing information with the congregation about new and old hymns will help them identify with the hymn. Using this book, which includes a paragraph on each hymn found in your hymnal, decide what you will share with the congregation when you introduce a hymn. Read the paragraph and read the scripture passage(s) on which the text is based, highlighting specific stanzas that point to that passage. Explain to the congregation where the hymn comes in the service and how it relates to what precedes or follows it. Tell them why you think the hymn is worth learning and why you enjoy it. Have the accompanist play the hymn once through as the congregation listens or hums and follows in their hymnals.

Now, have the song leader or cantor sing the first stanza as the congregation listens and hums; or have the choir (adult, children, or youth) sing the first stanza. Youth can assist teaching the congregation "El Shaddai" (123) while children may teach "We Are the Church" (558). Add an instrument to highlight the melody.

Have the congregation sing a stanza with the song leader or choir. If it sounds shaky, try a third stanza. If a specific part of the hymn is troublesome, rehearse that spot before singing the hymn again.

When the congregation sings the hymn in worship, use the choir to reinforce the melody line. Reserve part-singing for a time when the congregation sings more confidently, or when the choir sings alone.

Finally, use the opening voluntary (prelude), offertory, and closing voluntary (postlude) to reinforce new hymn tunes. Organ and piano arrangements for hymn tunes can be found in most music stores or you or your accompanist may create a free harmonization. *The Music Supplement* to the hymnal will also be invaluable. Other times for reinforcing new hymns are at gatherings such as fellowship dinners, Bible study, and church meetings. These are excellent times to sing favorites and learn new hymns. Use the same pattern suggested for Sunday morning.

Another method of introducing new hymns is through special programs. A Sunday evening or morning hymn festival is a great way of celebrating the rich hymnody found in our hymnal. To organize a hymn festival simply decide on a theme (a season of the Christian year such as Advent, Lent, or Easter; hymns by women; Wesleyan hymns; American hymns, or other theme); choose five to ten hymns (both old and new); intersperse the hymns with prayers and scripture readings (see the Indexes of Topics and Scripture); prepare the choir to sing a hymn arrangement; designate different stanzas to groups (choir, congregation, men, women, youth, children, Sunday School classes); prepare visuals relating to the theme; and ask persons in the congregation to participate in the leadership. Hymn festivals are a great way of getting everyone involved in the action. The Hymn Society of

America has several resources on organizing a hymn festival including an excellent guide, *Hymn Festivals*, written by Austin Lovelace. Contact the Hymn Society for further information.

C. THE HYMNAL AS AN ANTHEM RESOURCE

Many churches use the hymnal not only as a book for congregational singing but also as a source for choral anthems. The great diversity found in the hymnal—styles, historical periods, cultures—makes it an excellent source for hymn-anthems.

The hymnal contains a wide variety of hymns never before bound together in one book, including "God the Spirit, Guide and Guardian," "El Shaddai," "¡Canta, Débora, Canta!," and "Soon and Very Soon." Choirs of any-size congregation and of every kind will be able to find music that will suit their needs. The many styles represented here include gospel, chorale, chant, spiritual, traditional Hispanic, Asian, Native American, Afro-American, Southern harmony, folk, psalter tunes, and more. There are hymns for young and old alike, including a considerable number of hymns accessible for children and youth that speak their language, both musically and theologically, such as "Jesus, our Brother, Strong and Good," "I Sing a Song of the Saints of God," and "Jesus Loves Me."

There is a great amount of service music found in the hymnal, ranging from communion and baptismal responses to prayer and scripture responses to benedictions. See "Service Music" in the Index of Topics. A variety of languages is represented here as well. Spanish, French, German, and several Asian and Native American languages are provided. The choir may learn a hymn in a language different from their own and invite the congregation to sing along at the refrain.

Hymns, both old favorites as well as new additions can quite easily be arranged into anthems. In this book you will find suggestions on using hymns as anthems in the hymn paragraphs, such as "Serenity" (499). Use these descriptions and let them guide you as you prepare hymns for your choir to sing. The following are some basic ideas on arranging hymns for choirs:

- Designate different stanzas for men and women, boys and girls.

34

- Ask a soloist to sing a stanza (a cappella or with accompaniment).
- In a four-stanza hymn, play an interlude after the third stanza.
- Have a quartet sing a stanza from the back or balcony of the sanctuary.
- Add instruments on stanzas or interludes.
- Sing a hymn a cappella, such as "Heleluyan" (78).
- Sing a stanza a cappella in four-part harmony.
- Ask the congregation to join the choir at the refrain, as in "Are Ye Able" (530).
- Build the choir as you go—have children sing stanza one, youth join on stanza two, women on three, and all on four.
- Add more instruments on each stanza, as in "Lonely the Boat, Sailing at Sea" (476).
- Alternate piano and organ on stanzas with both playing the refrain.
- Teach interpretive movement to a group or to the congregation; this may include using simple sign language phrases that all may learn as in "Jesus Loves Me" (191).

As you begin using the hymnal as an anthem resource you will discover what will work best for your choir and what talents and resources are available in your congregation.

The hymnal is an excellent resource for all choirs. Use it as you would a Bible at Bible study. Begin your rehearsals with a hymn, use a hymn as a devotion, warm up with a hymn, and end rehearsal with a hymn such as "Blest Be the Tie That Binds" (557).

AMENS. The hymnal contains two choral Amens (902 and 904)—one by John Rutter and one by Peter Lutkin—taken from their settings of "The Lord Bless You and Keep You." The traditional two- and threefold Amens are also included (897–901, 903). Amens have not been included at the end of each hymn. Using the Amens found on p. 904B in *The Keyboard Edition* you may wish to add Amens for hymns whose final stanza is a trinitarian Doxology, for hymns which are prayers, for hymns whose music was composed with an Amen as essential to the tune, or any other hymn. For further information on the use of Amens, see Appendix 6.

CONCLUSION. Above all, sing! Congregational singing, joining voices and instruments to praise God, is our tradition, and it is our responsibility to continue this tradition. May you use *The United Methodist Hymnal* to strengthen congregational singing and through it offer God's grace to all creation.

> Glorious God, source of joy and righteousness,
> enable us as redeemed and forgiven children
>   evermore to rejoice in singing your praises.
> Grant that what we sing with our lips
>   we may believe in our hearts,
> and what we believe in our hearts
>   we may practice in our lives;
> so that being doers of the Word and not hearers only,
>   we may receive everlasting life;
> through Jesus Christ our Lord. Amen.

—Fred D. Gealy; altered by Laurence Hull Stookey

CHAPTER 3

THE HYMNS, CANTICLES, AND ACTS OF WORSHIP

57 O For a Thousand Tongues to Sing

Among the most celebrated of Charles Wesley's texts, traditionally the first hymn in our hymnals, it has become Methodism's "anthem." It proclaims the twofold aspect of Wesleyan theology: God's saving grace and invitation to Christian discipleship, and it is Charles Wesley's personal testimony, written on the first anniversary of his own heartwarming experience. Christians worldwide sing it as an opening hymn of praise and as an invitation to Christian discipleship.

58 Glory to God, and Praise and Love

This text, from which "O For a Thousand Tongues to Sing" is drawn, expresses the full evangelical fervor of that great hymn. In stanzas 1–6, Charles Wesley's heart overflows with praise as he remembers the dawning of his faith in God's justifying grace (Eph. 2:8). In stanzas 7–14, proclaiming this grace to others is emphasized. Those who recognize the seriousness of their condition will "feel their sins forgiven," and begin to anticipate "heaven below" through the power of love (sts. 15–18). Excellent for meditation, teaching, or antiphonal reading.

59 *Mil Voces Para Celebrar*

This favorite Wesley hymn is among recent translations by Methodist Bishop Frederico J. Pagura of Argentina. It may be used in either bilingual or English-speaking congregations who wish to experience worshiping through another language. Begin by teaching one stanza of the Spanish version to the congregation or choir, and sing that stanza in Spanish each time this hymn is used.

60 *I'll Praise My Maker While I've Breath*

In 1719 Isaac Watts published his monumental *The Psalms of David Imitated in the Language of the New Testament*. From that collection comes this paraphrase of Ps. 146, an exuberant paean of praise for God's goodness. It was a favorite of John Wesley's, who in his 1737 *Charleston Collection* altered it to its present form. Wesley used the hymn in his last sermon and then sang it on his deathbed—the significant words being from the first stanza: "I'll praise my maker while I've breath, and when my voice is lost in death, praise shall employ my nobler powers."

61 *Come, Thou Almighty King*

One of the most popular hymns for the opening of Christian worship, this text uses many names for God: King, Father, Ancient of Days, Incarnate Word, Spirit, Comforter, One in Three. It is also one of the best examples of a text's trinitarian organization with each of the first three stanzas addressing one of the persons of the Trinity: Father, Son, and Holy Spirit. The last stanza ties it together: "To thee, great One in Three."

62 *All Creatures of Our God and King*

This hymn is derived from the "Canticle of the Sun," written by Francis of Assisi during a time of great pain, suffering, and impending death. Francis, with his profound love of God's creation, was able even in adversity to join with nature in the praise of God. The text enumerates the facets of nature that praise God and then invites people "of tender heart" to join in the praise. The final stanza sums up the thought of the text with: "Let all things their creator bless, and worship him in humbleness." The phrases of the tune LASST UNS ERFREUEN may be sung antiphonally by the congregation and choir or between sections of the congregation. The tune also may be sung as a round by two or three groups in the congregation.

63 *Blessed Be the Name*

Ps. 72:19 is the basis for this well known chorus by Ralph Hudson. As a strong chorus of praise it can be appended to a variety of CM hymns (e.g., "O For a Thousand Tongues") or sung as a brief joyous affirmation and response to prayer or scripture reading.

64 *Holy, Holy, Holy! Lord God Almighty*

Early in the twentieth century this hymn was specifically recommended as an opening hymn in the Ritual for Holy Communion and still is often used for that purpose. This text, written to be sung after the Nicene Creed on Trinity Sunday, is an excellent example of the hymns Reginald Heber wrote for specific times in the Christian year. Drawing from biblical passages such as Rev. 4:8-11, in which the elders give homage to God, and from the vision in Is. 6, the text calls the worshiper to unite in praise with those of biblical times. Universally known and loved, it is ideal for use at the opening of Sunday morning worship and ecumenical celebrations.

65 ¡Santo! ¡Santo! ¡Santo!

The Spanish translation of this popular trinitarian hymn may be used in bilingual or ecumenical settings as well as in English-speaking congregations wishing to worship through another language. The translator, Bishop Juan B. Cabrera, was a talented hymnologist and translator who served the Spanish Reformed Church.

66 Praise, My Soul, the King of Heaven

Henry Lyte's paraphrase of Ps. 103 admonishes the soul to give praise to the everlasting and redeeming God and describes God as unchanging and "slow to chide and swift to bless." It provides a beautiful description of God who is both fatherlike and motherlike, tending and bearing us, merciful and gentle. The text invites angels and saints in heaven to join with us in the song of praise. The hymn may be sung antiphonally, with the choir singing the stanzas and the congregation singing the last two lines beginning with "Alleluia."

67 We, Thy People, Praise Thee

This joyful text, combined with the well-crafted tune attributed to Haydn, is widely used in Sunday Schools and is also suitable for use in congregational worship and choir festivals. The author, Kate Stearns Page, wrote this text for use as a school song. Let the keyboard introduce this hymn with the last five measures, then support it at a moderately brisk tempo, and if organ is used, with a bright registration.

68 When in Our Music God Is Glorified

This glorious hymn of praise combines the efforts of two distinguished Englishmen, Fred Pratt Green and Charles Villiers Stanford. Pratt Green, a retired British Methodist minister, wrote the text in 1971, inspired by the majestic tune by Stanford, first published in 1904. The text bears witness to the power of music to inspire and communicate faith, truth, and praise. Once learned by your congregation it is sure to be a favorite for any time of praise as well as for hymn and choir festivals. Feel two strong beats in each measure and provide a full, bright accompaniment for this majestic tune and do not slow down at the end of the stanzas.

69 *For True Singing*

This prayer may be used by choirs at rehearsal or before a service of worship, by congregations during a song service, or on other occasions of Christian praise through song. Its scriptural text particularly draws from Jas. 1:22, asking that we may sing not simply for pleasure but so that the joy God has given us may be manifested in good deeds.

70, 71 *Glory Be to the Father*

The *Gloria Patri* (Latin for "Glory Be to the Father") from the third and fourth centuries, also known as the Lesser Doxology, is derived from verses in the psalms and New Testament epistles. When we sing it, we join with centuries of Christians in praise of God. The *Gloria Patri* may be sung after the psalms or canticles to provide a trinitarian ending or as an act of praise following the opening prayer and on other occasions as an alternative to the Greater Doxology *(Gloria in Excelsis)*. The vibrant nineteenth-century tunes GREATOREX and MEINEKE are both widely used in United Methodist congregations.

72 *Gloria, Gloria*

Based on Lk. 2:14, the Angel's Hymn, this chorus is suitable for use at Christmas for a festival or for a praise response to scripture. This canon, or round, can be sung by two or four groups, each new group beginning where the numbers indicate. A brief rehearsal before the service will familiarize and encourage the congregation to participate in this lovely chorus.

73   O Worship the King

A free paraphrase of Ps. 104, this stirring text by Robert Grant tells of God's greatness seen in nature. The poet uses lofty images in describing God as "the Ancient of Days, Pavilioned in splendor." The hymn ends in a declaration of trust to the One who is our "Maker, Defender, Redeemer, and Friend."

74   Canticle of Thanksgiving (Jubilate)

Since the days of the Temple in Jerusalem, Ps. 100 has called the faithful to worship. The Latin word *Jubilate* ("rejoice" or "be jubilant") summarizes that the followers of God are filled with joy. The psalm remains one of the most constant, familiar, and lively invitations to sing a song in the presence of the God who is gracious and faithful and whose truth is enduring. This psalm is also found as 821 in *The United Methodist Liturgical Psalter* and in metrical paraphrase at 75. Let the organ and choir introduce the psalm response in unison with the congregation repeating it following the choir.

75   All People That on Earth Do Dwell

This metrical paraphrase of Ps. 100 is an effective hymn of praise and thanksgiving or an alternate setting of "Canticle of Thanksgiving" (74) and Ps. 100 in the Psalter (821). It is the earliest English metrical psalm setting still in wide use. The words are attributed to William Kethe, a Scottish Protestant who fled to the European continent during the persecution of Queen Mary (1553–1558). The well-known tune, OLD 100TH, attributed to Louis Bourgeois, was written for the French paraphrase of Ps. 134 found in the *Anglo-Genevan Psalter*, 1560.

76 *Trinity Sunday*

This prayer is intended for general use but particularly for Trinity Sunday (First Sunday after Pentecost). It acknowledges both the mysterious nature of God and the revelation of divine truth extending from the very person of God. The Church has received grace to worship God both as Unity and as Trinity. We ask to join the entire body of Christian believers in being steadfast in our faith.

77 *How Great Thou Art*

Stuart K. Hine's hymn, derived from Swedish, German, and Russian sources, speaks of the grandeur of God in nature. The wonder of this great God giving a son to die for our sins is expressed in stanza 3. Stanza 4 is a vow to praise God more fully in heaven. Primarily because of its soaring refrain, this hymn has a strong impact on many congregations. Surveys conducted by the Hymnal Revision Committee showed that among United Methodists it was of all hymns both the most loved and the most disliked.

78 *Heleluyan* (Alleluia)

This Muscogee-Creek hymn is often regarded by Creek Christians as their "tribal anthem." Never appearing before in a hymnal, it was transcribed into musical notation by a hymnal committee member specially for this hymnal. Sung at a variety of settings, historically, it is most often led by a male who begins each new stanza as others are completing the previous one. It is best sung without accompaniment and may be taught by rote with one person singing one line at a time and the congregation echoing or repeating what they hear. It is a good response for World Communion Sunday, Easter, Pentecost or Native American Awareness Sunday. The words "Yah-hay-ka-theis," meaning "I will be singing," may be substituted for measure 2.

79 *Holy God, We Praise Thy Name*

This metrical version of a portion of the *Te Deum* ("Canticle of the Holy Trinity," 80) was first published in German in an eighteenth-century Austrian hymnbook. Stanzas 1–4 are a summary of trinitarian theology calling all creation and history to join in praise of the Triune God. Stanzas 5–7 tell the story of Christ's saving work and the hope for everlasting life. It may be used throughout the year as a hymn of praise, or it may be substituted for the *Te Deum* in Morning Praise and Prayer. Choir and congregation may sing alternate stanzas of this joyful text.

80 *Canticle of the Holy Trinity* (Te Deum Laudamus)

This Latin hymn of the fourth or fifth century is an important link to the early Church, where it was prescribed by Benedictine Rule for early Morning Praise and Prayer (Matins) on every Sunday except during Advent, Lent, and feast days. Today it is used worldwide by Christians of many denominations and is especially appropriate and traditional in Morning Praise and Prayer. The text is a statement of praise to the Trinity and a prayer for sustenance (Is. 6:3). The concluding optional versicles and responses, comprising the third part of this canticle, were added in the fifth century (Ps. 28:10; 145:2; 123:3; 56:1, 3; 31:1).

81 *¡Canta, Débora, Canta!*

Recent Brazilian hymns have been an exciting addition to the rich, emerging Christian music of South America. This song by Luiza Cruz continues the tradition of music based on the heroes of the Old Testament. It sings the victory song of Deborah, the military leader in Jg. 5. Use this song to teach the story in Sunday School or as a strongly rhythmical reaffirmation of women in the Bible and the Church. This vibrant hymn has become the unofficial theme song of Methodist women in Brazil. All may sing the first line, "¡Canta, Débora, Canta!" with a choir or soloist singing the remainder in English, Spanish, or a combination of both.

82 *Canticle of God's Glory* (Gloria in Excelsis)

This fourth-century Christian hymn, often called by its original Latin title, *Gloria in Excelsis,* is also known as the Greater Doxology and the Angelic Hymn. Although the hymn begins with the Angel Song of Lk. 2:14, as a whole it is not based on a specific passage of scripture but summarizes many biblical passages. The first stanza praises God the Father; the second addresses Christ using two ancient hymns of the Eastern Church: *Agnus Dei* ("O Lamb of God") and *Kyrie Eleison* ("Lord, Have Mercy"); the third praises the Holy Trinity. This canticle has been sung in the service of Holy Communion; however, it is also appropriate for Morning and Evening Praise and Prayer. In this hymnal it appears in two different translations and musical settings: the traditional 1549 English translation, set to an old Scottish chant, and a new translation with musical response at 83. If your congregation is unfamiliar with this setting, let the choir or a soloist sing it the first time with accompaniment. The rhythm of the chant is dependent on the flow of the words, not note values. Organ registration should be bright and distinct for good congregational singing.

83 *Canticle of God's Glory* (Gloria in Excelsis)

This contemporary English version of the *Gloria in Excelsis,* the Angel Song (Lk. 2:14), was produced by the International Consultation on English Texts in 1975 and is now in common use. The text is printed in three stanzas, which may be read in unison by the congregation with or without the spoken or sung response. It is appropriate for Holy Communion as well as Morning and Evening Praise and Prayer. For a complete musical setting of the traditional English translation see 82. To introduce the response it should be sung once by the leader, then repeated by the congregation. The response may be sung without accompaniment. If accompanied, the organist or pianist will need to anticipate the congregation by bringing the cue note in during the last two words spoken by the congregation prior to their singing the response (R).

84   Thank You, Lord

Afro-American slaves knew well the products of "sowing" righteous seeds. They also learned to say, "thank you, Lord," before a blessing was returned. This simple, yet profound, utterance is an effective musical response for use at Holy Communion or following prayer.

85   We Believe in One True God

This metrical version of a portion of the Apostle's Creed by Tobias Clausnitzer was translated by Catherine Winkworth. The three stanzas describe some of the attributes of the persons of the Trinity: God as omnipresent and omnipotent; Jesus, "Mary's Son," who suffered on the cross for our salvation; the Holy Spirit upholding and comforting us in all our trials, fears, and needs. The hymn is appropriate for Trinity Sunday and general use. You may wish to read it in unison or responsively before singing it.

86   Mountains Are All Aglow

A hymn of thanksgiving for harvest, this text from Korea asserts that all blessings are from God who deserves all our praise and thanks. The last stanza probes deeply as the poet allegorically shows confidence in God's promise that in the planting of God's words, even in a barren heart, we still may expect seedlings to grow and bloom. Triple rhythm and syncopations ("is from our God") are typical of Korean folk styles, and Koreans find special excitement in singing it. Add drum (changgo) accompaniment to enliven the spirit of praise.

87   What Gift Can We Bring

Jane Marshall combines her gifts of poetry and music in this hymn written for the twenty-fifth anniversary of Northhaven United Methodist Church in Dallas, Texas. The hymn has a wider theme of thankful giving as it expresses thanks for the past, the now, tomorrow, and the present which we offer in joyful praise. The hymn would be useful for other church anniversary services emphasizing the themes of thankfulness and giving. A soloist may sing the first stanza (especially if the tune is unfamiliar), with the congregation singing the remaining stanzas. The hymn should be sung in unison with a full supporting accompaniment.

88 *Maker, in Whom We Live*

Demonstrating the trinitarian essence of Wesleyan praise in general, Charles Wesley originally titled this hymn "To the Trinity." The distribution of address in the first three stanzas sketches the panorama of trinitarian history—grounded in creation (Acts 17:28 and Lk. 2:14), centered in Christ (Rev. 7:10), carried forward by the Spirit (Tit. 3:5)—rising finally to the communal adoration of stanza 4. A natural choice for Trinity Sunday, the hymn is favorably set to the majestic tune DIADEMATA, whose soaring tune complements the rise and fall of the poetic line.

89 *Joyful, Joyful, We Adore Thee*

Henry van Dyke, a Presbyterian minister, writer, and diplomat, wrote this powerful text which combines three themes: the work of God seen in nature, the love of God seen in God's giving and forgiving, and the joy of love for one another to which God calls us. These themes are combined in the final stanza with the words: "Mortals join the mighty chorus, which the morning stars began." The tune HYMN TO JOY, derived from the finale of Beethoven's Ninth Symphony, adds an exultant mood to the joyful text. Note Beethoven's original syncopation at the beginning of the fourth line.

90 *Ye Watchers and Ye Holy Ones*

This exuberant hymn by Athelstan Riley calls the whole company of heaven and earth to praise God in mighty chorus. First, the orders of angels are invited, then Mary ("Thou bearer of th' eternal Word"), and finally, the souls at rest—patriarchs, prophets, apostles, martyrs, and all saints join with us concluding in a Doxology to the Trinity. Set with the soaring tune LASST UNS ERFREUEN and its resounding Alleluias, the hymn is a magnificent statement of faith. The Alleluias may be sung in four-part harmony.

91 *Canticle of Praise to God* (Venite Exultemus)

Venite Exultemus (Latin for "come let us praise") is a scripture song combining portions of Ps. 95 and 96, which praise God as creator, sustainer, sovereign, and judge. From early Church times to the present, this canticle has been widely used in daily worship and is most appropriately and traditionally used in Morning Praise and Prayer. The optional concluding praise to the Holy Trinity *(Gloria Patri)* also affirms the Church's claim to Hebrew scripture as its own expression of faith and praise to God. Anglican chant is a series of chords used to support a particular text. Several words may be sung to one chord, in which case the natural rhythm and syllable accents direct the flow of the music. Rehearse the congregation by speaking the text in unison, then practicing the tones on a neutral vowel, and finally combining words and music.

92 *For the Beauty of the Earth*

This litany of thanksgiving by Folliot Pierpoint was inspired by the beauty of the English countryside along the Avon River near Bath. The six stanzas of this litany enumerate the many joys of life—God's love, nature, senses, human love, the Church, and Jesus. The author's original refrain, "This our sacrifice of praise," from the communion service, is provided for optional use when this text is sung as a communion hymn. The hymn also may be sung responsively, with different stanzas sung by children, youth, women, and men, and the congregation joining at the refrain.

93 *Let All the World in Every Corner Sing*

On his deathbed in 1632 the great English poet George Herbert handed one final manuscript to his lawyer for possible publication. In that collection was this poem "Antiphon," so named because the antiphon, or refrain, appears at the beginning and end of the two stanzas. Erik Routley's tune AUGUSTINE uniquely expresses the call-and-response pattern of Herbert's poem by placing the antiphon consistent with the form of the text.

94 *Praise God, from Whom All Blessings Flow*

In this adaptation by Gilbert Vieira of Thomas Ken's famous Doxology (st. 14 of his hymn "Awake, My Soul, and with the Sun"), the first two lines are familiar and the remaining lines express praise to God in alternative and inclusive descriptions and forms of address. This is a long meter Doxology that can be sung to any tune marked LM (*see* Appendix 5). Set to the German tune LASST UNS ERFREUEN, however, it takes on added excitement and exuberance because of the interpolated Alleluias, which may be sung antiphonally.

95 *Praise God, from Whom All Blessings Flow*

Although this is commonly called the Doxology, there are in fact many Doxologies or expressions of praise to God. They are found in the Book of Psalms and elsewhere in the Old Testament. Trinitarian language appears in the late third century when the doctrine of the Trinity was in dispute. A doxological stanza was added to office hymns, and this practice was carried over into English hymnic tradition. This Doxology by Bishop Thomas Ken was originally the closing or doxological stanza for each of the three hymns he wrote for the scholars at Winchester College in England to sing every morning, noon, and night; the last of these is 682 in our hymnal. This is the Doxology most widely sung by American Protestants and is used in churches around the world. The sixteenth-century tune OLD 100TH was so named because it was used for a setting of Ps. 100, found at 75 in this hymnal.

96 *Praise the Lord Who Reigns Above*

A celebration of the eternal in and through the temporal, this hymn by Charles Wesley is based on Ps. 150. By doing the very thing it exhorts us to do—Praise!—the hymn is a beautiful example of how form and content entwine in the act of worship. With the lively tune AMSTERDAM, a favorite of John Wesley's, it is suitable for general use and especially fitting at the dedication of choirs and musical instruments.

97 *For the Fruits of This Creation*

This harvest hymn, originally entitled "For the Fruits of His Creation," is a song of joyful praise. Fred Pratt Green wrote this joyful harvest text to fit the tune EAST ACKLAM. The hymn to date has been included in fourteen hymnbooks. By stressing our responsibility to share our abundance with others—"the help we give our neighbor" and "our worldwide task of caring"—the hymn gives new meaning to Thanksgiving.

98 *To God Be the Glory*

This hymn has had great popularity both in Britain and in the United States. It is one of the five most requested "new" hymns to be included in the new hymnal. Fanny Crosby's words tell of the love of God through Jesus Christ; each stanza lists the "great things he hath done." William Doane's tune with its jubilant chorus invites all to rejoice and glorify God. If available, use both piano and organ, with the piano providing embellishment on the long notes. Divide the refrain between men and women with all singing "great things he hath done."

99 *My Tribute*

Andraé Crouch's refrain from his gospel song "My Tribute" makes for an effective prayer response. On special occasions, it works well as an introit or as an offertory response. It usually is sung very slow, the singer holding the right hand high, index finger pointed up, and swaying in a left to right "praising" motion on beats 1 and 3.

100 *God, Whose Love Is Reigning O'er Us*

This hymn of praise by Bishop William Boyd Grove of The United Methodist Church begins by proclaiming God as the source of all things. The second stanza recalls Abram's faith in offering Isaac as a sacrifice and Sarah's story as she bore a child when she was ninety. After remembering God's covenant to Abraham and Sarah, the third stanza speaks of the new covenant with Jesus, "Star-child born to set us free," leading to the final stanza which is a joyful exultation. John Goss's tune LAUDA ANIMA was written in 1869 for the hymn "Praise, My Soul, the King of Heaven." Let all sing the first stanza, a small group sing the second and third, everyone join at the "Alleluia," and full congregation and choirs on the fourth.

101 *From All That Dwell Below the Skies*

The first two stanzas of this hymn of praise are Isaac Watts's paraphrase of Ps. 117, while the last two stanzas are from an anonymous source. In his text Watts loosely paraphrased the following words: "O Praise the Lord, all ye nations: praise him, all ye people. For his merciful kindness is great toward us: and the truth of the Lord endureth forever. Praise the Lord." Watts casts the text into a rhyming metrical form.

102 *Now Thank We All Our God*

This seventeenth-century text by Martin Rinkart, translated by Catherine Winkworth, is one of our greatest and most popular hymns of thanksgiving for God's care and guidance. Written as a table grace, stanza 1 tells of how God has provided for us from our mother's arms to the present. Stanza 2 is a prayer for safekeeping and guidance, while the concluding stanza is a Doxology. The stately tune NUN DANKET is easily learned and appropriate as a hymn of praise throughout the Christian year.

103   *Immortal, Invisible, God Only Wise*

The text is based on 1 Tim. 1:17—"To the King of ages, immortal, invisible, the only God, be honor and glory for ever and ever." The poet, a minister of the Free Church of Scotland, uses the "light" to describe the invisible nature of God. The splendor of God's glory makes it impossible for mortals to see God's full greatness. The AABA form of the tune uses the first phrase three times, making this a very singable hymn for most congregations.

104   *Praising God of Many Names*

If we are dull and unimaginative in the forms of address to God, this prayer, written some seven centuries ago by a laywoman who took a vow of poverty, provides new options.

105   *God of Many Names*

God is a holy mystery, at the same time wonderful and awesome to contemplate. In this provocative text Brian Wren names God as Creator, as one who enters history particularly as God incarnate in Jesus Christ. Combining both prayer and praise, the text contains rich images appropriate for both singing and reflection. William P. Rowan's tune, composed as a carol, contrasts the stanzas and the refrain. Try giving the stanzas to solo voices singing in an almost ad-lib style, with the congregation singing the dancelike refrain.

Martin Luther King, Jr., wrote these words in a sermon preached at Dexter Avenue Baptist Church in Montgomery, Alabama, and at Ebenezer Baptist Church in Atlanta, Georgia. Laurence Hull Stookey, member of the Hymnal Revision Committee, constructed this litany for the hymnal from a sermon in King's book *Strength to Love*. Based on The Letter of Jude, vs. 24, King declares that God is able to do all things, to heal individuals, and to eliminate poverty, racism, and war.

107 *La Palabra Del Señor Es Recta* **(Righteous and Just Is the Word of the Lord)**

From Cuba comes this psalm, in folk-dance style, praising God's mighty works of creation and resolve to establish a just society. The interesting rhythm (3 against 2) is a style from Cuba called "Punto Guajiro." It provides the characteristic syncopated charm of much Latin-American music as does the tune's shift from minor to major and back to minor. Introduce this hymn by teaching the refrain to the congregation and asking the choir to sing the stanzas, either in English or Spanish or both.

108 *God Hath Spoken by the Prophets*

George W. Briggs, an Anglican priest and educator, published a number of books of hymns and prayers for children and was one of the founders of the Hymn Society of Great Britain and Ireland. This text first appeared in *Ten New Hymns on the Bible*, published in 1952 by the Hymn Society of America to celebrate the publication of the Revised Standard Version of the Bible. The tune, EBENEZER, by Thomas J. Williams, became very popular in Wales. For many years the tune was named TON-Y-BOTEL ("tune in the bottle"). This hymn is well suited for use either before or after the reading of scripture in worship. Sing the stanzas with strength and vigor but not too fast.

Creator, Sustainer, Redeemer, and Indweller are four attributes of God addressed in Bishop Rowthorn's powerful hymn. To praise the Creator, the author calls on sun, moon, stars, light, and "what lies hidden." God the Sustainer tenderly holds the mysteries of the earth. God the Redeemer embraces those rejected for creed or race and is made known where there is peace on earth. The shape note tune KEDRON, named for the Kidron valley running between Jerusalem and the Mount of Olives, was popular in nineteenth-century singing schools. It may be sung in unison with keyboard accompaniment or in canon (entering on the third beat of the second full measure) without accompaniment. On one or two of the stanzas men can sing a monotone C repeating the first two words of the stanzas.

110 *A Mighty Fortress Is Our God*

This is one of the ten most sung hymns in The United Methodist Church. Based on Ps. 46, this magnificent hymn expresses the struggle of good against evil, describing God, as our "fortress," "bulwark," and "helper." Sometimes called "the battle hymn of the Reformation," it combines Luther's skills as theologian, preacher, poet, and musician. Providing the people with the Bible, a catechism, and a hymnal in their own language was a common thread of the Evangelical reform movements of the fifteenth and sixteenth centuries, usually called the Reformation. What is unique about the contribution of Luther is his continuing influence in church music, liturgy, and theology for nearly five centuries.

111 *How Can We Name a Love*

God's infinite presence is so vast that it is difficult to communicate our thoughts about God. Brian Wren prompts us to see God in the faces around us and to think about God's constant care and love given us at birth. That is what God is like. It's setting to the tune TERRA BEATA ("This Is My Father's World") subtly furthers the expression of assurance and care.

112 Canticle of Wisdom

A prayer from the Apocrypha for the bestowing of wisdom, this text is attributed to King Solomon, who was often called the father of wisdom. The text echoes the pleas for wisdom found in Job, Psalms, Proverbs, and Ecclesiastes. The wisdom that comes from God is indeed "better than rubies; and all the things that may be desired are not to be compared to it" (Pr. 8:11, KJV). The Advent response "O Come, thou Wisdom from on high" is our constant prayer, for God's wisdom alone gives order to our lives. The canticle is particularly appropriate for Advent, Sunday School promotions, and installation of Sunday School teachers or other church officials.

113 Source and Sovereign, Rock and Cloud

This hymn, commissioned for *The United Methodist Hymnal*, contains thirty-nine names, descriptions, or metaphors for God. The author seems at first glance to have randomly compiled a list of names and attributes of Deity. However, on closer examination we see that he has carefully structured each stanza to conclude with a summary sentence that points to the Trinity. The refrain reminds us that no one single name is adequate to describe God, for God is more than one name, more than all these names. God is infinite. This powerful new text may be best introduced with the choir singing the stanzas and the congregation the refrain.

114 Many Gifts, One Spirit

This hymn rejoices in the rich diversity of gifts that God provides us. It also reminds us that there is but one Lord, one Spirit, and one Word, which through our gifts may be perceived in a variety of ways. Written in the style of a unison folk song with refrain, it is best accompanied by piano or guitar. First teach the refrain, then the stanzas.

115 *How Like a Gentle Spirit*

Who is God? What is God like? Our answer, couched in terms of human knowledge and Christian experience, is that God is love and that love is not narrow or meager or limited because God is without limits. The tune SURSUM CORDA provides a chantlike quality which gently carries the text. It may be taught by a soloist lining out each phrase, which is then repeated by the congregation.

116 *The God of Abraham Praise*

Based on the Jewish Yigdal, or Doxology, which expresses the thirteen articles of the Jewish creed (codified by Jewish scholar Maimonides, 1130–1205), this majestic text exemplifies concepts found in Hebrew Scripture, such as, "Jehovah, great I AM," "Holy, Holy, Holy," and "Almighty King." The tune LEONI is named for Meyer Lyon (Leoni), who arranged it from an old Hebrew melody. It is distinctive for its minor mode and its ascending line. The hymn reminds Christians of our linkage through Christ to Hebrew Scripture and our common heritage with our Jewish brothers and sisters. The text is restored here to those versions used in most Methodist hymnals from 1785 to 1935.

117 *O God, Our Help in Ages Past*

The greatness of God, the mortality of humanity, and the vastness of time are the main thrusts of this text based on Ps. 90. God was present before the hills stood; God has been our shelter and guide, and continues to be our hope for the future. Wedded to the stately tune ST. ANNE, this is among our finest general hymns of praise, but it is especially appropriate for times of remembrance and dedication.

118 *The Care the Eagle Gives Her Young*

The poet R. Deane Postlethwaithe, a United Methodist minister, uses an image from Dt. 32:11 and provides us with a loving picture of God who cares for us, tends us, challenges us to fly and grow, yet catches us when we fall. It is set to the only Scottish psalm tune attributed to a woman—Jesse Seymour Irvine. The tune gently carries the text, creating a hymn reminiscent of a lullaby. Try singing it with alternating voices singing lines 1–2 and 3–4.

119   O God in Heaven

Appropriate as an opening for worship, the three stanzas of this text are prayers to the persons of the Trinity, the one God we gather to worship: (1) God in heaven, for mercy, blessing, and unity; (2) Jesus, for our remembrance of his passion, resurrection, and redemption; (3) the Holy Spirit, for strength and help. The Filipino flavor of the melody enhances the beauty of this hymn.

120   Your Love, O God

This popular contemporary hymn from Sweden is already known to the many United Methodists who have sung it in *Supplement to the Book of Hymns* (1982). Anders Frostenson's text, translated by Fred Kaan, expresses God's unrestricted love in contrast to our own, which is often narrow and confining. Begin by teaching the refrain. Have a soloist sing stanza 1, then have everyone sing both the refrain and the remaining stanzas. It works well with guitar or Orff instruments. Stanzas 1 and 4 make a fine response of affirmation.

121   There's a Wideness in God's Mercy

Faber's text depicts the vastness of God's mercy, reflecting the influence of other Evangelical writers such as Cowper, Newton, and the Wesleys. In describing God, the poet uses everyday words, such as *mercy, kindness, justice, welcome,* and *healing,* and equates God's mercy to the wideness of the sea. Feel the melody in a stately two counts per measure, but do not rush the graceful eighth notes. The final stanza may be sung softly as a prayer of both confession and calm assurance.

122 *God of the Sparrow God of the Whale*

A profound theological statement in disarmingly simple words and tune. All of the images are biblical, but repeated reading and singing will uncover layers of meanings beneath the obvious symbols. The theme is "Thankful to Serve." The author, Lutheran pastor-theologian-poet Jaroslav J. Vajda, has written: "The text is meant to provoke answers from the users of the hymn as to why and how God's creatures (and children) are to serve him." Composed for this text, Carl Schalk's tune ROEDER weaves Vajda's series of statements and questions together with beauty and simplicity.

123 *El Shaddai*

This scripture song made popular by recording artist Amy Grant praises the eternal God. The Hebrew words *El Shaddai* mean "God Almighty"; *El Elyon*, "The Most High God"; *Adonai*, "Lord"; *Erkahmka*, "We will love you."

124 *Seek the Lord*

This paraphrase of the Second Song of Isaiah (Is. 55:6-11; *see* 125) by Fred Pratt Green is a succinct expression of Isaiah's views of God: (1) God as present and ready to forgive those who cease sinning and return to God (Is. 55:6-7). (2) God's own self-understanding, which is not to be judged by human standards, for God's ways and thoughts are not fully comprehensible; and God's faithful Word even in an unfaithful world (Is. 55:8-11). (3) God as love, forgiving and caring. This text was commissioned by the Hymnal Committee and is set to the tune GENEVA by George Henry Day. It is appropriate for Lent, Easter Vigil, services of commitment and dedication, the Love Feast, and Morning and Evening Praise and Prayer.

125 *Canticle of Covenant Faithfulness* (Quaerite Dominum)

Isaiah's threefold call to repentance proclaims that the time of salvation is at hand, that we should return to the Lord who is ready to forgive, and that repentance is necessary for entrance into God's kingdom. Isaiah's song is the Church's song to the world in every age and is appropriate for Lenten and Easter Vigil services and general use.

126 *Sing Praise to God Who Reigns Above*

Dt. 32:3: "For I will proclaim the name of the Lord. Ascribe greatness to our God!" is the basis for this seventeenth-century hymn. The poet extols God's goodness, power, love, salvation, healing, and faithfulness. We are called to praise God even though our way is toilsome and difficult. The sturdy tune MIT FREUDEN ZART may be new to your congregation and may be introduced using a call-and-response pattern (lining out).

127 *Guide Me, O Thou Great Jehovah*

Written during the great Welsh Revival of the eighteenth century, this hymn draws its images totally from the Bible as it compares the pilgrimage through life to the wandering of the Israelites through the wilderness: "Bread of Heaven" (manna), "crystal fountain" (water from the rock), "fire and cloudy pillar" (God's guide to the Israelites), "Jordan" (death), and "Canaan's side" (the heavenly reward). John Hughes's strong Welsh tune CWM RHONDDA enhances the strength and majesty of the text. This hymn is ideal as either an opening hymn of praise or closing hymn of sending forth. Teach altos and basses to sing the small notes in measure 12, then have everyone take a breath before singing the final two measures. It will become a tradition in your church!

128 He Leadeth Me: O Blessed Thought

Joseph Gilmore was inspired to write this hymn after lecturing on Ps. 23. The contemplative text, though not a paraphrase, does effectively draw on images from the psalm text, particularly God's leadership in life's journey. William B. Bradbury composed the tune and added the popular refrain.

129 Give to the Winds Thy Fears

John Wesley's 1739 translation of Paul Gerhardt's hymn first appeared under the title "Trust in Providence. From the German." The text is based on Ps. 37:5—"Commit thy way unto the Lord; trust also in him; and he shall bring it to pass" (KJV). The hymn also employs various biblical images of chaos (wind, waves, storm, night), recalling the Moravians' sense of assurance which so impressed Wesley as he sailed with them on the stormy voyage to Georgia in 1735. The message of the hymn is complemented by the familiar tune FESTAL SONG.

130 God Will Take Care of You

This hymn was written by Civilla D. Martin on a Sunday afternoon in 1904 while she was confined to a sickbed. Her husband W. Stillman Martin, when he returned from a preaching assignment, sat down at a pump organ and composed the tune appropriately called MARTIN. A hymn of comfort, it is useful in a variety of settings, including groups of older adults and others bearing burdens of illness and hardship.

131 We Gather Together

This Netherlands folk hymn from the sixteenth century celebrates Dutch independence from Spain as is evidenced in the phrases: "The wicked oppressing," "So from the beginning the fight we were winning," and the final phrase, "O Lord, make us free." In the United States the hymn has long been associated with the national holiday of Thanksgiving, but it is also sung appropriately at services dealing with God's leadership through difficult times or as a general hymn of praise.

132 *All My Hope Is Firmly Grounded*

This is a hymn of praise to the Creator and Sustainer of all creation: God, never-failing, constantly good, just, and caring. Written by Joachim Neander, a seventeenth-century pietistic German pastor and hymn writer, it appears here in a new translation by Fred Pratt Green, set to a beautiful tune by the twentieth-century British composer Herbert Howells. The final reference to "feeding" makes the hymn appropriate for Holy Communion as well as for general use.

133 *Leaning on the Everlasting Arms*

Consoling two friends who had recently lost their wives, A. J. Showalter quoted a scripture passage in his letters to them: "The eternal God is thy refuge, and underneath are the everlasting arms" (Dt. 33:27, KJV). He later wrote the music and words of the refrain, his friend Elisha A. Hoffman supplying the three stanzas. Depending on the mood of the service this hymn may be sung either at an upbeat tempo or at a slower swinglike tempo relaxing the rhythmic pulse and note values.

134 *O Mary, Don't You Weep*

This Afro-American spiritual of deliverance refers to Pharaoh's defeat as described in Ex. 14:28. It was popular near the end of the Civil War as a proclamation of freedom with a double meaning— one for the ears of slave owner and the other meant for the slaves. The "masked" message of release is a proclamation of freedom to "Mary"—Motherland Africa. We see in Mary (which in Hebrew is Miriam) both Miriam in Ex. 15:20-21 and Mary Magdalene in Jn. 20:11-18. Jesus' death and resurrection was a second Exodus, in which the powers of sin and death, like Pharaoh's army, were destroyed. Finally, Mary is each of us upon hearing or recalling the good news that God can deliver us from every form of slavery. Clapping on beats 2 and 4 will establish the style and rhythm. Piano, organ, or guitar may be used.

135   *The Canticle of Moses and Miriam* (Cantemus Domino)

In this scripture song, what is traditionally known as the Song of Moses (Ex. 15:1-18) and including the Song of Miriam (Ex. 15:21), is considered by some scholars to be the oldest poem in the Bible. Like many of the psalms, this canticle celebrates God's action in shaping history. It is a hymn of praise for Israel's deliverance from the Pharaoh and Egyptian bondage and is particularly appropriate after an Old Testament reading, for the Easter Vigil, and for the Easter season is general.

136   *The Lord's My Shepherd, I'll Not Want*

The anonymous writer of this metrical paraphrase from the 1650 *Scottish Psalter* has created beautiful poetry while adhering to the words of Ps. 23 (KJV). The tune CRIMOND, named after a village in northeast Scotland, greatly enhances the text. This hymn gained additional popularity when it was sung in 1947 at the wedding of Princess Elizabeth and Prince Philip, Duke of Edinburgh.

137   *Psalm 23* (King James Version)

This is the popular paraphrase of Ps. 23 (KJV) beloved for its continuity of thought, for vivid imagery (shepherd, pastures, paths, valley, table, God's house), and for expressing the personal nature of our relationship with God. The text conveys serenity and peace of mind rooted in an unswerving trust in God.

138   *The King of Love My Shepherd Is*

This popular nineteenth-century psalm paraphrase combines Ps. 23 with Christian references to "living water" (Jn. 4:10-11), "thy cross," "chalice," "grace," and "good shepherd" (Jn. 10:11), the parable of the lost sheep (st. 3) and the Lord's Supper (st. 5). Often sung at Holy Communion, the hymn may also be used when the psalm is suggested by the lectionary. Have the choir sing one or two of the six stanzas a cappella.

139   *Praise to the Lord, the Almighty*

One of Joachim Neander's sixty hymns, this great hymn of praise, translated by Catherine Winkworth, is based loosely on Ps. 103:1-6 and 150. Stanza 4 uses the powerful image from Dt. 32:11 of God as a mother eagle. This majestic tune sung with one pulse per measure demands strong instrumental support. Children can effectively help accompany the opening and closing stanzas using Orff instruments, accentuating the first beat of each measure.

140   *Great Is Thy Faithfulness*

Of all the hymns in *The Hymnal* of the Evangelical United Brethren Church that were not in *The Methodist Hymnal*, this was the one most often requested for inclusion in *The United Methodist Hymnal*. The theme of this text comes from Lam. 3:22-23: "The steadfast love of the Lord never ceases, his mercies never come to an end; they are new every morning; great is thy faithfulness." The tune FAITHFULNESS begins reverently, swelling with intensity and emotion in the refrain.

141   *Children of the Heavenly Father*

Caroline V. Sandell-Berg, often called the Swedish Fanny Crosby, began writing hymns after her father's drowning in 1858. This text is an affirmation of God's safekeeping in times of distress. The Swedish folk tune TRYGGARE KAN INGEN VARA (meaning "no one can be safer") has a long association with this text. The hymn is appropriate for children as they learn of God's love, and it also provides comfort at funerals and memorial services.

142 *If Thou But Suffer God to Guide Thee*

Though the Thirty Years' War (1618-1648) was for most of middle Europe a time of devastation, pestilence, and death, in Germany it was also a time of spiritual awakening and renewal as expressed in the writing of a number of great pietistic hymns. Many of these hymns greatly influenced John and Charles Wesley. In this hymn, God is our hope and strength; we are called to patience and waiting in God's time, to "sing, pray and keep God's way unswerving," echoing Ps. 55:22: "Cast your burden on the Lord." The archaic word "suffer" means "let" or "permit." A hymn of consolation and trust in God's care, it is particularly appropriate for use at funerals and memorial services.

143 *You Who Dwell in the Shelter of Our God*

This hymn by Roman Catholic hymn writer Michael Joncas evokes several biblical images of the providence and care of God. Drawing from the Psalms, God is a "shelter," a "shadow" (Ps. 91:1), and as in Ps. 94:22, "my God is the rock of my refuge." The refrain is based on Is. 40:31 and is the source for the tune name, ON EAGLE'S WINGS. Guitar accompaniment may be used effectively in place of keyboard. The refrain makes an excellent response to Ps. 91.

144 *This Is My Father's World*

Maltbie D. Babcock's frequent walks through the hills near his home inspired this hymn. Babcock saw God in elements of nature, such as rocks, trees, skies, seas, birds, light, flowers, and rustling grass. The text proclaims God as "the music of the spheres," the order and harmony of the universe. The hymn has enough depth for believers of all ages.

145 *Morning Has Broken*

Praising God for a new day and seeing behind today's sunrise to the first sunrise at creation is emphasized in this hymn made popular by Cat Stevens in the 1970s. "Springing fresh from the Word" recalls the accounts of creation in Gen. 1 and Jn. 1. Every morning reminds us of the first morning, and we rejoice that God recreates each new day. Congregations should note that the word "recreation" in the last line of the hymn refers to God's re-creating the world and should be pronounced "*re*-creation," not "recreation." The sweeping melody should be felt with one strong beat to the measure and sung in unison.

146 *At the Birth of a Child*

This act is intended for a service of worship when the birth of a child is announced. It normally would be used the Sunday after the birth takes place, rather than when the infant is presented for Baptism. The name of the child (or children) is to be inserted in the first sentence, and the names of the parents and the birth date may be added when this is not obvious from previous announcement. For example: ". . . a child, Elaine Ann, was born [on June 18th to Audrey and Joseph Trantz]. Rejoice. . . . " This act is adapted from rituals of African peoples, the Massai and the Akamba.

147 *All Things Bright and Beautiful*

Cecil Frances Alexander wrote poems for children that were paraphrases of articles in the Apostles' Creed. This text is based on article 2, "maker of heaven and earth." The English folk tune ROYAL OAK adds to the poem's simplicity and poetic beauty. Have a children's choir sing the stanzas with the congregation joining on the refrain. The hymn may also be used for services dealing with the environment and ecology.

148 *Many and Great*

This Dakota hymn from the *Dakota Odowan* (the Dakota Hymn Book) of the Northern Mississippi Valley is widely known and sung in the United States. YWCA groups in the first two decades of the twentieth century sang this hymn in the original language. The first and last stanzas were translated into English in 1929. The choir may introduce the hymn by singing the first stanza alone and adding the congregation on the second stanza.

149 *Cantemos al Señor* (Let's Sing unto the Lord)

Taken from the mass *Rosas Del Tepeyac* by Carlos Rosas, this exuberant hymn of praise based on Ps. 19 celebrates God's gifts of creation. Rosas directs the Mexican-American Cultural Center in San Antonio, Texas, a Roman Catholic institution devoted to new Hispanic contributions in music and liturgy. "Cantemos al Señor" is an appropriate processional hymn and may be accompanied with guitar, maracas or other rhythm instruments, and hand clapping.

150 *God, Who Stretched the Spangled Heavens*

Catherine Cameron's prayer to the Creator God is about God's creative powers shared with humankind. But it reminds us of our neglect of the lonely ones of our cities and warns us that, as the atom's secrets are probed, we have the choice of life's destruction or "our most triumphant hour." William Moore's lively tune HOLY MANNA is typical of the early nineteenth-century shape note tunes. It may be taught by first having the congregation sing it using *la* to familiarize them with the ABAA melody, then adding the text.

151 *God Created Heaven and Earth*

This popular Taiwanese hymn, whose text is based on Gen. 1:1-5 and whose tune is based on a traditional tribal melody, praises the great and merciful God for creating all things and providing for all our needs. It is also a witness and statement of faith to non-Christians, affirming the existence of only one true God. A flute doubling the melody will enhance the beauty of this hymn.

152 *I Sing the Almighty Power of God*

Isaac Watts, the "father of English hymnody," wrote some of the first hymns for children. This text is a colorful vision of the wonders of creation, expressed in a language meaningful to both children and adults. The text as it expresses God's power, wisdom, and goodness is also a succinct theological statement about God's nature. The English folk tune FOREST GREEN, harmonized by Ralph Vaughan Williams, is beautifully suited to the text and with its repetitive AABA form is easily learned.

153 *Thou Hidden Source of Calm Repose*

In fine Wesleyan fashion, this hymn revels in celebrating the "saving name" of Jesus through a succession of biblical images describing his presence and power. It appeared among the hymns "For Believers Rejoicing" in John Wesley's 1780 *Collection*, where it signified the overflowing of praise that occurs when Jesus' true identity is unveiled, even in the midst of suffering. The paradox of Christian joy and peace strangely resonates through the old Russian tune ST. PETERSBURG. After all sing stanza 1, have a small group or men alone sing stanza 2. Stanzas 3 and 4 should be sung by all as they are poetically linked together.

154, 155 *All Hail the Power of Jesus' Name*

Edward Perronet, who was an associate of the Wesleys, wrote this hymn which is a grand statement of praise inspired by Rev. 19:12 and 16. The text is set to two tunes: CORONATION by Oliver Holden, one of America's earliest tune writers, and DIADEM by James Ellor, an English hatter. The latter is a good example of a nineteenth-century "florid Methodist tune." This is one of the ten hymns most sung by United Methodists, and both tunes are widely used.

156 *I Love to Tell the Story*

During a long illness Katherine Hankey wrote an extensive poem about the life of Christ. At the end of the poem appear the words of the hymn "I Love to Tell the Story," which sum up her faith in Christ. She organized and taught Sunday School classes in London, wrote books of Bible lessons for Sunday School teachers, and supported foreign mission efforts. This is one of the ten most frequently used hymns in The United Methodist Church.

157 Jesus Shall Reign

This text based on Ps. 72 describes God's all-encompassing reign: God's kingdom spreads from shore to shore and lasts as long as the moon (Creation); people of all tongues are praising God. Because of its grand vision of the earth under Jesus' reign, it is considered to be one of our greatest mission hymns. Set to the sturdy tune DUKE STREET it may be used as an opening hymn of praise.

158 Come, Christians, Join to Sing

The original opening line of this children's Sunday School song, "Come, children, join to sing," was later altered to make the text inclusive of all ages. The simple and straightforward text can be sung in a call-and-response pattern, the "Alleluia! Amen!" phrases sung by the congregation while the other phrases are sung by the choir.

159 Lift High the Cross

The text by George William Kitchin and Michael Robert Newbolt exhorts Christians to lift up the cross as a symbol of the love of Jesus. The cross represents Christ's willingness to complete his redemptive role, even to his death. As a symbol of his sacrificial life, the cross challenges every believer to live a Christlike life. The strength of the text is complemented by the strength of its tune CRUCIFER, by Sydney Nicholson. A crucifer is one who carries a cross in church processions. This hymn is excellent for processing and recessing.

160, 161 *Rejoice, Ye Pure in Heart*

The text by Edward Plumptre relates to several scripture passages: Ps. 20:4, Ps. 147:1 and Phil. 4:4. The Philippians passage with Paul's exhortation to "Rejoice . . . , and again I say, Rejoice" (KJV), provides the theme for the hymn as Christians rejoice in the present, in the future, and in the life to come. The refrain with its exuberant command to rejoice offers several possibilities for antiphonal singing. The traditional tune for the hymn is MARION. The new tune, VINEYARD HAVEN, by Richard W. Dirksen, is widely acclaimed as one of the finest hymn tunes of our day.

162 *Alleluia, Alleluia!*

Donald Fishel's text in praise of Jesus Christ is set to a simple flowing melody. It acknowledges Jesus as our resurrected Lord, and we who "have been crucified with Christ" hear the promise of eternal life. The joyful refrain intertwines repeated Alleluias with brief phrases of thanksgiving and praise to the risen Lord. Have youth or a small choir sing the stanzas with all joining at the refrain.

163 *Ask Ye What Great Thing I Know*

This text is based on two statements of Paul's: 1 Cor. 2:2 ("For I decided to know nothing among you except Jesus Christ and him crucified") and Gal. 6:14 ("But far be it from me to glory except in the cross of our Lord Jesus Christ") set in a series of questions. The questions are answered by the words: "Jesus Christ, the crucified." The hymn easily lends itself to responsive singing, with the congregation singing the final phrase after the choir or soloist asks the questions. Choir and congregation should join together on the last stanza.

164 *Come, My Way, My Truth, My Life*

"The Call" by George Herbert was written as a devotional poem nearly two hundred years before hymn singing was permitted in the Church of England. Each stanza begins with key words, each of which is developed in a separate line of poetry. All of the words are descriptive of Christ (*see* Jn. 14:6) and make a moving prayer, calling on the Savior to enter our lives. This expressive tune by Ralph Vaughan Williams, originally a vocal solo, has been included in many recent hymnals. It may be sung as a call to prayer, response to a sermon, or during Communion. Have a soloist sing stanza 1 and all sing stanzas 2 and 3.

165   *Hallelujah! What a Savior*

This hymn by Philip P. Bliss takes its first line from Is. 53:3. In it Bliss describes the pain and humiliation Christ suffered for the sake of humanity but ends each stanza with a triumphant "Hallelujah! What a Savior!" This hymn in praise of Christ is typical of nineteenth-century gospel hymns sung at camp meetings: the slow beginning suddenly changes at the end when we proclaim, "Hallelujah! What a Savior!"

166   *All Praise to Thee, for Thou, O King Divine*

This hymn, based on Phil. 2:5-11, exhorts God's light to come into our darkened hearts and Christ's lowliness and salvation to enter through his death. The hymn is a call to fulfill Paul's request: "Fulfill my joy, that you be likeminded, having the same love, being of one accord, of one mind" (Phil. 2:2). The combination of this text with Ralph Vaughan Williams's tune SINE NOMINE, the author's own preference, is excellent, for the concluding Alleluias in each stanza affirm the Christian's ecstatic confession that Jesus Christ is Lord. Use it as a processional or recessional hymn.

167   *Canticle of Christ's Obedience*

Phil. 2:5-11 is one of the earliest hymns of the Christian church. Hymns 166 and 168 are based on this same scripture song. Paul calls to the Christians in Philippi to rise above their differences and have the mind of Christ. He presents two pictures of Christ: (1) in his original glory and (2) as he submitted himself in complete obedience to God's will and died on the cross in shame and rejection. The hymn is a call for our full surrender of self and possessions to God in humble obedience if we desire the mind of Christ. The hymn is appropriate for Lent, Holy Week, and services of commitment and dedication.

168   *At the Name of Jesus*

This hymn, based on Phil. 2:5-11 was first published in seven stanzas (*see* "Canticle of Christ's Obedience," 167). The text vividly portrays the contrast between Christ's exalted state and his suffering in his incarnation and passion. KING'S WESTON, a majestic tune of freshness and originality, was composed by Ralph Vaughan Williams in 1925 for this text. This is a good processional hymn, especially during the Easter season and when celebrating Christ's ascension.

169   *In Thee Is Gladness*

The text is by sixteenth-century German cantor Johann Lindemann, and the tune is by Italian priest-composer Giovanni Giacomo Gastoldi of the same century. The theme is gladness in the New Year, even in the midst of sadness. The exuberance of the text is perfectly matched by the lighthearted dancelike quality of the tune. Most appropriate for the first Sunday in January, it could well be coupled with Bach's famous chorale prelude based on this tune.

170   *O How I Love Jesus*

This U.S.A. folk tune, of unknown origin, typifies the musical style of early nineteenth-century campmeetings. The refrain was often sung with familiar common meter hymns such as "Amazing Grace!" A hymn of childlike trust, praise, and adoration, the simplicity of tune and repetition of text make it accessible for all congregations.

171 There's Something About That Name

This gentle, soothing tune and text by Bill and Gloria Gaither praises the name of Jesus with the reassurance that his name has given hope to believers through the ages in spite of the rise and fall of leaders and governments. It is a fitting congregational act of praise or prayer response.

172 My Jesus, I Love Thee

William R. Featherstone wrote this text at the age of sixteen. The text is a renunciation of sin in order to follow Jesus and states that "We love, because he first loved us" (1 Jn. 4:19). The tune GORDON was composed for this text by the Boston pastor Adoniram Judson Gordon. The last line of each stanza may be sung as a response by the congregation, with the first part of the stanza sung by a soloist or choir; or, it may be sung antiphonally, left and right, alternating phrases.

173 Christ, Whose Glory Fills the Skies

In his 1780 *Collection* John Wesley used portions of this hymn, originally titled "A Morning Hymn," as a prayer for the beginning of the Christian life. The imagery of light and darkness evokes the beginning of the life of faith with each new day and the inauguration of Jesus' ministry in history. Therefore, the hymn is a fitting hymn of praise, especially at Epiphany or on Transfiguration Sunday, or during the Easter Season. It is also appropriate as the opening hymn of Morning Praise and Prayer.

174 His Name Is Wonderful

Inspired by a worship service one Christmas Sunday morning, Audrey Mieir wrote the words to "His Name Is Wonderful" in the back of her Bible. The text is based on the passage from Is. 9:6: "His name shall be called Wonderful" (KJV); it praises Jesus as the "great shepherd" and "rock of all ages." The repetitive tune and the simple words of praise and adoration have helped to make this hymn a favorite among United Methodists.

175 Jesus, the Very Thought of Thee

Bernard of Clairvaux, a twelfth-century monk, was known for his self-giving consistent character and for his writings on a wide variety of religious subjects. *Jesu, Dulcis Memoria,* a long poem of mystical devotion contemplating the joy that Christ brings to the believer, is attributed to him. From this poem Edward Caswall extracted several stanzas and translated them as the hymn "Jesus, the Very Thought of Thee." John B. Dykes composed the tune ST. AGNES for this text. The text reminds us of the importance of contemplation and devotion in the life of the Christian.

176 Majesty! Worship His Majesty

While traveling in Britain, California pastor Jack Hayford took a special interest in the symbols of royalty, relating them to Christ and his Kingdom. "So powerfully did the sense of Christ Jesus' royalty, dignity and majesty fill my heart, I seemed to feel something new of what it meant to be His!" wrote Hayford. The text echoes the theme of Eph. 2:6, that God has "raised us up with him, and made us sit with him in the heavenly places in Christ Jesus." This chorus is the number one favorite in a survey taken among the United Methodist Renewal Services Fellowship.

177 He Is Lord

This traditional chorus supports the words of Phil. 2:9-11 which strongly proclaim the Lordship of Christ. It can be used in worship as an act of praise or affirmation.

178 Hope of the World

Georgia Harkness was a Methodist scholar, professor of theology, and champion of the ecumenical movement. "Hope of the World" was the winning entry in a competition sponsored by the Hymn Society of America in 1953 and was first sung at the 1954 meeting of the World Council of Churches at Evanston, Illinois. It is a prayer for our world filled with fear, physical and spiritual hunger, death, and despair. Christian spiritual virtues are expressed as the hope of the world. The author uses both contemporary and traditional language in this valuable hymn for today's church. The bright, sweeping tune VICAR accentuates the text's steady unfolding and its recurring theme of Christ, the hope of the world.

179 *O Sing a Song of Bethlehem*

Louis F. Benson's text deals with four geographical settings in the life of Christ: Bethlehem, where he was born; Nazareth, the place of his childhood; Galilee, the setting for most of his ministry; Calvary, where he died on a cross and rose from the grave. The charming English folk melody KINGSFOLD enhances the beauty of the words and may be introduced by teaching the three almost identical phrases 1, 2, and 4 first, then teaching the third phrase which is different.

180 *Jesus Es Mi Rey Soberano* (O Jesus, My King and My Sovereign)

Written by one of the beloved pastors of the Mexican Methodist Church, Vicente Mendoza, this traditional song celebrates the intimate joy of life with Christ. The third stanza has been used often to dedicate offerings, birthdays, and anniversaries. Many have found comfort in this text during times of struggle. Ask the congregation to meditate on the text before experiencing it with music.

181 *Ye Servants of God*

In response to early anti-Methodist attacks, this hymn first appeared in *Hymns for Times of Trouble and Persecution* (1744) under the heading "To Be Sung in Tumult." Despite present conflicts, and with assurance and strength from the future promised in

Christ, believers are invited to join here and now in the great song of praise foreseen in Rev. 7:9-12. Set to the stately tune HANOVER, it is suitable for the Season after Pentecost (Kingdomtide), especially on Christ the King Sunday.

182   *Word of God, Come Down on Earth*

Twentieth-century Scottish Jesuit priest James Quinn has written this text about the Word as introduced in the Gospel of John. Each stanza emphasizes the work of the Word—what God in Christ does in every area of our life. The extensive use of hidden scriptural references helps to bring new life to old ideas. Use this text for private meditation and study before singing it to this familiar tune, LIEBSTER JESU, also used with "Blessed Jesus, at Thy Word" (596).

183   *Jesu, Thy Boundless Love to Me*

Translated from the German during his sojourn in Savannah, this poem became to John Wesley a symbol of perfecting grace. He later quoted stanza 2 in *A Plain Account of Christian Perfection* as the "cry of my heart" upon leaving Georgia disillusioned and rejected. The hymn skillfully sifts the desires (st. 2) and fears (st. 3) of the heart in response to the singular love of Christ. The poem can be sung to ST. CATHERINE.

184   *Of the Father's Love Begotten*

The text of this hymn, one of our oldest, was written in a time of intense theological controversy as to whether Christ was truly God. The text states Christ has been since the beginning and will continue to be—the "Alpha and Omega," the beginning and the end. The plainsong melody may be sung effectively in unison without accompaniment. Use stanza 2 as an Advent call to worship and stanza 3 as a response to scripture, offering, or benediction.

185 When Morning Gilds the Skies

This anonymous German hymn is first and foremost a hymn of
praise, with the phrase "May Jesus Christ be praised!" appearing
twice in each stanza. It calls us to praise God throughout the day
and throughout all time. The hymn is often used for the opening of
morning worship.

186 Alleluia

This simple repetitive melody is easily learned by persons of all
ages. It may be used in worship as a congregational response to
prayer or scripture reading. Additional stanzas may be improvised, with a leader lining out the phrases.

187 Rise, Shine, You People!

This hymn of praise celebrates the power of Jesus Christ in human
lives. It bears witness to the light, life, and freedom Christ
graciously gives us and calls us to tell that story in the world. The
well-known church music composer Dale Wood was commissioned to write this sturdy tune. It is a hymn of witness, most
appropriate on occasions when Christian witness is being
emphasized. The first stanza may be used as a choral introit and
stanza 3 as a choral benediction.

188 Christ Is the World's Light

Jesus Christ as light (Jn. 8:12), peace (Eph. 2:14), and life (Jn. 1:4) is
the focus of this text by Fred Pratt Green. It also reminds us that
Jesus said, "He who has seen me has seen the Father" (Jn. 14:9).
Each stanza concludes with the song of the angels at Jesus' birth:
"Glory to God in the highest." The final stanza is a triumphant
Doxology in praise to the Trinity. Have different groups sing
different stanzas with all joining at "Glory to God on High!" Let a
children's choir or youth choir sing stanza 2 in unison.

189 *Fairest Lord Jesus*

This anonymous text is a glorious statement about Jesus, the ruler of nature who surpasses the beauty of the woodlands in spring, who shines brighter than the light of the sun, moon, and stars. It is appropriate for any season or occasion for praising the beauty and wonder of God's gracious gift of Christ Jesus.

190 *Who Is He in Yonder Stall*

This hymn by Benjamin Hanby is a traditional hymn of the former Evangelical United Brethren Church. It consists of questions and an answer. The stanzas inquire as to the identity of the person in the manger, the person who prayed in Gethsemane, the person in anguish at Calvary, the person who rose from the grave, and the person who is enthroned in heaven. The repeated refrain sung after each of the five stanzas answers all questions: " 'Tis the Lord . . . crown him, Lord of all."

191 *Jesus Loves Me*

This is perhaps the most universally known Christian song for children. It is a song of confidence in Jesus' love as revealed in the Bible: "for of such belongs the kingdom of heaven" (Mt. 19:13-14). In addition to the English text, the first stanza and refrain are printed in Cherokee, German, Spanish, and Japanese, Thus, all persons are invited to participate in singing of Jesus' love, which extends beyond the boundaries of race, language, and nationality. The eminent theologian Karl Barth, when once asked for a succinct statement of Christian faith and hope, replied "Jesus loves me, for the Bible tells me so."

192 *There's a Spirit in the Air*

This clear, exciting, and joyous hymn shows the Spirit living and working among us. The text addresses the problems of our time—hunger, homelessness, wrong. The repetition of the last two lines in alternate stanzas suggests a variety of presentations of this hymn as litany, with alternating voices. The text is set to a charming, singable medieval French melody. This Spirit-centered hymn is appropriate not only at Pentecost but for general use.

193 *Jesus! the Name High Over All*

A hymn of evangelical self-reflection and appeal, this text is based on Phil. 2:9-10. In his 1780 *Collection,* John Wesley placed this among the hymns "Describing the Goodness of God"—introductory hymns inviting people to repent and believe. The echo of John the Baptist in the final stanzas, "Behold, the Lamb!" (Jn. 1:29), suggests its use during Advent or when the Baptism of the Lord is celebrated.

194 *Morning Glory, Starlit Sky*

W. H. Vanstone is a priest and highly respected theologian of the Church of England, a graduate of Oxford who studied in New York and was influenced by Reinhold Niebuhr and Paul Tillich. His text speaks of the many gifts of God's love, coming to a climax in God's self-giving in Christ.

195 *Send Your Word*

As a response to the chaotic situation of the modern world caused by the failure of human words in communication (not unlike the consequence of the Tower of Babel), author Yasushige Imakoma asks God to send the incarnate Word, who alone has the "healing power of love" to guide us, to free us, and to lead us to God's new world. Pastor Imakoma has dedicated his life to serving the blind in Japan. Both the text and the tune were written for the second volume of the Japanese hymnal *Sambika (Hymn of Praise)* in 1965. Children may introduce this hymn, singing stanza 1 accompanied by flute or recorder, while the adult choir sings stanza 2 in four-part harmony, adding the congregation on stanza 3.

196 Come, Thou Long-Expected Jesus

This beloved Advent text by Charles Wesley touches the full range of biblical memory and human hope, evoking the promise of Christ's coming to transform human life in the present. The tune HYFRYDOL ("good cheer") by the Welsh composer Rowland H. Prichard is one of the finest tunes from the late nineteenth century and as arranged is a fine part song. Let the choir sing stanza 1 in parts as a call to worship each Sunday in Advent.

197 Ye Who Claim the Faith of Jesus

This fine hymn about the birth of Jesus is especially appropriate for use during Advent or on Annunciation Day (March 25), when the Church celebrates the angel's announcement to Mary. The blessedness of Mary, our honor and thanks for Mary, and the Song of Mary (see "Canticle of Mary," 199) are woven together in this beautiful text. Congregations will enjoy this lyrical tune, which inverts the direction of the melody at each phrase.

198 My Soul Gives Glory to My God

Miriam Therese Winter's paraphrase of the Song of Mary (*Magnificat*, Lk. 1:46b-55), set to the tune MORNING SONG, emphasizes the active nature of God. God's visitation to Mary signifies that justice is dispensed to all. God casts down the proud and rich and lifts up the humble and poor, a recurring promise of the Incarnation in every age and the central focus of God's loving covenant. Mary's song is a song of justice, calling all who sing it to be just. Give stanzas 2 and 4 to women, stanza 3 to men and have all sing stanzas 1 and 5. As an introduction, play the melody, adding the full harmony on the last phrase.

199 Canticle of Mary (Magnificat)

The Gospel of Luke records this Song of Mary, sung during her visit to Elizabeth, mother of John the Baptist. Mary's song has become the Church's song around the world, where it is traditionally sung at Evening Praise and Prayer. Its summary of Old Testament faith and God's promise to Israel expresses the past, present, and future hope of the humble, poor, and hungry. The response (Is. 40:5) affirms the Church's ongoing task to be a present-day expression of the hope that "all flesh shall see it together."

200 Tell Out, My Soul

This frequently published text by Timothy Dudley-Smith, written in 1961, is based on Luke 1:46b-55 (see "Canticle of Mary"). The recurring phrase "Tell out my soul, the greatness of . . ." (from the New English Bible) in stanzas 1 through 3 serves to make Mary's song the song of all believers, who proclaim with her the greatness of the Lord and of God's name and might. Stanza 4 provides the fitting climax by declaring "the glories of God's word," just as Mary's song ends with the remembrance of God's promise to Abraham and his children. Unlike other settings of the Magnificat which are gentle, this hymn combines a powerful tune with a powerful paraphrase into an exciting hymn of praise.

201 Advent

During the season of Advent we recall the role of the prophets in preparing for the coming of Messiah, particularly their teaching and exhortation. We look ahead to the celebration of Christmas Day and to the time when the Lord, who came in humility to Bethlehem, will come in glory.

202 *People, Look East*

French carols are popular because of their rousing rhythms and beguiling melodies. Eleanor Farjeon, an English poet, provided this text for the *Oxford Book of Carols*. The carol expresses the hope and excited expectation of Christ's coming. Christ is called Love, Guest, Rose, Star, and Lord. Sung to this merry traditional French melody, it will be a favorite among children and youth as well as adults.

203 *Hail to the Lord's Anointed*

James Montgomery took Ps. 72 as the basis for this vivid hymn on the reign of Jesus. The text is a beautiful statement of the righteousness of God's reign, the fulfillment of God's promise of righteousness in Jesus, and the vision of the King's reign as universal and eternal. Set to the majestic German tune ELLACOMBE this hymn is appropriate during Advent.

204 *Emmanuel, Emmanuel*

Bob McGee's setting of "Emmanuel" is based on Mt. 1:23: "and his name shall be called Emmanuel (which means, God with us)." The tender melody invites all to join in singing this chorus of expectation. It is appropriate especially for Advent worship services as a response to the scripture or call to prayer.

205 *Canticle of Light and Darkness*

One of the dominant themes of Advent and Christmas is light. Alan Luff's adaptation of the anticipation of light from Hebrew Scripture (Is. 9:2, 59:9-10; Ps. 139:11-12; Dan. 2:20, 22), combine with the New Testament epistle 1 Jn. 1:5 to summarize the messianic hope: the coming of God's light into the world. When human attitudes are bleakest, when persons lament their hopeless groping in darkness, God, who is light, comes to turn worldly darkness into light. This is both an ancient and contemporary hope which, as two of the responses emphasize, is perpetually fulfilled in the coming of Christ.

206 *I Want to Walk as a Child of the Light*

Kathleen Thomerson, a United Methodist music director and organist, cites several passages of scripture that inspired this text. The theme is best summarized in Eph. 5:8: "For once you were darkness, but now you are light in the Lord; walk as children of light." References to Jesus as light, star, and sun lend themselves to a variety of liturgical uses, including Advent, Epiphany, Baptism, and confirmation services. The tune has a strong yet transcendent quality which complements the metaphor of Christ as light.

207 *Prepare the Way of the Lord*

This chorus from the Taizé community in France was designed to be sung during Advent as a call to worship. The text comes from Is. 40:3 and 52:10. It is a four-part round, with each new group entering as parts 1, 2, 3, and 4 are reached by the first group. It would be effective to introduce the song to the congregation by placing the choir in four sections around the congregation, to give the round a spatial as well as an aural dimension.

208 *Canticle of Zechariah* (Benedictus)

This is a shorter form of Lk. 1:68-79, which records that Zechariah, father of John the Baptist, at his son's circumcision affirms God's promise to fulfill the covenant of liberation made with Abraham and to raise up a Savior from the house of David. Just as John prepared the way for the true Messiah by preaching repentance, so the Church today should prepare the way by proclaiming repentance in all it is and does: affirming God's promise, covenant, salvation, and freedom. This canticle is appropriate during Advent, before New Testament readings, as a song of praise at

Holy Communion, at Morning Praise and Prayer, or at a funeral as the casket is carried from the church.

209   Blessed Be the God of Israel

A paraphrase of the "Canticle of Zechariah" (Lk. 1:68-79, see 208), this hymn of praise for the Incarnation emphasizes three primary themes: liberation—God has fulfilled the covenant of liberation made with Abraham (Lk. 1:68-70); salvation—Christ has come as the personification of God's grace to reclaim humankind (1:69-70); restoration—prisoners of sin and darkness will be restored to freedom, light, and peace (1:77-79). It is appropriate before New Testament readings, as a song of praise at Holy Communion, for Advent, or for funerals and memorial services. The hymn, written in rhyming couplets, makes an excellent responsive reading.

210   Toda la Tierra (All Earth Is Waiting)

Advent calls for the vigorous, positive tone of hope that this new hymn from Spain provides. The text mingles phrases from Is. 7:14 and 40:3-5 with words of hope for today's world. The marchlike tempo and melody is repetitive and easy to learn. Encourage the congregation to begin each stanza at moderate volume, then to sing out on the high notes of the third line which climaxes the message.

211   O Come, O Come, Emmanuel

This venerable Advent hymn has its origins in the Middle Ages. Various names for the Messiah are used in each stanza to express the fulfillment that Christ brings. The plainsong melody may be sung by a soloist or choir with the congregation joining at the refrain with the word "Rejoice!" The eight antiphons printed following this hymn can be read effectively when the hymn is sung, each antiphon being read before its corresponding hymn stanza is sung.

212 *Psalm 24* (King James Version)

Ps. 24 is divided into three distinct sections. Verses 1-2 proclaim God's dominion over creation. Verses 3-6 (like Ps. 15) are a liturgy for the entrance of worshipers to the Temple, which ask and answer the question, "Who may be admitted to worship?" Verses 7-10 are a liturgy for God's entrance to the Temple. Worshipers find that God has claimed their lives, and that involves moral responsibility, of which they are reminded upon entering worship. The idea of the people in the presence of God is at the heart of this great psalm. This is the same faith as that of Advent and Passion/Palm Sunday, which hails the coming of Christ. The psalm is appropriate for the opening of worship, for Advent, Passion/Palm Sunday, or general use.

213 *Lift Up Your Heads, Ye Mighty Gates*

This hymn by seventeenth-century pietist Georg Weissel is one of the great hymns for Advent. The first stanza, based on Ps. 24, speaks of the King coming in glory. Other stanzas exhort the Christian to "fling wide the portals of your heart," that it may be a temple of the King and lists the results of Christ's coming to the believer's heart: inner presence, grace, and love. During Advent the hymn is appropriate particularly for the opening of worship. Use this hymn as a response to the reading of Ps. 24, or intersperse reading the psalm and singing the hymn: Read verses 1-2, sing stanza 1; read verses 3-6, sing stanza 2; read verse 7, sing stanza 3; read verses 8-10, sing stanza 4.

214 *Savior of the Nations, Come*

This powerful Advent text places the marvel of Christ's birth within the context of Jn. 1 and the whole of Christ's life, death, resurrection, and ascension. St. Ambrose, to whom it is attributed, was the father of Western hymnody elected to be bishop while still an unbaptized candidate for church membership. It was translated into German by Martin Luther. The tune, basis of many chorale preludes including some by Johann Sebastian Bach, traces its origin back to plainsong.

215　To a Maid Engaged to Joseph

The Annunciation, when the angel Gabriel came to Mary, is the topic of this text first published in 1984 by Gracia Grindal, a Lutheran poet and author. Often in our rush to Christmas we overlook this first important step for Mary in understanding and participating in God's Incarnation. The text presents the Gospel (Lk. 1:26-38) without embellishments or elaboration, making it very effective for use in the place of the Gospel lesson of the day.

216　Lo, How a Rose E'er Blooming

This German carol, set to a familiar sixteenth-century melody, is based on Is. 35:1-2 and in its extended form related all the events in Lk. 1 and 2 and Mt. 2 about the birth of Jesus. The much loved adaptation into five stanzas by Theodore Baker tells of the prophecy of Isaiah, the shepherds, the angels, Bethlehem's manger, and Christ—human and divine—the people's Savior.

217　Away in a Manger

The origin of this Christmas gem is unknown. It first appeared in 1885 in an American Lutheran publication *Little Children's Book for Schools and Families*. The tune AWAY IN A MANGER, composed by James R. Murray, is notable for its modest nature, which mirrors the simplicity of the text. The text describes the lowly state into which Jesus was born. A child's prayer for safe-keeping concludes this hymn, which may be used for children's Christmas services, Christmas pageants, and Christmas Eve services.

218 *It Came upon the Midnight Clear*

Written during a period of strife and unrest in America (1849), this well-known text by Edmund Sears emphasizes the social implications of the coming of the Prince of Peace and the angels' message of peace and goodwill (Lk. 2:8-14). One of the first carol-like hymns composed in United States, it has been included in most major hymnals since the late nineteenth century. This hymn was written by a Unitarian pastor who believed in the divinity of Christ and thus was able to write one of the most beloved hymns on the birth of Jesus.

219 *What Child Is This*

This lovely Christmas text written by William C. Dix is to be sung after the reading of Mt. 2:1-12 and Lk. 2:6-20. The first two stanzas are questions: "What child is this?" and "Why lies he in such mean estate?" The questions are answered by the refrain: "This, this is Christ the King." The well-known English folk tune GREENSLEEVES , dating from the Renaissance, continues to be a favorite.

220 *Angels, from the Realms of Glory*

James Montgomery wrote this text in 1816 to appear on Christmas Eve in the *Sheffield Iris,* which he edited. The poem is based on Lk. 2:8-20; Mt. 2:1-12; and Mal. 3:1. The hymn is an ideal call to worship "the newborn king," as it invites all visitors in the Christmas narrative to "come and worship." It is appropriate as a Christmas processional hymn, and the stanzas may be sung by a choir, with the congregation joining in the refrain. In a Christmas pageant, the angels may enter as stanza 1 is sung; the shepherds may process during stanza 2; the wise men may enter on stanza 3, and finally Anna and Simeon may join the assembly during stanza 4.

221 *In the Bleak Midwinter*

Christina Rossetti's poem places the scene of Christ's birth in the cold winter of England. This artistic liberty strengthens her emphasis on the state of the world into which Jesus was born and the rude conditions that surrounded his birth. The winter mood is set through the use of short, descriptive words to suggest the cold, contrasted in the third stanza with the description of the hosts of heaven who gather to worship Christ. The last stanza summarizes our response to Christ's coming in this statement of faith: "What can I give him, Poor as I am? . . . Yet what I can I give him: Give my heart."

222 *Niño Lindo* (Child So Lovely)

This enchanting traditional Christmas carol from Venezuela is an *Aguinaldo,* a song sung by carolers hoping to receive little treats or gifts called *aguinaldos.* The text represents the devotion inspired in a youngster viewing the Christ Child. Ask the congregation to sing quietly, and use contrasting Latin-American percussion, claves and maracas in the alternating triplet/duple rhythm.

223 *Break Forth, O Beauteous Heavenly Light*

Johann Rist (1607–1667) wrote more than six hundred hymns, covering a wide variety of theological subjects. They were sung with enthusiam by Protestants and Catholics alike in seventeenth-century Germany. This hymn gained popularity through its use by Bach in his *Christmas Oratorio.* Fred Pratt Green's translation of stanzas 2 and 3 is a poetically sensitive presentation of the mystery of Christ's birth in a rude stable. The poignant conclusion invites, "Come dearest child into our hearts and leave your crib behind you." Sing at a moderate tempo that allows the rich inner harmonies to be heard without seeming rushed. Try the middle stanza a cappella with choir or congregation.

224 *Good Christian Friends, Rejoice*

In the Middle Ages carols developed in which Latin words were combined with the vernacular and sung to secular tunes. These carols were often "macaronic"—meaning a mixture of elements from various sources. It was in this context that this carol was written. The joyful, childlike tune IN DULCI JUBILO ("in sweet jubilation") has for four centuries been popular with the Church and its people. The happy message of the text and its appealing, rhythmic tune invite us to rejoice. Flute, finger cymbals, and other rhythm instruments will add to the festive nature of this tune.

225 *Canticle of Simeon* (Nunc Dimittis)

This Gospel canticle is one of the three songs from Luke most commonly used for worship in the early Christian church. The other two are the canticles of Zechariah (208) and Mary (199). The theme of this canticle is promise and fulfillment. God fulfills the promise to Simeon that he should not die "before he had seen the Lord's Christ" (Lk. 2:26). Because promise and fulfillment are also the pattern of Christian daily life, this canticle is traditionally said or sung after the reading of scripture in Evening Praise and Prayer or at private worship before bedtime. It is also appropriate at funeral or memorial services.

226 *My Master, See, the Time Has Come*

This text is a paraphrase of Lk. 2:29-32, the "Canticle of Simeon" (225). Simeon's prayer becomes the prayer of all the faithful who experience God's promise of salvation fulfilled in their lives. When Christians truly see the salvation of the Lord through the eyes of faith, they depart this life in joy; the fulfillment of salvation in their lives is a testimony to the light God has revealed to all nations. This hymn may be used for Evening Praise and Prayer or for funeral and memorial services.

227　The Friendly Beasts

Between the tenth and early seventeenth centuries, it was customary in France on January 14 (Feast of the Ass) to pay tribute to the animal that carried Mary to Bethlehem and the child Jesus to Egypt. The dancing triple time and the animal theme led to a longer narrative text which includes other beasts that probably were at the manger and gave their gifts to the Christ Child. This is excellent for a children's choir.

228　He Is Born

Christmas calls for carols, many of which come from folk traditions with no known author or composer. Among the many delightful French carols *Il Est Ne* is a special favorite. The opening refrain could be enhanced by adding available instruments (flute, oboe, violin). The words are simple yet profound. The three stanzas could be sung by three soloists, with choir and congregation singing the refrain in either English or French or both. In the absence of "oboe and bagpipes," finger cymbals (or triangle), tambourine, and/or drum can be added on the refrain.

229　Infant Holy, Infant Lowly

This simple Polish carol is unusual in its short phrases of four syllables, followed by a phrase of seven, each mentioning an element of the Christmas story. This meter, plus a clever rhyme scheme, makes the text poetically attractive. The first stanza gives the setting of the manger and the coming of the angels, while the second tells of the shepherds who heard the message and responded. The folk melody w zlobie lezy, with its short sequential phrases and lullaby quality, is a gem among Christmas hymns. It may be sung quietly and prayerfully, with very light accompaniment. A beautiful hymn for children as well as for adults.

230 *O Little Town of Bethlehem*

On Christmas Eve in 1865, Phillips Brooks visited Bethlehem and made a journey on horseback to the shepherds' field. The recollection of his view of Bethlehem in the distance that night inspired him to write this text, first sung at a Sunday School Christmas service in 1868. The stanzas outline the hope of the world, the story of Jesus' birth, the spiritual blessings brought by the Child, and end with a prayer that Christ will be born in our hearts—Emmanuel, "God with us."

231 *Christmas*

This Christmas prayer links the birth of Jesus with our new birth whereby we are redeemed from sin and enabled to lead new lives. The prayer picks up the theme from the final stanza of "O Little Town of Bethlehem" (230):

> O holy Child of Bethlehem,
> Descend to us, we pray;
> Cast out our sin, and enter in,
> Be born in us today.

232 *When Christmas Morn Is Dawning*

A delightful song for Christmas which begins with the wish of many Christians—that they had been present at the stable that first Christmas morning with Jesus, Mary, and Joseph. We pray that we may not sin by scorning his lowly birth, and we express our need for Christ's love to guide us to the end. Set to this gentle German folk tune, the hymn is ideal for children as well as for adults. The repeated words at the end of each stanza are a beautiful echo which may be sung by the congregation, choir, or children.

233 *En el Frio Invernal* (**Cold December Flies Away**)

Though part of modern-day Spain, the northeastern region of Catalonia has always maintained its own rich culture, language, and music. This enchanting carol, based on Is. 35:1-2, reflects the sentimentality of many European carols of past centuries, with nature echoing the human joy of Christ's birth. The repeated melody in the final measures suggests the tradition of the madrigal song; teach that last line first and the rest will seem easy to the congregation.

234 *O Come, All Ye Faithful*

This magnificent Christmas hymn's origin is shrouded in mystery, although scholars have determined that it is probably the work of eighteenth-century composer John F. Wade. It is an invitation to join in praise of the newborn king, a statement of Jesus' divine and human nature, and an invitation to join the heavenly choirs singing "Glory to God in the highest!" The memorable refrain with its gradually rising melodic line ends the hymn in a triumphant mood. It is an effective Christmas processional hymn with the last stanza especially appropriate for Christmas Day. The original Latin words of the first stanza are included in this edition.

235 *Rock-a-Bye, My Dear Little Boy*

This translation by Jaroslav J. Vajda of a traditional Czech carol joyfully imagines Mary singing softly as she cradles her child in her arms. The text reflects Mary's amazement that this child, the gift of God, "here in my arms lies so peacefully curled." The final couplet is a foreshadowing of what is destined to happen to this child at Calvary. The gentle shape of this Czech folk melody will facilitate the learning of this hymn.

236 *While Shepherds Watched Their Flocks*

This is the only hymn text by Nahum Tate that remains in current use. A paraphrase of Lk. 2:8-14, the story of the angels' appearance to the shepherds, it is one of the finest examples of scripture paraphrase in the hymnal, with simple, straightforward language that is faithful to the biblical text. The hymn is especially appropriate for Christmas Eve services. The Hymnal Committee has restored the tune CHRISTMAS to its earlier version.

237 Sing We Now of Christmas

"Noel!" meaning "News!" referring to the good news of Christ's birth, typifies this joyful Christmas carol. The tune FRENCH CAROL is used also with the Easter carol "Now the Green Blade Riseth" (311). Try stanza 1 sung by all, stanzas 2 and 3 by half the congregation, and stanzas 4 and 5 by the other half, with all joining in the refrain. Even small children can learn the refrain and take part.

238 Angels We Have Heard on High

This anonymous French carol, which is thought to date from the 1700s, is based on Lk. 2:6-20. The French tune GLORIA traditionally has been associated with this text. The jubilant refrain typifies the nature of the carol with its dancelike quality and its blending of languages, and here it proclaims "Glory to God in the highest." Use a melody instrument to reinforce the tune.

239 Silent Night, Holy Night

This beloved carol was written for Christmas Eve in 1818 by assistant pastor Joseph Mohr and organist Franz Gruber, at Saint Nikolaus Church in Oberndorf, Austria, perhaps because the organ failed to play. It probably was first sung by children accompanied by guitar. The text provides the setting of the birth of Jesus, tells of the shepherds who were visited by the heavenly hosts, and speaks of the coming of Jesus as the "dawn of redeeming grace." The last stanza addresses the star, asking for light as we sing with the angels. The first stanza hymn may be sung in the German, perhaps with guitar accompaniment, to recreate the simplicity of that first performance.

240 Hark! the Herald Angels Sing

This is one of Charles Wesley's most widely known and loved texts. The original title was "Hymn for Christmas-Day." The invitation to join with the angelic chorus (Lk. 2:8-14) is deepened in stanza 2 with the reference to prophetic fulfillment, "offspring of a virgin's womb" (Mt. 1:22-23; cf. Is. 7:14). The celebration of Jesus' birth, as "Prince of Peace" and source of "light and life" is enhanced by this sprightly tune which Mendelssohn never intended to be sung to a sacred text.

241 That Boy-Child of Mary

This delightful Christmas text is set to a traditional dance tune of Malawi, adapted by Tom Colvin, a missionary pastor in Africa for over twenty years. The text in simple language names Jesus in the African tradition of naming children. It tells us of his birth in Bethlehem and of our hopes for his life among us. A wonderful hymn for children, it may also be sung with alternating voices on the stanzas—left/right, men/women, or adults/children.

242 Love Came Down at Christmas

Christina Rossetti was an important nineteenth-century British poet, much of whose poetry displays a deeply religious and sometimes mystical tone. This Christmas hymn stresses the love present in God's gift at Christmas; the word "love" is used eleven times in three short stanzas. The last stanza states that because of God's love shown to us, "love shall be our token." The simple Irish tune GARTON is well-suited to the text and may be sung at a moderate tempo supported with a full sound.

243 De Tierra Lejana Venimos (From a Distant Home)

This Puerto Rican Epiphany carol, based on Mt. 2:1-12, will be a favorite at traditional Christmas plays and carol services, as well as at Epiphany. Each king may sing a stanza as a solo. Add tambourine, claves, maracas, and finger cymbals. Give the congregation a strong first beat at the start of each line from which the quick notes can bounce off. A good alternative to "We Three Kings."

244 'Twas in the Moon of Wintertime

A carol preserved through the oral tradition of the Huron people of the St. Lawrence River Valley in Canada, it is thought to be among the earliest songs using Native American images and symbols to tell the birth story of Jesus. The French Jesuit priest Jean de Brebeuf founded a mission among the Huron and died among them in 1649, massacred during a war between the Iroquois and the Huron. A variety of instruments may be used including flute, drum, and finger cymbals.

245 The First Noel

This traditional English carol is a seasonal favorite because of the tune's beautiful lilting quality and triumphant refrain. The text is a simple retelling of the story of the shepherds (Lk. 2:8-14) and wise men (Mt. 2:1-12). The star and light are the unifying themes of the carol. The emphasis on light and the story of the wise men make the hymn appropriate for Epiphany. The carol may be sung by a soloist with the congregation joining at the "Noel" refrain. Note that *Noel* means "news," referring to the good news of Christ's birth.

246 Joy to the World

This significant hymn for the celebration of Christmas by Isaac Watts is a paraphrase of Ps. 98:4-9. The psalm is an expression of joy over the marvelous works of God. Watts gives it a fresh interpretation, praising God for the salvation brought through the babe of Bethlehem. The tune by the pioneer U.S.A. music educator Lowell Mason is derived from two motifs found in Handel's *Messiah*.

247 O Morning Star, How Fair and Bright

This "Queen of Chorales," as it is often called, is one of our most beloved Epiphany hymns. The text is alive with references to the light that Jesus brings into the world. Numerous names for Jesus, such as Morning Star, Sovereign, Root of Jesse, David's Son, Lord and Master, heavenly Brightness, Light divine, and Crown of Gladness, make this hymn a treasury of rich metaphors for Jesus. This hymn is particularly appropriate for Epiphany (January 6) but is also suitable for general use.

248 On This Day Earth Shall Ring

This is an example of choir music that can become popular with congregations. The driving rhythmic tune set to a story of Christ's birth (see Lk. 2:6-14; Mt. 2:1-12) was arranged by the famous British composer Gustav Holst in 1925. It is a perennial favorite for festivals of lessons and carols, with different groups singing different stanzas and all joining in the refrain. *Ideo* (pronounced *ee-day-o*) means "therefore"; *Gloria in excelsis Deo* means "Glory to God in the highest."

249 There's a Song in the Air

The first two stanzas of this picturesque Christmas text by Josiah Holland tell in simple words the basic elements of the Christmas story. Stanza 3 brings the Christmas story into the present by expressing the meaning of the event to the world through the ages. The final stanza is the worshiper's response to the Incarnation: "We rejoice in the light and we echo the song, . . . and we greet in his cradle our Savior and King." The tune CHRISTMAS SONG was written for the 1905 Methodist Hymnal by Karl P. Harrington, who was a member of that hymnal commission.

250 Once in Royal David's City

Anyone who has heard the recording of the Festival of Lessons and Carols at King's College Chapel in Cambridge, England, knows how effective this hymn can be when a boy's solo voice sings stanza 1, and the choir and congregation join in a grand crescendo through the rest of this majestic hymn. The author, Cecil Frances Alexander, wife of an Anglican bishop, wrote many hymns to teach the articles of the Apostles' Creed to children. This particular hymn deals with "born of the Virgin Mary." A beautiful effect can be achieved if the third stanza is sung by children alone, or by children and the women in the congregation.

251 Go Tell It on the Mountain

"Go Tell It on the Mountain" is a Christmas hymn that directly calls us to spread the "good news," suggesting the social implications of the birth of Jesus Christ. Afro-American slave-poets conceived the refrain in such a way that it places the singer at the scene of the event. The three stanzas used here were adapted by John Work, who was a collector and researcher of spirituals shortly after 1900. This spiritual traditionally is sung joyfully in full voice.

252 When Jesus Came to Jordan

The parallel accounts of Jesus' baptism given in Mt. 3:13-17, Mk. 1:9-11, and Lk. 3:21-22 are combined in this text. The first two stanzas tell of Jesus' coming to the Jordan River to be baptized by John the Baptist. He came not to be pardoned but to share with those who seek repentance and those who are tempted. When the Spirit of God descended on Jesus like a dove, this marked the beginning of his ministry on earth. Stanza 3 is a prayer that the Holy Spirit will be ours and give our lives direction and purpose. Appropriate for the First Sunday after Epiphany, it should be sung with a feeling of two strong beats per measure. The two distinct sections in each stanza may be sung by alternating groups.

253 Baptism of the Lord

While appropriate at any Baptism or the Reaffirmation of the Baptismal Covenant, this prayer is especially intended for use on the Sunday of the Baptism of the Lord (the Sunday following January 6). The prayer first presents meanings of Jesus' own baptism; he was thus proclaimed God's Son and anointed with the Holy Spirit. The prayer then connects our baptism with his: We are baptized into his name and are joined in covenant with him. We are called to confess him boldly, and for this task of faithful witness we ask God's help.

254 *We Three Kings*

This Epiphany carol is based on the account of the visit of the wise men to Jesus in Mt. 2:1-12. It is traditional to speak of them as kings, although the Bible does not do so, and also to assume that there were three of them, one bearing each of the three gifts. In the text, each king presents a gift and mentions the symbolism of the gift. Gold represents the crown for the newborn King. Frankincense is for a God worthy to be worshiped by all. Myrrh is a spice used to anoint the dead, prophesying the death and suffering of Jesus. Framing the central theme, the first and last stanzas, along with the refrain, complete this Epiphany text with the symbols of the star and light.

255 *Epiphany*

The Feast of the Epiphany (January 6) proclaims the unity of God's people. The magi were Gentiles who came seeking the King of the Jews. This prayer incorporates biblical themes appropriate to the day and alludes to Acts 17:26; Mt. 2:2 and 1:23; Eph. 3:6; and Is. 60:3.

256 *We Would See Jesus*

J. Edgar Park began each stanza of this hymn with the words from Jn. 12:21 (KJV): "We would see Jesus." Each stanza represents important events in Jesus' life and ministry, showing examples for today's Christian. The text deals with Jesus' birth and growing up as an obedient child and tells of Jesus' teaching and healing ministry. "Follow me!" is Jesus' call to each of us and a fitting conclusion to this hymn about Jesus' ministry.

257 We Meet You, O Christ

This text by Fred Kaan, a pastor and hymn writer, is rich in scriptural and expanded images of Christ which reflect our everyday lives. We meet Jesus—the gardener of this garden, the earth—in many disguises as he identifies with the earth and with the struggles of its inhabitants. The cross is repeatedly called a "tree," as in Acts 5:30, 10:39, and 13:29. Christ's death and resurrection are a unity, as "the tree springs to life and our hope is restored." Set to a new tune by Carl Schalk, it is appropriate for Good Friday, Easter, or general use. Feel one beat to the measure and have the choir sing the third stanza a cappella, perhaps in C minor.

258 O Wondrous Sight! O Vision Fair

This translation by John M. Neale of a medieval Latin text is based on the story of the Transfiguration of Christ (Mt. 17:1-8; Mk. 9:2-8; and Lk. 9:28-36). With Peter, James, and John, Jesus went up into a high mountain. There his face became radiant and his clothes "became white and dazzling." There appeared Moses, representing the law which God had given Israel, and Elijah, representing the prophets. This hymn is appropriate for Transfiguration Sunday (the Sunday before Ash Wednesday) or whenever the story of the Transfiguration is read and preached.

259 Transfiguration

For use on Transfiguration Sunday (the Sunday before Ash Wednesday), this prayer sets forth themes for that day. In the revelation of Messiah in his glory, Jesus is proclaimed as the One who fulfills the Hebrew scriptures. We ask that we may receive his light and may thus share in both his suffering for the sake of the world and in his glory. The prayer is based on Mt. 17:1-8; Mk. 9:2-8; and Lk. 9:28-36.

260 *Christ, upon the Mountain Peak*

This contemporary text attempts to capture the worship and adoration experienced by the disciples who saw the Transfiguration of Christ (Mt. 17:1-8; Mk. 9:2-8; Lk. 9:28-36). The majesty and wonder of the text by Brian Wren, a British hymn writer and pastor in the United Reformed Church, is captured in the tune SHILLINGFORD by Peter Cutts. This tune illustrates the text—striding up the mountain peak—and at the Transfiguration, transposed to another key—striding down again. A soloist or the choir should introduce this hymn with the congregation singing the "Alleluias." Most congregations will "catch" the tune after hearing it sung a few times.

261 *Lord of the Dance*

Sydney Carter's folk hymn, written in 1963, is especially popular with youth and young adults. The "dance" is interpreted to be life lived in its fullest abundance, or as Carter defines it, "the image of all faith." The stanzas choreograph the life of Christ, with the refrain inviting the singers to "Dance, then, wherever you may be." Carter adapted the tune from the nineteenth-century Shaker melody SIMPLE GIFTS. The Shakers, who grew to considerable numbers in prosperous communal villages in the century following American independence, regularly used formation dances in their worship. This was the single hymn added to the proposed hymnal at the 1988 General Conference. When the hymn had been considered previously, concern had been expressed that stanza 3 might be interpreted as stating that Jewish leaders, rather than Pilate and the Roman soldiers, killed Jesus; it is imperative that this inference not be made.

262 Heal Me, Hands of Jesus

This text on healing is a poignant plea to find peace again by restoring hope, removing fear, learning forgiveness, admitting sin, dispelling guilt, and removing anxiety. The stanzas begin with the key words "Heal," "Cleanse," "Know," "Fill." The tune may need to be introduced by a soloist or choir. The reccurring downward melodic pattern is an aid to learning and memory. This hymn may be used for healing services or whenever the theme of the service is healing.

263 When Jesus the Healer Passed Through Galilee

This contemporary text recalls a few of the many stories of Jesus' healing ministry: Jesus' healing in Galilee (Lk. 4:31-41), the healing of the paralyzed man (Lk. 5:17-26), the healing of Jairus' daughter (Lk. 8:40-42, 49-56), the healing of blind Bartimaeus (Mk. 10:46-52), the cleansing of lepers and casting out of demons (Lk. 17:11-19; 4:40-41), and the healing ministry of the disciples (Mt. 10:5-15). Today our congregations are filled with persons in need of spiritual, mental, and physical healing. This hymn may be used in a service of healing or when preaching on the hymn's biblical texts. Sing it antiphonally with choir or soloist and congregation.

264 Silence, Frenzied, Unclean Spirit

Here is a powerful fresh look at Mk. 1:21-28 and Lk. 4:31-37. Demons, then and now, come under Christ's power and healing. The tune combines with the text to portray the authority of Christ in battling the demons and ends with a more lyrical melody of healing. The hymn may be used between the Gospel reading and the sermon. Try it with solo, choir, and congregation singing the three stanzas respectively.

265 O Christ, the Healer

The prolific British Methodist author Fred Pratt Green, who has written more than two hundred hymns since his "retirement" as a

Methodist minister, has been called the modern Charles Wesley. This hymn, while written for healing services, also expresses our deeper needs for wholeness, better self-understanding, mental health, an end to pride, and a sense of community that will reach out to all humankind. The text is nicely wedded to the sixteenth-century German tune ERHALT UNS HERR. A stanza may be read aloud as the tune is played, or stanzas 2 and 4 may be sung by the choir.

266 *Heal Us, Emmanuel, Hear Our Prayer*

Addressing Jesus as Emmanuel (meaning "God with us") the text comprises a petition for Christ's healing touch; Christ's conversation with the father of the epileptic boy he healed (Mk. 9:14-29); Christ's healing of a woman who, having suffered with a hemorrhage for twelve years, comes to touch the hem of his garment (Mt. 9:20-22; Mk. 5:25-34; Lk. 8:43-48). The text concludes with our hope for healing as we, too, reach out to touch Christ's robe. Cowper's beautiful words may be accentuated by having stanzas 3 and 4 sung in unison by men or by women. The last stanza may be sung in a round, unaccompanied, with the second voice entering one full measure after the first.

267 *O Love, How Deep*

This strong, stirring melody, written as a ballad to celebrate the victory of King Henry V of England over the French at Agincourt, is an effective setting for the celebration of the life and deeds of Christ "for us"—words that begin four of the stanzas. Thought to be a precursor to Christmas and Epiphany carols, the original Latin text dates from the fifteenth century and has been attributed to Thomas à Kempis, a priest from Holland. Its narrative style can be presented antiphonally, dividing the stanzas between various groups with varying musical treatments.

268 *Lent*

Lent, a time to reflect upon our wilderness journey through this world to the eternal land of God's glory, begins with the account of

Jesus' own sojourn and temptation in the wilderness. This prayer takes up those themes, reminding us that we are heirs of the Hebrew people and children of the same God who guided and delivered them.

269   Lord, Who Throughout These Forty Days

This text by Claudia Hernaman recalls Jesus' fasting in the wilderness for forty days and nights and the temptations posed by Satan (Mt. 4:1-11; Mk. 1:12-13; Lk. 4:1-13). Each stanza mentions the struggles of Jesus and concludes with a prayer—for strength to conquer sin, to learn to live, to abide in Christ, and, after this life, to attain "an Easter of unending joy." The tune LAND OF REST is a delightful U.S.A. folk tune. Appropriate for Ash Wednesday, the First Sunday of Lent, or later in Lent.

270   The Lord's Prayer

The Lord's Prayer is found in Mt. 6:9-13. Here it is set to a simple ancient chant formula that is easy to sing. It can be used whenever the Lord's Prayer is used in worship.

271   The Lord's Prayer

The late Duke Ellington included this popular West Indian folk hymn in his *Sacred Concert II*, in which he used the traditional style of having a soloist singing lines 1 and 3 and the congregation singing—"Hallowed be thy name." This setting can be used whenever the Lord's Prayer is used in worship. It may be sung without any accompaniment, with simple improvised harmony by the choir and congregation, or with a few rhythm instruments to add flavor.

272   Sing of Mary, Pure and Lowly

In this twentieth-century text, Roland Palmer successfully and beautifully combines the themes of Mary, Christ the Son of God, the joyous birth, the sorrowful death scene, and Christ's love for his mother. The tune, written by Skinner Chávez-Melo in 1985, enhances the beauty of the text. It can be introduced effectively as a solo, using stanza 1 in a carol service. Such a gracious, lyric melody might be introduced by a children's choir singing the first stanza. Men, or boys of a youth choir, could sing stanza 2, with the entire congregation joining in on the last stanza.

273 *Jesus' Hands Were Kind Hands*

This contemporary text by Margaret Cropper, set to the old French tune AU CLAIR DE LA LUNE, recalls incidents from scripture when Jesus touched people with his hands. The first stanza describes the kind hands of Jesus as he healed, blessed, washed, and saved "those who fall." The second stanza is a prayer that those who sing this hymn may be open to opportunities of service and use their hands in strong and gentle ways to do good, as Jesus did. Use piano, organ, autoharp, or guitar to accompany this simple tune.

274 *Woman in the Night*

From his birth to his resurrection, Jesus touched the lives of women. This text takes eight biblical incidents of women in contact with Jesus: Mary giving birth to Jesus (Lk. 2:6-7), the woman in the crowd who touches Jesus' garment (Mk. 5:24-34), the woman at the well (Jn. 4:7-30), the woman at the feast (Lk. 7:36-50), Martha in her house (Lk. 10:38-42), the women on the road who have traveled far and wide to witness to the Lord, the women at Calvary (Jn. 19:25), and the women at Jesus' tomb (Lk. 24:1-11). Jesus' attitude toward women, who were "nonpersons" in his time, gives power and freedom to all, so that we may see one another as Christ sees us. The refrain invites: "Women, children, men, Jesus makes us free to live again." The form of the tune HAIZ, by Charles H. Webb, written for this hymnal, suggests solo or choir stanzas and congregational refrains which may be sung more briskly than the stanzas.

275 The Kingdom of God

Based on Jesus' parable of the mustard seed in Mt. 13:31-32 and
Mk. 4:30-32, Gracia Grindal's text likens the kingdom of God to a
very small mustard seed. This "smallest seed . . . grows into the
largest plant . . . so birds can rest inside its crown of leaves." The
final couplet is repeated in all four stanzas, reversing the words of
Jesus, that the mustard seed "is like the kingdom of God and a
mystery." Have the children sing this hymn in Sunday worship
after reading the Matthew passage. All may join singing at the last
phrase of each stanza.

276 The First One Ever

This ballad-style song by Linda Wilberger Egan tells of the women
who were the first to know about important events in the life of
Christ. Mary was the first to know that she was to bear the Christ
(Lk. 1:26-38, 45). The Samaritan woman at the well was the first to
know that Jesus was the Messiah (Jn. 4:7-26). The three women
who came to the tomb were the first to know that Christ had risen
from the dead (Lk. 24:1-11). One or several soloists, with guitar
accompaniment, can present this song effectively.

277 Tell Me the Stories of Jesus

William Parker's Sunday School text captures the imagination of
children as they ask to hear the stories of Jesus. The text describes
Jesus' blessing of them and his triumphal entry into Jerusalem
from the viewpoint of a child. Here it is the *child* who says: "Yes, I
would sing loudest hosannas, 'Jesus is King.'" The last stanza is
appropriate especially for Passion/Palm Sunday.

278 Hosanna, Loud Hosanna

This joyful children's hymn comes from the pen of Jeanette
Threlfall, an Englishwoman whose life was filled with pain and

misfortune. Her hymn is based on the Mk. 11:1-10 account of Jesus' triumphant entry into Jerusalem. The text concerns the experience of the children who followed the procession through Jerusalem. It recounts Jesus' blessing of the children and tells that the children sang his praise. It ends as a hymn for today's worshiper, as the Church takes up the children's song of old.

279 *Mantos y Palmas* (Filled with Excitement)

This joyous hymn for Passion/Palm Sunday by Rubén Ruiz Avila, a Mexican Methodist, was honored at the 1980 InterAmerican Choral Festival in Mexico City. Help the congregation sense the excitement of Jesus' approach to the Holy City by starting with the refrain at the word "Hosanna"; this section also can be sung simultaneously with the stanzas. Use Latin-American percussion, playing the same rhythm beneath the word "Hosanna." As with all bilingual hymns, the English and Spanish may be sung at the same time.

280 *All Glory, Laud, and Honor*

Theodulph, Bishop of Orleans (750–821), wrote this text while in prison. The original Latin hymn, designed for long Palm Sunday processions, contained thirty-nine two-line stanzas. This translation by John Mason Neale is a most appropriate processional hymn for Passion/Palm Sunday as it contrasts Jesus' festive entry into Jerusalem with the foreshadowing of his passion. The procession can be made more meaningful by carrying suitable banners and involving children. Palm branches may be provided for the entire congregation.

281 *Passion/Palm Sunday*

This prayer, appropriate for Passion/Palm Sunday, can also be used at other times as a corporate or private prayer. At the beginning of Holy Week it is appropriate to ask that we share with our Lord—first, by being obedient to God's will, as Jesus was in his suffering and death; second, by having a part in his Resurrection victory, which we celebrate most fully later.

282 'Tis Finished! The Messiah Dies

Originally published in *Short Hymns on Select Passages of Holy Scripture* (1762), the watchword of this Charles Wesley hymn echoes Jesus' last cry from the cross, "It is finished" (Jn. 19:30). The finished character of Jesus' sacrifice implies not only the end of his suffering but also the fulfillment of Old Testament worship (st. 2; cf. Heb. 9:1–10:22) and the permanent disposition of saving grace (sts. 3–4; cf. Rom. 5:8-9; 1 Cor. 15:54-57). Set to OLIVE'S BROW it evokes a counterpoint of praise and confession. The hymn lends a particularly evangelical note during Lent and on Good Friday.

283 Holy Thursday

This prayer may be used in private devotion before or during the Service of Holy Communion on Holy Thursday. It reminds us that one of the central meanings of this sacrament is thanksgiving (*eucharist*). Even as we remember the suffering and death of Jesus, we look beyond his anguish to the bread and wine with their promise of eternal life through Christ, whose resurrection we will celebrate three days hence.

284 Good Friday

This prayer is intended for use on Good Friday but can also be used in any service that focuses upon Christ's atoning work. The prayer asks God to look with favor upon us, for whom Christ was willing to die. It implies that the Savior died not merely because of historical circumstances (something *they* did to him) but for the sake of all sinners (what *we* have done), so that we might be redeemed.

285 *To Mock Your Reign, O Dearest Lord*

The intriguing line "They could not know, as we do now" is the heart of this masterpiece by retired British pastor Fred Pratt Green. The crown of thorns becomes the crown of victory; the mocking purple cloak becomes a robe of mercy for our nakedness; the ridiculous reed becomes the scepter of the Kingdom. This hymn should be required reading by the congregation before worship each Sunday during Lent. Its intensity of language and tightness of construction also mark it as a great hymn for Holy Week services. Sing this sturdy tune in a moderate tempo, with a feeling of two strong beats per measure; however, do not rush the eighth notes.

286 *O Sacred Head, Now Wounded*

This anonymous Latin Passion hymn is one of the classic and best loved of all the chorales. It describes Jesus' head surrounded with a crown of thorns (Mt. 27:27-31; Mk. 15:16-20: Jn. 19:1-5) and his face, once radiant but now pale with anguish. We are reminded that he suffered and died for our sins. Set to the chorale melody that is used five times in Bach's *St. Matthew Passion*, this text uniquely expresses the meaning of Good Friday for the Christian.

287 *O Love Divine, What Hast Thou Done*

A poignant meditation on the cross, this text was originally entitled "Desiring to Love." John Wesley placed it among the hymns "Describing the Goodness of God" in his 1780 *Collection*, where it served to ground and illustrate the call to repentance. It is appropriate during the season of Lent, especially Holy Thursday or the Service of Tenebrae. The sense of penitential gratitude deepens with the gravity of the scene remembered and is enhanced by the brooding rhythm of the melody, SELENA.

288 *Were You There*

Afro-American slave-poets asked the question "Were you there?" In this spiritual, the response is so overpowering that performers cry out in bitter anguish as if they have been transported, standing trembling out of pity and utter shame at the crucifixion scene. The stanzas recount the events at Calvary and at the tomb. This spiritual traditionally is sung softly and inwardly to one's self with much expression and feeling. The personalized "oh" (pronounced), at the beginning of the refrain is, at times, sung outwardly to express anguish. "Were You There" is a passion spiritual that makes a perfect musical summary at the conclusion of the Good Friday worship service.

289 *Ah, Holy Jesus*

This profound text on the passion of Christ, based on an eleventh-century Latin meditation, was written by Johann Heermann in the seventeenth century during the devastation of the Thirty Years War. It expresses the deeply personal thoughts of the poet about the crucifixion. For example, he writes, "For me, kind Jesus" and "I crucified thee." Johann Crüger's tune HERZLIEBSTER JESU gives ideal support for the inflection and mood of the text. The hymn is valuable for worship during Holy Week and especially Good Friday. The text may be read aloud or silently during worship as a meditation to allow the deeply spiritual nature of the text to touch the worshiper. Use the organ or other instrument for meditative interludes between the singing of the stanzas to allow for contemplation of the text.

290 *Go to Dark Gethsemane*

James Montgomery, champion of liberal causes in the early nineteenth century, here portrays the final events in the life of Christ—the agony in Gethsemane, the trial, the crucifixion and resurrection—and thus is well suited for use during Holy Week. In addition, the text gives instructions in Christian living by using Christ as the example for praying, suffering, dying, and rising. The sense of the text is active, urging the Christian, to "go," "see," "adore," and "hasten." The various stanzas may be used on Holy Thursday, Good Friday, or Easter.

291 *He Never Said a Mumbalin' Word*

This is one of a host of Afro-American spirituals addressing the crucifixion of Jesus Christ. The crucifixion theme captured the hearts and minds of slaves because it offered them a real hope for eventual resurrection from the yoke of bondage. Slaves readily identified with the rejection and despisement dealt Jesus, because they, too, daily experienced a similar fate. The refrain—"and he never said a mumbalin' word, not a word"—refers to Jesus' silence at the sedition trials. This spiritual is sung softly and mysteriously.

292 *What Wondrous Love Is This*

Some of the greatest contributions of the U.S.A. to hymnody are the folk hymns of the early nineteenth century. This is a good example of the beauty of melodic line and simplicity of thought often found in these hymns. This one is a meditation on Christ's love—so great that he would give up his crown for a sinner's soul. The repetition of the words and the rise and fall of the lines emphasize the meaning. The hymn is appropriate for Lent and Holy Week or general use.

293 *Behold the Savior of Mankind*

This poem by Samuel Wesley, father of John and Charles, is one of the few papers that survived the Epworth rectory fire of 1709, when John Wesley was rescued as a "brand plucked out of the burning." It first appeared in Wesley's hymnbook *A Collection of Psalms and Hymns* (Charleston, 1737) under the title, "On the Crucifixion." In July 1738, Charles Wesley sang it with condemned criminals at Newgate prison in London. By placing the reader imaginatively at the foot of the cross, the poem becomes a deeply self-involving meditation on the meaning of Jesus' passion. The spiritual drama of this text belongs in the movement from Lent to Easter. It might be read antiphonally, for example, in the Service of Tenebrae on Holy Thursday, or on Good Friday.

294 *Alas! and Did My Savior Bleed*

This text is a profound personal contemplation by Isaac Watts on the meaning of the cross. It has been used effectively as a commitment hymn at revival services. The great hymn writer Fanny Crosby was moved to conversion during the singing of the words, "Here, Lord, I give myself away," her soul filled with "celestial light." The text is sung to contrasting tunes; the tune MARTYRDOM has a more stately, introspective mood, while HUDSON is more outgoing in the style of a gospel hymn and refrain. Worship leaders may choose the style most appropriate for a particular service.

295 *In the Cross of Christ I Glory*

In Gal. 6:14 Paul wrote, "But far be it from me to glory except in the cross of our Lord Jesus Christ, by which the world has been crucified to me and I to the world." In 1825 John Bowring was inspired by this passage to write this text on the centrality of the cross. Its message is that the cross is for all times, "towering o'er the wrecks of time." In times of joy the cross adds radiance; in times of sorrow the cross provides peace. The text through its repetition of the first stanza as the last gives emphasis to Paul's words.

296 *Sing, My Tongue, the Glorious Battle*

This translation of a sixth-century Latin hymn tells of the life of Jesus and exhorts us to sing of the resurrected Christ, who "as a victim, won the day." He comes in the fullness of time, and the cross is a "sign of triumph." In the concluding Doxology we sing praise and glory "while unending ages run." The majestic French carol tune PICARDY complements this powerful text.

297 *Beneath the Cross of Jesus*

Elizabeth Clephane of the Free Church of Scotland was known for her sunny personality and her concern for the poor to whom she gave most of her income. Written shortly before her death, this text is a meditation on the cross and its importance in the faith of the believer. The text's numerous scriptural allusions indicate the poet's deep knowledge of the Bible. The hymn may be used in services contemplating the cross, such as on Good Friday, or as a hymn of commitment, particularly during Lent.

298, 299   *When I Survey the Wondrous Cross*

Many have called this hymn by Isaac Watts the greatest hymn in the English language. When Watts contemplated the cross he saw all his accomplishments as nothing. He refers to Gal. 6:14, "God forbid that I should glory, save in the cross of our Lord Jesus Christ" (KJV), then vividly describes the suffering of Jesus by directing the attention to the head, hands, and feet of Jesus. Watts believed that Jesus demands from us "my soul, my life, my all." This is a most meaningful hymn for use on Good Friday.

300   *O the Lamb*

This is one of many anonymous songs that appeared during the early ninteenth-century American campmeetings. These camp-meeting songs are predecessors of the later gospel songs but are less standardized and more like folk songs. Both words and music were arranged in 1980 for publication in *Supplement to The Book of Hymns* by Ellen Jane Lorenz. She is well-known for her work with the Lorenz Publishing Company, was music editor of *The Hymnal* (1957) of The Evangelical United Brethren Church, and in her retirement has done extensive research into early American campmeeting songs. This song is well suited for use during more somber and penitential times such as Lent.

301   *Jesus, Keep Me Near the Cross*

According to Fanny Crosby, her lack of sight seemed to help her more fully focus on the spiritual aspects of life. She never felt handicapped, feeling instead that spiritual blindness was more tragic than physical blindness. This meditation on the power of the cross contains an interesting prayer from one who was sightless:

"Near the cross! O Lamb of God, Bring its scenes before me." The author pictures in her mind's eye the vision of Christ dying on the cross. The symbol of light is found in stanza 2: "There the bright and morning star sheds its beams around me," and concludes with the promise to watch and wait, hope and trust, forever.

302   *Christ the Lord Is Risen Today*

This is the most widely used Easter hymn among United Methodists. It expresses the meaning of eternal life and the significance of our participation in Christ's victory over death and the fear of the grave (st. 3; cf. 1 Cor. 15:15). The restored final stanzas join to celebrate praise and love as signs of resurrection power already joining earth and heaven. The anonymous tune EASTER HYMN was known and used by early Methodists.

303   *The Day of Resurrection*

John of Damascus, of the eighth-century Eastern church, where great importance was placed on Easter worship, was one of the great hymn writers of his era. This hymn was traditionally sung at midnight at the beginning of Easter Day, with lighting of candles, brilliant music, and shouts of "He is risen!" The first stanza uses the symbolism of the Passover for the resurrection, calling Easter "the passover of gladness."

304   *Easter People, Raise Your Voices*

William M. James is a black United Methodist pastor widely known in New York City for his pioneering multi-ethnic and street ministries. In his sermons he preaches that every Sunday is a new Easter. The stanzas presented here are 1, 3, and 5 of James's original text and exhort the faithful to sing the Lord's praises, triumph over every evil foe, and witness to the power of God. This stirring hymn should be sung as a rousing march as voices reach a climax at "Alleluia! Alleluia!" Here the accompanist may wish to drop out, reentering at the last two measures.

305 *Camina, Pueblo de Dios* **(Walk on, O People of God)**

Cesareo Gabaraín is a contemporary Catholic composer from Spain. The text places us in the footsteps of Christ on the road to Calvary and the Kingdom, making it useful for Lent, Holy Week, Easter, or Holy Communion. Teach the refrain to the congregation first, with a crescendo at the end of each stanza, thus carrying the voices back to the refrain as our Christian response to the rebirth and resurrection proclaimed in the stanzas.

306 *The Strife Is O'er, the Battle Done*

This anonymous Latin text is based on Col. 2:15, which depicts the struggle between life and death. The text is notable for its three short rhyming phrases, followed by an Alleluia, which suggests possibilities for antiphonal singing. Each stanza carries out the contrast between death and resurrection: The battle is contrasted with God's triumph; the legions of death are dispersed by Christ; the three sad days are compared with the joy of the resurrection; and, the wounds of Christ enable his servants to live with him forever. The opening line of Alleluias may be sung as an introduction by the choir.

307 *Christ is Risen!*

This resurrection text by Brian Wren is packed with wonderful biblical images of the newness and life which Christ brings to our world—a tree growing in the desert with "healing leaves of grace," people walking from "caverns of despair" into a morning of gladness, the triumph of Christ over the world's "demonic chorus." Paired with a familiar Polish carol tune (which is also set to "Infant Holy, Infant Lowly," 229), the text has a reflective joy appropriate for the Easter season or for Communion.

308 *Thine Be the Glory*

This Easter hymn by Edmond Budry, pastor of the Free Church in Vevey, Switzerland for thirty-five years, begins with a line of praise to the risen Lord, repeated after each stanza in the refrain. It tells of angels who rolled the stone away; alludes to Jesus' greeting to the women at the tomb: "Lovingly he greets thee, Scatters fear and gloom"; and refers to the doubting of Thomas: "No more we doubt thee, glorious Prince of life!" With its stately tune taken from Handel's oratorio *Judas Maccabeus*, the hymn presents a majestic mood for Easter worship. Enhance the melody by introducing it with a trumpet.

309 *On the Day of Resurrection*

This contemporary hymn is based on the account of Christ's appearance to two travelers on the road from Jerusalem to Emmaus (Lk. 24:13-35). It tells of the experience in the present tense, reminding us that in our pilgrimage, Jesus is with us and, in his own way, makes himself known to us. Then, like the two who returned to Jerusalem to tell the eleven of the resurrection, we too must share the news that Christ is risen and "is through us made known." Vary the registration of this six-stanza hymn and use alternating groups to sing the stanzas. The last two stanzas should be sung by all.

310 *He Lives*

Presbyterian pastor Alfred H. Ackley in 1933 was asked by a young Jew, "Why should I worship a dead Jew?" "But Jesus lives!" was Ackley's response, and the result of that conversation was this hymn. The stirring tune enables the singer to proclaim with conviction a living and present Christ. The last stanza may be used as a congregational sending forth following the benediction on Easter Day.

311 *Now the Green Blade Riseth*

This Easter hymn by Anglican priest J. M. C. Crum uses the analogy of the seed becoming a new plant with the resurrection of

Jesus (cf. 1 Cor. 15:35-44). The hymn compares the seemingly lifeless seed in the ground to the dead Christ buried in the tomb. The final stanza carries the comparison further by saying that when our hearts are cold, grieving, or in pain, Jesus' touch can revive them. A short refrain ends each stanza: "Love is come again like wheat that springeth green." The unusual tune is a traditional French Christmas carol.

312 *Hail the Day That Sees Him Rise*

Originally titled "Hymn for Ascension Day," this Charles Wesley text focuses upon Jesus' ascension (Acts 1:9), striking a balance between praise for Christ's exaltation (Ps. 24:7) and grateful response for Christ's continuing presence and commitment to world and Church (Mt. 28:20; Acts 2:33). The intended balance of the theme is further confirmed in the symmetry of the tune, LLANFAIR. This hymn is especially appropriate for Ascension Day or Ascension Sunday. Use a brass instrument or an organ trumpet stop to introduce and highlight this melody.

313 *Cristo Vive* (Christ Is Risen)

From Argentina comes this beautiful Easter text with its swinging, marchlike rhythm. The tune by Pablo Sosa, professor of sacred music at Union Theological Seminary in Buenos Aires, underscores this powerful text. In addition to the joyful announcement of Christ's resurrection, the text urges us to share the good news that the reign of God is replacing the dominion of death in our lives, too. Teach to the congregation a phrase at a time, singing with a full, vibrant sound.

314 *In the Garden* (I Come to the Garden Alone)

This tender text and tune by C. Austin Miles, written in 1913, has been shown consistently by surveys to be among the top ten favorite hymns of United Methodists, despite the fact that it was not in our previous official Methodist or Evangelical United Brethren hymnals. The text, based on Jn. 20:1-18, tells of Mary Magdalene's recognition of the risen

Christ on Easter morning. In worship, the singer is allowed to enter into the personal joy of Mary as she enters the garden tomb and is the first to know of Jesus' resurrection—a joy "none other has ever known." Often sung just as a solo, this popular hymn also can be sung by the congregation alternating unison and part-singing, men and women.

315 *Come, Ye Faithful, Raise the Strain*

As a basis for this text on the resurrection, the eighth-century theologian and poet John of Damascus uses the Canticle of Moses and Miriam (*see* 135) from Ex. 15. He borrows the image of the Hebrews' release from captivity and their crossing the Red Sea to describe the redemption brought through Christ's resurrection in stanza 1: "Loosed from Pharaoh's bitter yoke Jacob's sons and daughters; Led them with unmoistened foot Through the Red Sea waters." This joyful text is enhanced by the exultant tune ST. KEVIN by English operetta composer Arthur S. Sullivan.

316 *He Rose*

This Afro-American spiritual commemorates the crucifixion, burial, and resurrection of Jesus Christ, our Lord and Savior. It includes the actions of Joseph, Mary, and the angels who rolled away the stone from the entrance of the tomb. Slave-poets set the singer at the scene of the events. It is at the same time set in the past and present and is both communal and personal. This lively spiritual is sung with unrestrained joy. It makes an effective opening for Easter Sunday worship.

317 *O Sons and Daughters, Let Us Sing*

This Easter text by Jean Tisserand begins with the invitation to sing because of Christ's triumph over death and ends with "Alleluia! Alleluia!" The following stanzas narrate the Easter story, telling of the women who came to the tomb, the angel who spoke to them, Jesus' appearance to the apostles, the doubts of Thomas and his belief after touching the wounds of Jesus. The tune is a fifteenth-century French folk tune. The medieval characteristics of the melody may be enhanced through unaccompanied singing or with the use of hand drums, tambourines, or finger cymbals. Stanzas 1 through 5 are especially appropriate for Easter Sunday; stanzas 6 through 9, for the second Sunday of Easter.

318   Christ Is Alive!

This marvelous Easter text by Brian Wren was written in April 1968 and sung at Easter services—ten days after the assassination of Martin Luther King, Jr. at the church where Wren was pastor. It reminds us that the Easter event and the Christ who rose are not far away from our lives. Christ is alive; he suffers with us yet lives and comes to us with good news, "with joy, with justice, love and praise." The tune TRURO adds joy and vigor to the text, together forming a celebrative Easter hymn.

319   Christ Jesus Lay in Death's Strong Bands

Martin Luther wrote this Easter hymn based on earlier German and Latin hymns. The tune CHRIST LAG IN TODESBANDEN, by Johann Walther, was influenced by the Latin sequence *Victimae Paschali Laudes* and the German melody CHRIST IST ERSTANDEN. The hymn became one of the most beloved among Lutherans. A vivid portrayal of the struggle between life and death in Christ's resurrection, the hymn is also well-known as the basis for J. S. Bach's Cantata No. 4, *Christ lag in Todesbanden*. One of the strongest and most powerful chorales, it may be sung by alternating stanzas between choir and congregation, and by singing a cappella or with accompaniment.

320   Easter Vigil or Day

This prayer celebrates the victory of Jesus Christ over death and asks that by the power of the Holy Spirit we may die and rise with our Lord to a righteous life. Although designated for use at the Easter Vigil or on Easter Day, this prayer is appropriate for use on any Lord's Day, because, rightly understood, every Sunday is an occasion on which we "celebrate the day of our Lord's Resurrection."

321 Sundays of Easter

This prayer sets in cascading form a series of joys. The joy of the resurrection should give us joy in our lives of service to God. Further, these joys point toward the ultimate joy of eternal life. Thus, Christian faith, life, and hope are bound together. The prayer is suggested for use in congregational worship on any of the Sundays of the Easter season. It can, however, be used on any Sunday, since each Lord's Day is a commemoration of the resurrection.

322 Up from the Grave He Arose

This hymn portrays the contrast between the death of Jesus and his resurrection. Each of the stanzas about his death is sung to a somber tune in a low register, while the refrain is rhythmic and ascends to an exciting climax on the words "Up from the grave he arose." The dramatic contrast makes this an effective hymn for Easter worship. Written and composed by Robert Lowry, an important figure in nineteenth-century gospel music, the hymn has found its place in the standard repertory.

323 The Ascension

This prayer is for Ascension Day (the fortieth day of the Easter season) or for the Sunday following that Thursday. The prayer embodies the meaning of the ascension: The living Christ, who before his resurrection was bound to a few hundred square miles for roughly thirty years, is present with us at all times and in all places. The ascension declares Christ's dominion and power throughout creation and beyond. We pray for the faith to live by these truths.

324 Hail Thee, Festival Day

Fortunatus, a sixth-century Italian who became Bishop of Poitiers, wrote a 110-line poem on the resurrection, from which this hymn is taken. There are three stanzas for Easter, three for Ascension, three for Pentecost, and four for general use; thus the hymn can be sung on various festive days of the Christian year. Ralph Vaughan Williams created this festival setting in which the choir sings the stanzas, with the refrain sung by all. Suggestion: teach the stanzas to children and youth choirs and have them lead the singing. Keep the tempo brisk and the mood festive.

325 *Hail, Thou Once Despised Jesus*

This strongly doctrinal text is attributed to John Bakewell, who moved to London as a young man, fell under the influence of John and Charles Wesley and eventually became a Methodist preacher. It begins with the suffering and humiliation of Jesus and contrasts those sharply with his glorification. The last stanza echoes the words of Rev. 4:11.

326 *The Head That Once Was Crowned*

Based on Heb. 2:9-10, this hymn contrasts the shame of the cross with the exaltation of the risen Christ. The contrast begins in the first line, comparing the crown of thorns with the crown of glory. It tells of the cross, the source of grace which brings salvation, and claims that those who suffer for Christ on earth will reign with him in heaven. The last stanza completes the contrasts by saying that the shameful cross is life, health, hope, and wealth to those who follow Christ. Thomas Kelly, who wrote the text, was a nineteenth-century Irish evangelist who devoted his energies and money to helping the poor.

327 *Crown Him with Many Crowns*

Matthew Bridges, a nineteenth-century Anglican, was inspired by Rev. 19:12, "and on his head are many diadems [crowns]." Later rewritten by Godfrey Thring, the four stanzas itemize the characteristics of the risen Lord: "The Lamb upon his throne," "The Lord of life," "The Lord of peace," and "The Lord of love." The familiar tune by George Elvey was named DIADEMATA, in keeping with the spirit of the text.

328 *Surely the Presence of the Lord*

In Lanny Wolfe's words and music the singer can "feel," "hear," and "see" evidences of a holy Presence. This chorus lends itself to a variety of uses in worship, including a song of gathering, a choral introit, and an opening act of praise.

329 *Prayer to the Holy Spirit*

Here we address God in one of the titles familiar to Native Americans, Great Spirit. The entire prayer is adapted from that tradition. God's revelation through creation is a particular focus of this prayer, as we ask for wisdom and purity of life. The prayer is useful in a variety of circumstances, but particularly when the glory of God's creation is being celebrated.

330 *Daw-Kee, Aim Daw-Tsi-Taw* (Great Spirit, Now I Pray)

This prayer from the Kiowa nation, a people found mostly in the South Central region of the United States, is a plaintive plea for God's presence in our lives. Libby Littlechief and Charles Boynton, mother and son, have transcribed the prayer into notation and English. The ethereal tune should be sung easily and calmly using the notation only as a guideline. Have a soloist sing it once as a call to prayer, then sing it again after the prayer as a solo, choral response, or congregational response. Use a recorder instrument or flute on the melody.

331 *Holy Spirit, Come, Confirm Us*

Vatican II encouraged Roman Catholics to write hymns in their native tongues. The contemporary British poet Brian Foley has given us a fine text on the Holy Spirit, built around four words that describe the work of the Spirit: *"confirm," "console," "renew," "possess."* The last two stanzas freshly emphasize the holiness of the Spirit. Although especially suitable for Pentecost, this hymn may be sung throughout the year.

332 *Spirit of Faith, Come Down*

Invoking the prevenient and converting grace of the Holy Spirit, this Charles Wesley hymn was originally published in *Hymns of Petition and Thanksgiving for the Promise of the Father* (1746). Placed among the hymns "Praying for a Blessing" in John Wesley's 1780 *Collection,* it is essentially a prayer of the believing community on behalf of those who await the "witness" of the Spirit (1 Cor. 2:12; Rom. 8:16). A fitting hymn of praise to the Holy Spirit, this is also appropriate in the context of invitation to Christian discipleship.

333 *I'm Goin'a Sing When the Spirit Says Sing*

Many believe this spiritual to be a reaction to formal worship patterns that did not allow for spontaneous expression. The basis for such a reaction may be found in the teaching of Paul in 1 Cor. 14:15: "I will sing with the spirit and I will sing with the mind also." "I'm Goin'a Sing" is a popular summer camp song and takes well to hand clapping. This jubilee-type spiritual is well known in the United States with regional variations. This version is adapted from a recording of several veteran singers at St. Mark's UMC, Harlem.

334 *Sweet, Sweet Spirit*

Author and composer Doris Akers was the choir director for the Sky Pilot Radio Church in Los Angeles. As the choir prepared for worship services one Sunday morning, she prayed: "I know there's a sweet, sweet spirit in this place." The phrase stayed with her throughout the worship service, and the next day she wrote both words and music of this hymn, which praises the sweetness and goodness of the Holy Spirit known to Christians as they worship together. Feel two beats per measure. If accompanied by the piano, embellish the long notes and ends of phrases in the gospel style. Keep the rhythm moving.

335 *An Invitation to the Holy Spirit*

This prayer to the Holy Spirit uses three metaphors: wind, fire, and dew. As we remember the cleansing, refining, and refreshing activity of the Spirit, we ask God to work in human lives. This may be used as an opening prayer or prayer for illumination, especially on special days such as Pentecost and ordinations. It is also suitable for private devotions.

336 *Of All the Spirit's Gifts to Me*

Fred Pratt Green, a retired British Methodist pastor, based this text on three fruits of the Spirit mentioned in Gal. 5:22: love, joy, and peace. The middle three stanzas describe the Spirit's graceful interaction with us; the final stanza moves us from individual appropriation of the gifts to corporate sharing of them. The hymn is especially fitting in a service that focuses on the gifts of the Spirit, but it also is suitable for general use. The stepwise melody and simple rhythm accentuate the final phrase in each stanza. The last stanza may be used as a sung benediction.

337 *Only Trust Him*

Written for his collection *Salvation Melodies No. 1*, 1874, John H. Stockton's text reflects the style of the campmeeting song. Stockton's original refrain had the words "Come to Jesus" rather than "Only trust him." The change, made by Ira Sankey because he felt that the words "Come to Jesus" were trite and overused, has been retained in successive hymnals. The hymn is useful as one of invitation and commitment.

338 *Where He Leads Me*

A simple and inviting hymn of quiet trust and commitment by E. W. Blandy and J. S. Norris. The Savior is calling us to "Take thy cross and follow me" (Mk. 8:34), and we respond with firm resolve: "Where he leads me I will follow" (Mt. 8:19). This hymn may be especially meaningful during Lent.

339 *Come, Sinners, to the Gospel Feast*

This text by Charles Wesley, based on Jesus' parable of the great supper (Lk. 14:16-24), declares the central conviction that salvation is offered "to all." The essential point, "ye need not one be left behind," is echoed in every stanza. Set to the tune HURSLEY, it may be used as an invitation hymn which proclaims and celebrates the inclusiveness of the Christian community.

340 Come, Ye Sinners, Poor and Needy

This popular text by Joseph Hart first appeared in his collection *Hymns Composed on Various Subjects* in 1759. It is a straightforward appeal to unbelievers and a strong statement about salvation by grace alone. The refrain refers to the parable of the prodigal son (Lk. 15:11-32). The sinner is the prodigal son, and Jesus is the father who is ready to save. Stanzas 2 and 3 begin with language and imagery from Is. 55:1 and Mt. 11:28 respectively. Set to RESTORATION from *Southern Harmony* (1835), it is an often-used hymn of invitation.

341 I Sought the Lord

This anonymous text, written about 1890, beautifully expresses the truth that we can seek and love God because God first seeks and loves us. The quiet and meditative tune PEACE reinforces the message of the words. In introducing this hymn, it may be helpful for the pastor to comment on its message and then for a solo voice to read or sing the hymn, while the congregation has a chance to study and meditate on the words.

342 Where Shall My Wondering Soul Begin

This is generally thought to be part of Charles Wesley's conversion hymn (see historical note in the hymnal). Originally titled "Christ the Friend of Sinners," the poem begins in praise for the personal assurance of salvation and then in stanza 4 turns to the proclamation of the gospel to all who acknowledge themselves as sinners. Appropriate for the celebrations of Aldersgate or Heritage Sunday, this poem can be either read antiphonally or sung to the tune ST. PETERSBURG (*see* 153).

343 Come Back Quickly to the Lord

This text, based on the parable of the prodigal son (Lk. 15:11-32) and also calling to mind Mt. 11:28, was written during World War II by Young Taik Chun, a pastor in the Korean Methodist Church and editor of the Korean Christian Literature Society. The English translation is by Sang E. Chun, his son and a United Methodist pastor, and Ivy G. Chun, Young Chun's granddaughter. This hymn may be used as an invitation to Christian discipleship or in any service where the emphasis is upon the compassion, patience, and forgiveness with which Christ, with open arms, calls and waits for us to return and receive God's love, healing, and peace. Sing it in a gospel style at a moderate tempo.

344 Tu Has Venido a la Orilla (Lord, You Have Come to the Lakeshore)

Hear Christ's call to discipleship in this lovely, imploring melody by the Spanish composer Cesareo Gabaraín, as arranged by Skinner Chávez-Melo, a church musician in New York City. This hymn is appropriate for commissioning services, reception of members, or times of commitment. Reinforce the beautiful swaying rhythm with light chording on guitar or keyboard.

345 'Tis the Old Ship of Zion

"Ship of Zion" is one of many occupational enterprise spirituals employing an agent of transportation. Such agents are interchangeable: chariots, ships, boats, wagons, trains, oxen, horses. In slave poetry, these agents are almost always a means of transportation to the Promised Land. Very often, slave-poets employed a "mask" to conceal the true nature of a message. This invariably happened when the poet intended the message only for the ears of other slaves. Many an implied "landing" site is a factual geographic reference. Here, "Ship of Zion" may have been named for Marcus Garvey's flagship of the short-lived Black Star Line. The spiritual traditionally is sung very slowly. The melody resembles that of the spiritual "Gimme Dat Old-time Religion."

346 Sinners, Turn: Why Will You Die

Originally published in *Hymns on God's Everlasting Love* (1742) and based on the plea of Ezek. 18:31: "Why will ye die, O house of Israel!" (KJV), this poem also appeared in John Wesley's 1780 *Collection* as a hymn "Exhorting, and Beseeching [Sinners] to Return to God." Each of the first three stanzas connects the theme of repentance to some aspect of the work or character of the triune God: Maker, Savior, Spirit. The poem could be read antiphonally as a congregational call and response to the manifold and inviting grace of the "suffering God."

347 Spirit Song

Author and composer John Wimber wrote "O Let the Son of God Enfold You" in a few hours' time, during which he recalls he received "something which in a very real sense was dictated to me." This hymn, composed as an altar call, is intended not only for those experiencing conversion but also for believers, that they too may fully receive the promises of Christ. As in the gospel style, a soloist or choir may sing the stanzas while the congregation joins at the refrain. Try singing the refrain a cappella as a response to prayer, letting everyone improvise harmony.

348 Softly and Tenderly Jesus Is Calling

The first stanza of this familiar invitation hymn expresses an image of Jesus similar to the father in the parable of the prodigal son (Lk. 15:11-32): Patiently Jesus is waiting and watching, "watching for you and for me." Subsequent stanzas speak of the urgent need for repentance, and the mercy, pardon, and love that Christ offers. The refrain, reminiscent of a gentle lullaby, welcomes prodigals home. Appropriate as a hymn of commitment, it is often used also at funeral and memorial services.

349 Turn Your Eyes upon Jesus

Both text and tune were written by Helen H. Lemmel, daughter of a British Wesleyan Methodist pastor, who later emigrated to the

United States. The text is simple and forthright, directing us to center our eyes and spirit on Jesus. Her tune reinforces the reverent, sincere attitude of the text. The hymn is especially effective as an invitation to Christian discipleship or a call to prayer.

350 *Come, All of You*

"Come, all of you" is a Thai hymn. It uses such images as food and drink for the poor and hungry and thirsty (Is. 55:1-2; Rev. 22:17), rest for the "bearers of burden" (Mt. 11:28), peace for the troubled (Jn. 14:27). The tune is from a Thai folk song, *"Soi Son Tud."* It is clearly an invitation to Christian discipleship. Introduce it using a flute or recorder.

351 *Pass Me Not, O Gentle Savior*

Fanny Crosby and William Doane collaborated on many gospel songs, including this one composed in 1868. Born in 1820 and blinded at the age of six weeks, Fanny Crosby began writing verse at the age of eight; and by the time she died at the age of ninety-four she had written between 8,000 and 9,000 gospel song texts. She also taught at the New York City School for the Blind. Over the years this has been a favorite invitation hymn at revival services. Do not clip the dotted-note rhythm of the tune.

352 *It's Me, It's Me, O Lord* (Standing in the Need of Prayer)

Afro-American slave-poets dealt with this personal petition in very much the same manner that Fanny Crosby did in "Pass Me Not, O Gentle Savior" and Charlotte Elliott did in "Just As I Am." In this work, slave-poets expressed a personalized "me" to distinguish the personal from the collective petition. The tune PENITENT is named for the penitent thief on the cross at Calvary, who spoke up for himself to the Lord and was rewarded with a promised place in paradise.

353 *Ash Wednesday*

This prayer draws upon scriptural themes for the beginning of
Lent: Gen. 3:19; Ps. 51:10; and 1 Th. 2:12. It identifies the cross as
the center of redeeming and reactivating power for our broken
lives. Although specifically written for Ash Wednesday, the prayer
may be used publicly or privately on any occasion when sin,
repentance, and renewal are the pertinent themes.

354 *I Surrender All*

Judson W. Van Deventer wrote this text to commemorate the time
when, after a long struggle, he dedicated his life to active Christian
service. The tune SURRENDER was composed for this text and
complements the hymn's message of complete trust and assurance. It is especially effective when used before a time of prayer or
as an invitation to Christian discipleship.

355 *Depth of Mercy*

Originally titled "After a Relapse into Sin," this Charles Wesley
text was first in the section of John Wesley's 1780 *Collection* headed
"For Mourners Convinced of Backsliding." We identify with Paul
as "the chief of sinners" (1 Tim. 1:15) and turn to the Master we
"afresh have crucified" (Heb. 6:6). The depth of conviction is
sounded in the pleas even for the *desire* to repent. This hymn may
be used as a prayer of confession and is appropriate during the
season of Lent, especially on Ash Wednesday, or on other
occasions when the emphasis is upon repentance.

356 *Pues Si Vivimos* (When We Are Living)

The first stanza of this quiet, affirming hymn comes to us from
unknown Christians in Mexico, where it has circulated orally for
several years. The tune is easy to learn and is especially appropriate
for funerals, graveside committals, benedictions, closing prayer
circles, memorial and baptismal services, or any celebration of
beginnings and endings. Sing a cappella or with guitar. An
additional stanza, "Shalom to You," can be found at 666.

357 *Just As I Am, Without One Plea*

At the time of her conversion, Charlotte Elliott was told by a friend: "You must come as you are, a sinner, to the Lamb of God who takes away the sin of the world." As she remembered the anniversary of her conversion and recalled the words of her friend she wrote this text. The text alludes to Jn. 6:37: "All that the Father gives me will come to me; and him who comes to me I will not cast out." It has become one of the most widely used hymns of invitation.

358 *Dear Lord and Father of Mankind*

In 1872 John Greenleaf Whittier wrote a poem entitled "The Brewing of Soma," in which he compares the noisy and hysterical camp meetings and revivals that took place in his neighborhood to the religious rites of pagans, in which they worked themselves into a drunken stupor. The final lines of that poem, from which this text is taken, are a beautiful prayer for inner peace, reflecting Whittier's simple inward Quaker faith. With the tune REST, written for this text in 1887 by Frederick C. Maker, this hymn has become a favorite in many denominations, including those with a strong campmeeting and revival heritage.

359 *Alas! and Did My Savior Bleed?*

See 294.

360 *Freedom in Christ*

As Paul understood, "the last enemy to be destroyed is death" (1 Cor. 15:26), and the dread of death consumes much of our energy. We try to ignore this fact and in the process complicate our lives still further by denying reality. This prayer asks that we may be freed from the fear of death, for only so can we live the joyous life Christ has won for us in his resurrection. The evidences of

God's goodness all about us are signs of deliverance, and we ask to be always aware of these gifts from God. The prayer, which may be used either in public or private, is by Rubem Alves, a contemporary Presbyterian theologian and teacher in Brazil.

361 Rock of Ages, Cleft for Me

The metaphor "Rock of Ages, Cleft for Me" possibly comes from two scripture passages: Is. 26:4 and Ex. 33:22. The theme is the gospel message that Jesus' suffering and death alone provide the way to salvation. The water and blood which gushed from his side provide life everlasting, just as the water from the rock provided physical life for Hebrews wandering in the desert. Augustus M. Toplady, a staunch Calvinist and contemporary of the Wesleys, carried on an open feud with John Wesley over the role of free will in salvation. This hymn is his response to John Wesley's views, but Methodists soon made it their own and have loved it ever since. Thomas Hastings wrote the tune TOPLADY in 1830 for this text.

362 Nothing but the Blood

Images from the book of Revelation are the basis for this text by Robert Lowry, a nineteenth-century Baptist pastor in Pennsylvania and New York. This hymn is a strong affirmation of the pardoning of sins found only through the redeeming blood and sacrificial love of Jesus Christ. Lowry's tune is light and joyous, expressing the believer's ultimate hope.

363 And Can It Be that I Should Gain

Published in *Hymns and Sacred Poems* (1739) under the title "Free Grace," this is one of two Charles Wesley hymns (the other being "Where Shall My Wondering Soul Begin") that have been identified with his *Journal* entry for May 23, 1738: "At nine I began a hymn on my conversion. . . . " As such, it would also have been sung a day later "with great joy" on the occasion of John Wesley's

Aldersgate experience. In his 1780 *Collection*, John Wesley placed it among the hymns "For Believers Rejoicing," expressing the confidence of justifying grace and new birth. The "no condemnation" of stanza 5 echoes the breakthrough of Rom. 8:31. Though connected with Aldersgate Sunday, the hymn is also appropriate for any evangelical occasion. The marchlike quality of the tune SAGINA is well suited to the boldness and confidence of the text.

364   *Because He Lives*

In 1974, "Because He Lives" was named "Best Gospel Song of the Year" by the Gospel Music Association. It was one of the five new hymns most requested by United Methodists for inclusion in the new hymnal. William J. Gaither wrote its tune RESURRECTION and co-authored the text with his wife, Gloria. Presenting a message of justifying grace and pardon and proclaiming new life through the resurrection of Jesus Christ, this personal expression of faith echoes the words of hope found in Jn. 14:19: "Because I live, you will live also."

365   *Grace Greater than Our Sin*

Julia H. Johnston, a Presbyterian laywoman from Peoria, Illinois, here expresses the words of Paul in Rom. 5:20: "But where sin abounded, grace did much more abound" (KJV). It is a hymn of forgiveness and pardon, offering hope and redemption to believers through the "grace that is greater than all our sin!" The gentle, reassuring tune, MOODY, complements this text. Repeat the refrain after the last stanza without accompaniment, everyone singing softly.

366   *For Guidance*

This Korean prayer acknowledges that looking to God is like looking in a mirror and seeing ourselves as we really are, with all our faults. It asks God not to abandon us but to dwell in us and guide us. It is an appropriate prayer of confession by individuals or congregations or may be a prayer for illumination.

367 He Touched Me

"He Touched Me" is one of William J. Gaither's best known and loved gospel hymns. It was one of the five new hymns most requested by United Methodists for inclusion in the new hymnal. Based on the stories of Jesus' cleansing the leper (Mt. 8:3; Mk. 1:41; Lk. 5:13), the text testifies to the healing power of Jesus' touch. The singer personally acknowledges that, whatever the sickness of soul or body, the Savior can cleanse and make us whole.

368 My Hope Is Built

The faith in Jesus' blood and righteousness to sustain the believer is the focus of this hymn by the English Baptist pastor Edward Mote. Through all the trials of life, faith built on "the solid rock" gives the believer hope. This metaphor along with that of "sinking sand" are found in the parable of the wise man who built his house on the rock and the foolish man who built his house on the sand (Mt. 7:24-27). The tune entitled THE SOLID ROCK with its bold leaps was written by the gospel hymn composer William Bradbury.

369 Blessed Assurance

Fanny Crosby, the blind nineteenth-century gospel hymn writer, wrote over 8,000 texts. Her ability to write hymns almost spontaneously is shown in the way this hymn came about. Her friend, Phoebe P. Knapp, composed the tune and played it for Crosby. Immediately Crosby said that the tune suggested the words "Blessed assurance, Jesus is mine" and within a short time had completed the entire text. As one of the ten most popular hymns among United Methodists, this hymn is widely used both for evangelistic crusades and revivals.

370 *Victory in Jesus*

Eugene M. Bartlett wrote both text and tune in 1939. The text is a
personal statement of salvation through the redeeming blood of
Christ. Singers readily identify with the themes of the "precious
blood's atoning" and "the old redemption story" which gives
"victory in Jesus." The triumphant tune HARTFORD, named for the
Arkansas town where Bartlett lived, encourages all to join in
singing this popular hymn of assurance.

371 *I Stand Amazed in the Presence*

Charles H. Gabriel's joyous text of assurance closely follows
Lk. 22:41-44, Christ's prayer in the Garden of Gethsemane. The
personal emphasis on Christ's bearing "my sins and sorrows" is
echoed in the refrain: "How marvelous! How wonderful is my
Savior's love for me!"

372 *How Can We Sinners Know*

This Charles Wesley text is a concise summary of Wesleyan
theology. Originally titled "The Marks of Faith," the questions in
stanza 1 are answered in turn with reference to God's justifying
grace in stanza 3 and sanctifying grace in stanza 5. Finally, these
two aspects of Wesleyan doctrine are summed up in another
favorite scriptural formula: "and both the witnesses are joined, the
Spirit of God with ours" (Rom. 8:16).

373 *Nothing Between*

In this hymn of Christian perfection, Charles A. Tindley teaches us
how to clear the path in order to make the soul and Savior one.
Worldly ways must be renounced even if friends and the world
may turn against you. Triumph is realized only through hard trials
and much tribulation. The hymn is especially appropriate when
sung during the serving of Holy Communion.

374 Standing on the Promises

The promises of God sustain the believer in every situation of life; that is the subject of this gospel song by Kelso Carter, a Methodist pastor active in the late nineteenth-century Holiness movement. God's promises do not fail even in times of doubt and fear. They bind Christians to Jesus through love, helping us to overcome problems and sin in daily life. Simple and repetitive in its message and exuberant in its musical style, it is a favorite of many evangelical Christians.

375 There Is a Balm in Gilead

The prophet Jeremiah carried God's message to the people of Israel, predicting the conquest and ruin of their country at the hands of the Babylonians. Jeremiah's rather gloomy warnings went unheeded by the people. Their negative response tested his faith, and he began to doubt his own words, Jeremiah felt rejected by the Lord, and out of disappointment cried out: "Is there no balm in Gilead? Is there no physician there?" (Jer. 8:22). Slave-poets, with the assurance of knowing, acquired from Christian learning and experience, responded to Jeremiah's despairing queries with profound conviction. Indeed, "Doctor" Jesus is alive and well and does heal the sin-sick soul. This spiritual traditionally is sung moderately slow with intense feeling.

376 Dona Nobis Pacem

Dona nobis pacem means "Give us peace." Spiritual peace, peace in our homes, peace in our world—all can be supplied through the love of God in Christ. This traditional Latin canon (or round) beautifully gives us an image of that peace. Simple enough to be learned by children and sung as a round by a congregation, it is appropriate as a prayer hymn or benediction.

377 It Is Well with My Soul

In 1873, Chicago lawyer Horatio G. Spafford sent his wife and four daughters on a European trip, with plans to join them later. His family sailed on the SS *Ville du Havre,* which was struck by another ship and sank. Mrs. Spafford survived, but the daughters were lost. She cabled her husband from Cardiff, Wales: "Saved alone." Spafford sailed to meet his wife and wrote this text near the scene of the tragedy. The languid melody by Philip P. Bliss is learned easily. The beautifully written refrain should be well supported by the choir and organ or piano.

378 Amazing Grace

John Newton was referring to his own life and experience when he wrote this monumental hymn. He had been a slave trader but was converted under the influence of George Whitefield and the Wesleys. He was later ordained and became both a leader in the evangelical wing of the Church of England and a vigorous opponent of slavery. His tombstone epitaph sums up his experience: "John Newton, clerk, once an infidel and libertine, a servant of slavers in Africa, was, by the rich mercy of our Lord and Saviour Jesus Christ, preserved, restored, pardoned and appointed to preach the faith he had long labored to destroy." This tune has become a favorite among Native American churches, and is sung with a variety of texts in their native languages, of which five are provided in the hymnal. The anonymous sixth stanza has been added to the hymn by popular request.

379 Blow Ye the Trumpet, Blow

In this great hymn of justifying grace, the biblical themes of atonement and the year of jubilee (Lev. 25:8-24) become an invitation to the whole world to receive through "the precious blood of Christ" (1 Pet. 1:19) a salvation that cannot be bought or earned. The hymn is well suited to the evangelistic and invitational context of revival, as well as to the expression of the assurance of faith that is relevant in every season. The rousing tune LENOX amply demonstrates the triumphant spirit of the words.

380 There's Within My Heart a Melody

This joyous text combined with an uplifting tune invites everyone to sing. The text speaks of a melody within the heart because the name of Jesus "keeps me singing as I go." A life of discord becomes harmonious when "Jesus swept across the broken strings, stirred the slumbering chords again." Luther B. Bridgers, a Georgia Methodist pastor, wrote both words and music after losing his wife and children in a house fire.

381 Savior, Like a Shepherd Lead Us

Time has yet to reveal the true author of this popular text. Some have attributed it to Dorothy Thrupp while others believe it is the work of Henry Lyte. Although this text was written for young people (see Ps. 63:1—"O God, thou art my God; early will I seek thee" [KJV]), it has become a favorite of all age groups. Its theme was inspired by Jn. 10:3: "he calls his own sheep by name and leads them out." The tune BRADBURY traditionally is sung in an easy, moderately flowing manner.

382 Have Thine Own Way

Adelaide Pollard, an activist in various Christian causes, penned this text during a time of personal despair. The message centers on completely forsaking self and submitting to God's will. The poet uses the image of God as the potter and the self as the clay to be molded (Is. 64:8; Jer. 18:3-6), thus setting the tone for the entire hymn. With George Stebbins's tune ADELAIDE, this hymn is one of the most frequently sung invitation hymns.

383 *This Is a Day of New Beginnings*

Any day of significance in the life of a church is an appropriate one on which to sing this hymn. It may be the first Sunday of a New Year, a church anniversary, or any day that maybe a "day of beginnings." Each stanza suggests new opportunities that point us to new experiences. In stanza 3 there is the suggestion cf Paul's exhortation to the church at Corinth (2 Cor. 5:17). Stanzas 4 and 5 each end with a reference to Rev. 21:5. Stanza 5 makes the hymn appropriate for Holy Communion. This contemporary text by Brian Wren is complemented by the tune NEW BEGINNINGS, written specifically for this text by Carlton R. Young. Have the choir sing the first two stanzas (while the congregation reads or hums along) with all singing the remaining stanzas.

384 *Love Divine, All Loves Excelling*

In the section "For Believers Groaning for Full Redemption" in John Wesley's 1780 *Collection,* this Charles Wesley text sounds the depths of Christian praise and perfection. Perfecting grace is centered in Christ's presence by the Spirit (Jn. 14:16-23; 20:22), yet it involves an ever-deepening process—"changed from glory into glory" (2 Cor. 3:18; 5:17)—which is finally communal and cosmic in scope (Rev. 4:9-11). This is one of the ten most widely sung hymns among United Methodists. It is suitable for general use but may find special meaning on one of the Sundays of the Easter season, anticipating Pentecost.

385 *Let Us Plead for Faith Alone*

A concise summary of the Wesleyan understanding of faith, this Charles Wesley hymn holds together biblical themes that have sometimes been pushed apart. Salvation is by "faith alone" (Eph. 2:8-10), yet this always implies a "faith which works by love" (Gal. 5:6; Jas. 2:18). As such, this hymn could serve as a peculiarly Wesleyan celebration of the great theme of "faith and works" (Reformation Sunday). The simplicity of the tune, SAVANNAH, is well suited to the simple beauty of the text.

386   Come, O Thou Traveler Unknown

Long acclaimed among Charles Wesley's best, this poem dramatically expresses the struggle of faith. The pivotal image is that of Jacob wrestling with the angel (Gen. 32:24-32); only now, the image is applied to the struggle that often attends the birth of faith. In Wesley's 1780 *Collection*, the hymn appears in the section "For Mourners Brought to the Birth." As a struggle with *and* by grace, focused throughout on the One whose "name is Love," the hymn is also appropriate as a prayer for revival and renewal.

387   Come, O Thou Traveler Unknown

"Wrestling believers may obtain glorious victories, and yet come off with broken bones; for 'when they are weak, then they are strong, weak in themselves, but strong in Christ' (2 Cor. 12:10)." So wrote Matthew Henry, a biblical scholar who had a strong influence on Wesley, in his *Commentary* on Gen. 32:24-32. As Jacob wrestled with the traveler unknown at Peniel, so Charles's poem wrestles with God's nature, as seen in each stanza. Use it as a meditation by first reading the scripture passage, then reading or singing the full poem.

388   O Come and Dwell in Me

An invocation of the Spirit's sanctifying and perfecting presence, this Charles Wesley text originally appeared as three separate items in *Short Hymns on Select Passages of Holy Scripture* (1762). The presence of the Spirit brings liberty (2 Cor. 3:17; Rom. 8:21) and renewal (2 Cor. 5:17), and is confirmed through the witness of a life spent pleasing God (Heb. 11:5; 13:21). The text is well set to the simple tune ST. MICHAEL. This hymn is apt whenever the emphasis is on the Holy Spirit and particularly at Pentecost.

389 Freely, Freely

Carol Owens's hymn of rebirth and response is best known by its refrain, "Freely, Freely," based on Jesus' words in Mt. 10:8 "Freely ye have received, freely give" (KJV). The stanzas acknowledge the gift of being born anew "in Jesus' name" and the responsibility we have to share the love and power Jesus has freely bestowed (Mt. 28:18-20). Feel the melody with one strong beat to the measure, and for variety, have the women sing the first stanza and the men, the second.

390 Forgive Our Sins as We Forgive

Rosamond Herklots has taken a phrase from the Lord's Prayer (Mt. 6:12) and used it as a measure with which we examine our lives, pointing us toward a deeper understanding of the entire prayer. Set to the prayerful early U.S.A. tune DETROIT, it may be used as a call to prayer or as a response to confession or sermon.

391 O Happy Day, That Fixed My Choice

This text by the eighteenth-century English hymn writer Philip Doddridge was originally titled "Rejoicing in Our Covenant to God" and was suggested by 2 Chr. 15:15—"And all Judah rejoiced at the oath" (KJV). It emphasizes the importance of the salvation experience before expounding on God's gifts of joy and security in the life of the believer. The refrain was added probably from campmeeting sources. It is especially useful for baptisms, confirmations, and evangelistic services.

392 Prayer for a New Heart

A prayer for a new heart is perpetually appropriate to Christian people, whether assembled in worship or separated for mission in the world. This text is a particular treasure, first because of its beauty of construction and simplicity of form, and second because its author exemplified so well the words he wrote. As international diplomat and secretary-general of the United Nations, Dag Hammerskjöld demonstrated what it means to have a heart that sees, hears, serves, and abides in God. In the public reading of the prayer, attention needs to be given to the opening phrases: God is over us as sovereign Lord; God is one of us as incarnated servant in Jesus. But most of all, God exists in full reality and power. The verb "art" appears in italics in the third line as an indication that this existence of God (alluding to Ex. 3:14) is a central Judeo-Christian affirmation, to be emphasized by the very way we speak the words.

393 Spirit of the Living God

Daniel Iverson was pastor of Presbyterian churches in the southeastern United States. His chorus "Spirit of the Living God" is a prayer for rebirth and renewal based on Acts 11:15: "The Holy Spirit fell on them just as on us at the beginning." A pleading quality to the music imparts the sincere desire of the singer to be used and filled by the Holy Spirit. This chorus makes an effective prayer for illumination, call to prayer, or prayer response. Have the choir sing it once, then repeat with everyone singing.

394 Something Beautiful

This text by Gloria Gaither is a strong testimony to the transforming power of Jesus Christ. The tune by William J. Gaither provides a flowing, contemporary gospel sound. This chorus offers words of hope and assurance and may be used following the prayer of confession. Accompany on piano, playing embellishments while the organ sustains the congregation.

395 Take Time to Be Holy

William Longstaff's familiar text is a good expression of Christian holiness (see 1 Pet. 1:16: "You shall be holy, for I am holy"). The

Christian should pray, study the Word, associate with Christian brothers and sisters, and help the weak. This closeness will bring a calm to the soul and serenity to life and will prepare the Christian for eternal life with God.

396   O Jesus, I Have Promised

John E. Bode wrote this as a confirmation text for three of his children in 1866 and based his text on Lk. 9:57: "I will follow you wherever you go." The words express the wonder of a child setting out on a new adventure. In the stanzas are expressed a promise to follow if Christ is near to guide, prayers for strength to resist temptations, and Jesus' promise made to those who follow him to the end. The hymn is appropriate at confirmations, baptisms, or reaffirmations of the baptismal covenant.

397   I Need Thee Every Hour

In 1872 Annie Hawks, a mother and homemaker, wrote this text out of her daily experiences and need for God's presence. One day while working in her home, she was overcome with a sense of nearness to God and the words "I need thee every hour" came to her mind. She showed the text to her pastor, Robert Lowry, a prominent poet and musician, who set the words to music. Although the thought of the hymn is very simple, its words strike a responsive note for the Christian. It is a favorite hymn of devotion.

398   Jesus Calls Us

Author of many hymns for children, Cecil Frances Alexander chose to teach the basic tenets of faith through her poetry, in this instance the Apostles' Creed. The second stanza originally read, "As of old Saint Andrew heard it," and the hymn was entitled "Saint Andrew's Day." In later editions, "Saint Andrew" in the second stanza was changed to "th'apostles." Set to the familiar tune GALILEE, it is appropriate as a hymn of commitment and sending forth.

399 Take My Life, and Let It Be

There may be no other hymn sung by our church that better addresses the commitment of one's talents and possessions. Frances Havergal's text is based upon Rom. 12:1: "I appeal to you therefore, brethren, by the mercies of God, to present your bodies as a living sacrifice, . . . which is your spiritual worship." The gifts that are to be committed in service to God and neighbor are life, moments, hands, feet, voice, lips, silver and gold, intellect, will, heart, love, and self.

400 Come, Thou Fount of Every Blessing

Robert Robinson, a pastor influenced by both Whitefield and Wesley, wrote this exuberant exhortation of praise in 1758. The term "Ebenezer" in the second stanza refers to the passage 1 Sam. 7:12: "Then Samuel took a stone and set it between Mizpah and Shen, and called the name of it Ebenezer, saying, Hitherto hath the Lord helped us" (KJV). Ebenezer is the Hebrew for "Stone of Help." The tune NETTLETON provides a joyful mood to this well-loved hymn of providence and grace.

401 For Holiness of Heart

This personal prayer identifies the heart as the center of our fear and our yearning and asks to be perfected by divine love. Written by a leading American black theologian and poet, it speaks authentically to our humanity and our striving after God.

402 Lord, I Want to Be a Christian

Many slaves embraced the religion of their owners. These slaves found hope and comfort in a merciful God who sent Moses to deliver the household of Israel out of bondage. Converted slaves became more excited about their religion when they encountered Jesus Christ and had sufficient cause to revere and savor passages such as Jn. 8:31b-32: "If you continue in my word, you are truly disciples, and you will know the truth, and the truth will make you free." Such sentiment provided slaves with visions of a brighter tomorrow where ultimate release would occur. In contrast to many owners who practiced a part-time religion on Sunday with their mouths and tongues, converted slaves desired to practice a full-time religion every day with their hearts and minds. This spiritual is universally appealing, as it continues to speak to all practicing Christians with freshness.

403   For True Life

At the heart of this prayer there is a striking request: "Do not punish me . . . by granting that which I wish or ask." Can answered prayer be punishment? The great Spanish mystic Teresa of Avila knew it could be—should God grant our foolish requests. The prayer is clearly an expansion of Jesus' petition in Gethsemane: "Not my will, but thine, be done" (Lk. 22:42). Therefore we ask to be governed by God's wisdom not our own, dying to self and living in Christ.

404   Every Time I Feel the Spirit

The theme of this spiritual was inspired by Rom. 8:15-17. Paul taught that the children of God are heirs of God and as such are fellow heirs with Christ. Unknown slave-poets chose scenes from the lives of Moses and Elijah to illustrate what Paul meant by heirs. The word "shine," in stanza 1, refers to brightness. The "train," in stanza 2, is an image commonly found in spiritual poetry. Here, a train has been substituted for Elijah's chariot. Hand clapping will enhance the singing of this upbeat spiritual.

405   Seek Ye First

This text was born out of Karen Lafferty's own struggle to seek God's will for her life. After attending a Bible study on Mt. 6:33:

"Seek ye first the kingdom of God" (KJV); she returned home and picked out the simple melody to accompany the stanzas on her guitar. The song quickly became a favorite with youth and young adults and remains popular today. Lafferty describes it as "a song in which people can put God's desire for their lives above their own."

406 *Canticle of Prayer*

This canticle was adapted by Alan Luff from the Revised Standard Version of Rom. 8:26 and Lk. 11:9-10 during the Scottish Churches' Consultation on Church Music which took place at Dunblane in 1962. The tune was composed in 1969 and, with the text, appeared in *New Songs for the Church: Book 2, Canticles* (1969). The introduction was added by John Wilson in 1978. The antiphon is sung by the congregation and the verses by the soloist. Keep a slow one beat per measure throughout.

407 *Close to Thee*

Fanny Crosby was often inspired to write words to existing tunes. This is the case with this text inspired by the tune CLOSE TO THEE, composed by Silas Vail. The text centers on the Christian's need to walk with God. The Christian does not need ease, worldly pleasure, or fame but only the presence of God to lead the way through life. This walk with God will lead the Christian through "the vale of shadows" and eventually through "the gate of life eternal." Sing this rousing tune joyously. For contrast, try singing stanza 3 softly with no accompaniment on the refrain.

408 *The Gift of Love*

This paraphrase of 1 Cor. 13:1-3 and adaptation of a traditional English melody (O WALY WALY) by Hal Hopson is a very singable congregational hymn. Stanza 3 is a prayer voiced to the Holy Spirit that love may control our every action; for "by this we worship, and are freed." Appropriate at Pentecost and weddings, it may accompanied with piano, organ, or guitar. Try adding a flute, violin, or handbells to enhance the melody.

143

409 *For Grace to Labor*

This, one of the briefest of all prayers, is also one of the deepest in its meaning. Two particular uses should be noted. First, this is notably fitting as the closing prayer in a series of petitions; if the petitions have been made by a leader or by individuals within the congregation, this may then be a unison prayer spoken by the whole congregation. Second, this prayer, so easily memorized, can become an important resource for individuals in their personal devotional lives. The author was Sir Thomas More, the statesman, author, and martyr whose life was celebrated in the play and motion picture *A Man for All Seasons*.

410 *I Want a Principle Within*

Originally titled "For a Tender Conscience," this Charles Wesley hymn eloquently expresses the Wesleyan experience of sanctifying grace. The central biblical allusion is to Ezek. 11:19—"And I will give them one heart, and put a new spirit within them." In the 1780 *Collection*, John Wesley placed this among the hymns "For Believers Watching," where it signified the diligence of Christian discipleship. The carefree tune GERALD has endured, perhaps because it somewhat relaxes the strenuousness of the text. Sing the second stanza in two parts, using only the upper voices ending on a unison D.

411 *Dear Lord, Lead Me Day by Day*

Adapted from a very popular Filipino folk song, "Planting Rice Is Never Fun," Francisca Asuncion transformed the original phrase "bent from morn till the set of sun" into "praise from morn till the set of sun," suggesting the intimate relationship between work and celebration. The act of praise is also an act of prayer, with no time limit or boundary of space. It is a commitment to serve the whole of humanity with the confidence of God's love. This hymn is especially suitable for youth or children. Guitar accompaniment will greatly enhance its lively folk style. Begin by teaching the simple refrain to the congregation with children singing the stanzas.

412 *Prayer of John Chrysostom*

This prayer is attributed to the leading preacher and bishop of the fourth century—John "the golden tongued." Used as we conclude corporate worship, it acknowledges that it was God's grace that brought us together to make our prayer in common. We also recall the promise of Mt. 18:20, that Christ is present in the midst of the worshiping assembly. Then we ask God to grant our prayers according to divine wisdom, presumably denying us any petitions we have made out of selfishness or misguided faith. The present and the future are linked in the concluding lines of the prayer. Thomas Cranmer provided a version of this prayer for the Church of England in 1544. This petition traditionally has been used at the end of Morning Prayer but is suitable for the conclusion of any congregational service.

413 *A Charge to Keep I Have*

This Charles Wesley text first appeared in his 1762 *Short Hymns on Select Passages of the Holy Scriptures* as a paraphrase of Lev. 8:31-36, where Moses charges Aaron to remain steadfast in his duties, lest Aaron die. The key phrase is Lev. 8:35: "Keep the charge of the Lord" (KJV). Charles Wesley's text summons Christians today to accept God's call "to serve the present age" And like Moses, Wesley reminds us that God will hold us accountable to the mission with which we have been charged. A hymn frequently sung at camp meetings during the early nineteenth century, it remains popular at Annual Conferences, Charge Conferences, mission events, and services of dedication and consecration. This text may be read in unison as a congregational prayer, followed by its singing.

414 *Thou Hidden Love of God*

John Wesley translated this text, probably at Savannah in 1736 at the outset of his friendship with the Moravians, and titled it

"Divine Love. From the German." It was included in his 1780 *Collection* among the hymns "For Believers Groaning for Full Redemption." VATER UNSER, a sturdy German chorale melody, was one of Wesley's favorites, and he set this text to it in his *Foundery Collection* of 1742.

415 *Take Up Thy Cross*

Charles Everest, a nineteenth-century Episcopal priest in Connecticut, begins his text by quoting Jesus (Mt. 16:24-25). The poet elaborates upon the scripture by stating that though the cross will be heavy, God will provide the strength. We are not to be ashamed of the cross but should think of the suffering and shame that Jesus bore on our behalf. The cross is to be carried until death when it will be exchanged for a glorious crown. The hymn is appropriate for use in Lent or as an invitation to Christian discipleship.

416 *Come Out the Wilderness*

A slave named Nat Turner led a rebellion in Virginia in 1831. Later declaring that he had been inspired by the voice of God, he warred with what he believed to be the Philistines. This slave-preacher then retreated into a forest covering. When he was flushed out and captured, he emerged nightly preaching repentance and stating that he was "leaning on de Lawd." News reporters on the scene engaged in open dialogue with Nat Turner, unaware that they were documenting the birth of this American folk song. The calls and responses in this text are unique among Afro-American spirituals in that they were first printed in a local newspaper. The spiritual traditionally is sung in a relaxed and unhurried manner.

417 *O For a Heart to Praise My God*

Taking up the petition of Ps. 51:10: "Create in me a clean heart, O God; and renew a right spirit within me" (KJV), this Charles Wesley text is essentially a prayer for sanctifying and perfecting

146

grace. John Wesley placed it among the hymns "For Believers Groaning for Full Redemption" in his 1780 *Collection*. The stanzas are a catalog of Christian virtues such as meekness, humility, purity, and culminates with love as the cardinal virtue.

418 We Are Climbing Jacob's Ladder

"Jacob's Ladder" is derived from the dream story in Gen. 28:10-17. Slave-poets extracted elements from this story to develop a theme on Christian perfection. Play as a bright march, changing key each succeeding stanza up a half step as an effective means of variation to highlight the spiritual's meaning.

419 I Am Thine, O Lord

Fanny Crosby had a remarkable ability to write hymn texts simply on the suggestion of a thought or a passage from scripture. One evening while visiting William H. Doane, the topic of conversation was nearness to God. Crosby, inspired by Heb. 10:22: "Let us draw near with a true heart in full assurance of faith," wrote this text. Doane later set it to music.

420 Breathe on Me, Breath of God

Edwin Hatch was a widely known Oxford scholar and theologian. This text demonstrates his simplicity of faith and thought. The word for spirit in both Hebrew and Greek is the same as that for breath. Thus, the Holy Spirit is the "Breath of God," which gives life to the believer. This idea is carried out through the text to the final stanza's emphasis on eternal life. The tune TRENTHAM provides an appropriately meditative setting as a call or response to prayer or for devotional use. Suitable for general use, it is especially appropriate at Pentecost.

421 *Make Me a Captive, Lord*

Paradox is found in almost every phrase of George Matheson's text on Christian freedom. Inspired by Eph. 3:1 where Paul writes of himself as a "prisoner for Jesus Christ," its overall message is that true freedom is found only in complete commitment to Jesus. Sung to the well-known tune DIADEMATA, the hymn has a powerful message. The phrase, "it varies with the wind," has caused controversy as to whether it is an "eye" rhyme and pronounced wind, as in a breeze, or whether it is an allusion to a mechanical device that one winds, thus rhyming with find. Decide for yourself.

422 *Jesus, Thine All-Victorious Love*

Based on Rom. 5:5: "The love of God is shed abroad in our hearts by the Holy Ghost" (KJV), this text is a prayer for sanctifying grace. The way of sanctifying grace is not without struggle, yet the struggle rests finally upon the promises of the Spirit's refining presence. The tune AZMON is an appropriate tune for this powerful text.

423 *Finding Rest in God*

Here are juxtaposed two closely related statements, one very ancient, from Africa, the other, modern, from India. The first is one of the most famous prayers and affirmation of all time, from the opening of *The Confessions* of St. Augustine. Sundar Singh, knowing well this fourth-century statement, commented upon it in his own meditation. These passages may be employed for individual devotion. In corporate worship they may be used in a variety of ways. One such way is for the congregation to speak the prayer of St. Augustine in unison, with the leader then reading the commentary by Singh. This could be a preparatory act before prayer, or an act to open the entire service of worship, whether on the Lord's Day or a weekday. These acts may also be used in conjunction with the singing of the hymn "Thou Hidden Love of God" (414), for the close of that hymn's first stanza alludes to this prayer of St. Augustine.

424 *Must Jesus Bear the Cross Alone*

The question in the first line of this text by Thomas Shepherd challenges the singer, "Must Jesus bear the cross alone?" The origin of the stanzas is obscure, and they have been subject to alterations over the centuries. This text has remained a favorite at Holy Week as the singer contemplates, "there's a cross for everyone, and there's a cross for me."

425 O Crucified Redeemer

This text by Timothy Rees, written early in this century, reminds us that Christ is crucified anew by the sins of our time. Calvary is everywhere, as our neighbors here and abroad bleed in wars, and in the everyday battles for the necessities of life, "where might is right and self is king." Set with the somber Welsh tune LLANGLOFFAN, the hymn is a prayer for awareness and change from selfishness to the reign of Christ's love. Have the beautiful melody played through before singing using an instrument with a warm rich sound to highlight the melody.

426 Behold a Broken World

Timothy Dudley-Smith, an Anglican bishop, is one of several British hymn writers whose hymns are appearing in most new hymnals. The theme of this text is an ancient one, the prayer for peace, and combines the prayers of the prophets with Christ as Prince of Peace. The words could be read as a prayer by pastor or congregation; or, stanzas 1 and 6 could be sung, and the middle four read. Max Miller's tune MARSH CHAPEL is named for the chapel at the United Methodist Boston University School of Theology, where he is organist.

427 Where Cross the Crowded Ways of Life

Frank Mason North wrote this standard hymn about the Christian's responsibility to the city. The city was New York in 1905. He was influenced by Mt. 22:9: "Go therefore to the thoroughfares, and invite to the marriage feast as many as you find." The text enumerates the many needs of people in an urban setting and tells us that Jesus never recoiled from people in desperate need but showed compassion. The last two stanzas are one thought: The city needs the presence of Jesus until all people on earth learn Christ's ways of service and the city of God comes upon earth.

428 *For the Healing of the Nations*

In this prayer for peace and justice we glimpse the new heaven and new earth of Rev. 21:1–22:5. The text calls to us to "rise and pledge our word" for the healing of the nations, to face our own pride and divisions (stanza 3), and to grow in the divine image in which God has created us. This text, one of Fred Kaan's most widely used, is matched with the strong and popular Welsh tune CWM RHONDDA.

429 *For Our Country*

Christians who disagree with the policies of their governments often are regarded as being disloyal, if not treasonous. One such was Toyohiko Kagawa, an outstanding Christian leader and pacifist, who spoke out against the militaristic policies of imperial Japan during the 1930s and 1940s. His prayer for Japan has been adapted for use by persons of any nation. It shows the deep concern that can characterize those who feel constrained to criticize their native lands. This is intended as a corporate prayer, particularly on patriotic occasions.

430 *O Master, Let Me Walk with Thee*

Washington Gladden, a pioneer of the social gospel movement, wrote this text in 1879 as a devotional poem for a magazine he edited. The theme of the poem is that walking with Jesus involves serving others. Just as Jesus ministered to the sick and spiritually needy so should we help the "slow of heart" and guide the "wayward feet." Further, the walk with Jesus extends into the future in our eternal life with the master. Very useful as a hymn of commitment.

150

431 *Let There Be Peace on Earth*

A prayer with text and tune by Sy Miller and Jill Jackson for peace throughout the world, this hymn recognizes that the prospect of peace begins with each individual. The recognition that all are God's children and should walk together each day in a harmonious relationship should control our lives every day, as we strive to live peaceably with those about us. Use piano or piano and organ accompaniment to reinforce the rhythm and maintain a constant tempo.

432 *Jesu, Jesu*

Tom Colvin, former Church of Scotland missionary in Malawi and Ghana, has provided a text about neighbors, reminiscent of Christ's words to the questioning lawyer that he should love God with heart, soul, strength, and mind, and his neighbor as himself (Lk. 10:25-28). Jesus' washing of the disciples' feet (Jn. 13:1-17) is an example for us of how to serve God and neighbors. "This is the way we should live with you." The text is set to a folk tune from Ghana. This hymn is especially appropriate on Holy Thursday, for services commemorating Jesus' footwashing, or any service of reconciliation. Congregations will enjoy singing this hymn together; however, you may wish to designate stanzas to children, youth, men, and women.

433 *All Who Love and Serve Your City*

The late Erik Routley, one of this century's most outstanding hymnologists, wrote this hymn in 1966 after reflecting on the riots in the Watts district of Los Angeles. It reflects Jesus' deep concern for those residing in cities and calls us to make Christ known in daily living. A hymn of social concern, it ends with the prophetic view of the City of God found in Ezek. 48:35: "And the name of the city henceforth shall be, The Lord is there."

434 *Cuando el Pobre* **(When the Poor Ones)**

J. A. Olivar and Miguel Manzano, the poet and composer respectively, are former priests from Madrid who have created many new congregational songs in Spain since Vatican II. The text is based on Jesus' parable of the last judgment (Mt. 25:31-46), and the refrain also suggests the Emmaus story (Lk. 24:13-35) when it affirms God's companionship on life's journey. The text reminds us that those in the greatest need are often those through whom God most powerfully ministers to us. Sing this hymn when emphasizing missions and social concerns. Have a soloist or choir introduce this hymn by singing the first two stanzas, with all singing the remaining stanzas. If it is sung in Spanish, the congregation may wish to join at the refrain in English.

435 *O God of Every Nation*

This hymn won a contest sponsored by the Hymn Society of America in 1958 for a text on the "New World Order." The author, William W. Reid, Jr., a United Methodist pastor, gives us a strong prayer for peace in our strife-torn world and prays that war and the sounds of war will cease. The familiar strong Welsh tune LLANGLOFFAN matches the mood and tone of the words and provides a powerful hymn for services on the theme of world peace.

436 *The Voice of God Is Calling*

This hymn uses the call of God—"Whom shall I send, and who will go for us?"—from Is. 6:8 as a call to respond to the needs of people in our world. These needs are seen everywhere—in cot, mine, slum, field, mart, and city street. We respond but can succeed only if we allow God to magnify our weakness. The last stanza is a prayer for deliverance from ease, plenty, pride, and low desire. The hymn was written in 1913 by a Unitarian pastor strongly committed to social action and it still has a message for today's church. This stately tune should be played in a steady moderate tempo, supported by a full sound from the organ or piano.

437 *This Is My Song*

Lloyd Stone of Hawaii begins this text as a prayer for peace, as he tells of love for his country where his heart, hope, and dreams are. He also acknowledges that persons from other lands, who love their country and have similar hopes and dreams, experience the same blue sky and the beauties of nature. The last stanza, written by Georgia Harkness, a Methodist theologian, is a prayer that God's will may be done on earth, with all serving Christ and nations living in peace. This hymn is appropriate for Worldwide Communion and Independence Sundays and other patriotic, civic, and international celebrations.

438 *Forth in Thy Name, O Lord*

Originally titled "Before Work" and entered among the hymns "For Believers Working" in John Wesley's 1780 *Collection,* this Charles Wesley text describes the full range of sanctifying grace that touches every sphere of human experience. The basic thought is that of 1 Cor. 2:2, to know nothing "save Jesus Christ" (KJV), and in all things to prove God's "good and perfect will." It is a natural hymn for Labor Day Sunday. The marchlike quality of the tune, DUKE STREET, provides bracing energy for the words.

439 *We Utter Our Cry*

Fred Kaan, whose hymns often forcefully speak to present-day issues, wrote this text for the opening service of a Christian World Conference on Life and Peace in 1983. It is an impassioned protest against the evils of the world, including possible atomic annihilation, and a passionate plea for peace. The closing line is a masterpiece.

440 *Let There Be Light*

The theme of world peace too often has inspired wordy hymns. This text is built around six striking short imperatives, with stanzas

4 and 5 quoting from the Lord's Prayer. Canadians Frances W. Davis and Robert J. B. Fleming, author and composer respectively, have succeeded in combining a most unusual meter and an unrhymed text with a singable tune. Notice how the last stanza combines all the key words in the preceding stanzas. If organ is used, vary the registration to reflect the essential idea of each stanza.

441   What Does the Lord Require

Albert F. Bayly, distinguished twentieth-century British hymn writer and minister in the United Reformed Church, based this text on Mic. 6:6-8. He relates the prophet's ancient questions about what the Lord requires to contemporary situations and sees them in the light of God's revelation in Christ. The gifted twentieth-century British hymnologist Erik Routley composed the tune for this text. Routley was editor of *Rejoice in the Lord*, of the Christian Reformed Church in America, and a major consultant to *The Hymnal 1982* of the Episcopal Church.

442   Weary of All Trumpeting

This hymn will speak eloquently to those who are weary of political and military posturing. The author, Martin Franzmann, a Lutheran theologian, professor, scholar, and poet, calls on us to follow the way of the cross and all that this means. The paradox of triumph through suffering is mirrored in the stark yet powerful tune by Hugo Distler, a brilliant German composer who was driven to suicide by the oppression of the Nazi authorities. The organ (with full and bright registration) or piano should forcefully support this great tune, emphasizing its strong martial rhythm.

443   O God Who Shaped Creation

United Methodist pastor William W. Reid, Jr., long active in the Hymn Society of America, wrote this text based on Gen. 1:1-3,

26-27, expressing God's eternal love and care for all of us wayward children, always seeking us with motherlike compassion. The tune TUOLUMNE, named for an Indian territory in California, was written by Dale Wood, eminent American composer and editor. This text was commissioned especially for *The United Methodist Hymnal* by the Hymnal Revision Committee.

444 O Young and Fearless Prophet

Ralph Harlow wrote this hymn in 1931, during the Great Depression. First used at a student conference, and controversial because of its strong stand on social issues, the text depicts Christ as the "young and fearless prophet" who served others while the cross loomed before him. The third stanza, opposing militarism, has been restored to its original wording (except that "unity" has been substituted for "brotherhood"). The fourth stanza, protesting greed and wealth of some while many go hungry, was rejected by previous Methodist hymnals with the view that "the church is not ready to sing that yet"; it is here included for the first time. The last stanza prays that we may hear above our noisy world the call of Christ to serve God by serving others. The vigorous tune may be sung by all or it may be varied by having a reader speak stanza 2 and a soloist sing stanza 4.

445 Happy the Home When God Is There

The characteristics of a happy Christian home are enumerated in this text by Henry Ware, a nineteenth-century Unitarian pastor from Massachusetts. These qualities include God's presence, Christian teaching, parental example, prayer, praise, love of the Bible, and love for one another. In the last stanza the text moves beyond the family and speaks of love for all outside the family. While the hymn describes an ideal seldom totally achieved, Christian families may find such an ideal helpful in these times when the values of family life are threatened. It is especially effective when used at services that emphasize the family and for parent-child dedication services.

446 *Serving the Poor*

Mother Teresa, the humanitarian nun of Calcutta, has set in a few lines a moving prayer for all who serve the poor. The arresting opening words identify the need for a sense of humility rather than of superiority by all who would labor on behalf of those who suffer. In a service of worship this prayer is particularly useful in conjunction with other prayers for the homeless, the hungry, and the dispossessed.

447 *Our Parent, By Whose Name*

This text is a prayer in which each of the three stanzas is addressed to a person of the Trinity, asking blessing and guidance for families. It reminds us that God is the model for our parenting; Jesus, our model for growth; and that the Holy Spirit dwells in our homes. F. Bland Tucker was an Episcopal priest and poet who served for over twenty years at Old Christ Church in Savannah, Georgia, the parish served by John Wesley. This hymn is appropriate for the Festival of the Christian Home, Mother's Day, or Father's Day.

448 *Go Down, Moses*

"Go Down, Moses" was the most widely known and sung spiritual during the midnineteenth century. Its twenty-seven or more stanzas were as powerful as abolitionist oratory. "Moses" may have been sung first by the Hutchingson Brothers, a black quartet, at Cooper Union in New York City on the occasion of an emancipation speech delivered by President Lincoln in 1863. It remains a popular favorite, beloved because of its stirring melody and strong message recounting the entire Exodus story. The tune has been named for ex-slave and underground railroad conductor Harriet Tubman, who was known as "the Moses of her People." The eleven stanzas presented here should be sung very broadly and boldly with brilliance.

449 *Our Earth We Now Lament to See*

Originally titled "For Peace" and published in *Hymns of Intercession for All Mankind* (1758), this Charles Wesley text illustrates how early Methodists made the connection of praying for the world and protesting the evils of war. The satanic and "unnatural" images in stanza 2 (Rev. 9:11; Jer. 7:31; 32:35) are contrasted with the scriptural themes of God's creation and reign in stanzas 3 and 4, which ground the Christian commitment to "follow after peace."

450 *Creator of the Earth and Skies*

This text by Donald Hughes pleads for wisdom through God's truth and strength. We confess that our ignorance of God makes us trust ourselves, and the lack of love for God results in hatred and "evils wrought by human pride." Hence we plead for God's knowledge to "end this worldwide strife." Jeremiah Clark's tune UFFINGHAM carries the text well with its strong minor tune.

451 *Be Thou My Vision*

This eighth-century Irish hymn is a prayer for the vision of God throughout life. The text is a personal prayer as we acknowledge God to be "my light . . . my treasure . . . Ruler of all." The lovely Irish melody SLANE with its ABCD form (all four lines are different) enhances the text. Slane is a hill ten miles from Tara in Count Meath, Ireland, associated with St. Patrick's struggle against Druid priests.

452 *My Faith Looks Up to Thee*

This text by Ray Palmer looks to Jesus as our source of faith. It acknowledges Jesus as the source of faith, prays for strength through the difficulties and sorrows of life, and asks for faith and trust at the hour of death. Set to Lowell Mason's devotional tune OLIVET, it has become one of the most widely used hymns of faith. This text is also meaningful when read in unison by a congregation.

453   More Love to Thee, O Christ

This prayer by Elizabeth Prentiss is the result of her own physical suffering and mental anguish expressed in the words: "Let sorrow do its work, Come grief or pain." Even in sorrow, grief, and death our prayer shall be, "More love to thee." This hymn may be used for a meditative prayer or as a hymn of commitment.

454   Open My Eyes, That I May See

This text prays for openness to God's leading—for open eyes to see the truth, for open ears to hear the truth, and for an open mouth to bear the truth. The believer waits, ready to do God's will. This hymn may be used as a prayer for illumination or as part of the prayer time in worship.

455   Not So in Haste, My Heart

Bradford Torrey's text admonishes us to wait patiently on the Lord, because "He never comes too late." Note the unusual construction; the first line of each succeeding stanza repeats the final line of the previous stanza to reemphasize the truth of the line. The tune from Austria, DOLOMITE CHANT, is interesting in its alteration of 2/4 and 3/4 time, enhancing the mood of the text. Once the congregation knows the tune, have them experience it a cappella, which will enhance the melody and the beautiful suspension at the end of each stanza.

456   For Courage to Do Justice

This prayer for openness to the needs of others is appropriate in a variety of settings. It is especially apt just before or after singing the hymn "Open My Eyes That I May See" (454), for it gives that hymn a social dimension that may otherwise be overlooked. This is one in a series of prayers for peacemaking by the South African author and social reformer Alan Paton, who drew his inspiration from the prayer of Saint Francis, "Lord, make me an instrument of thy peace," found as 481 in the hymnal.

457 *For the Sick*

This prayer for those who are ill may be used in corporate worship, particularly after the names of sick persons have been mentioned. It is also appropriate for private devotion. We pray not only for the sick but also for those who help them, bearing in mind medical personnel, clergy, friends, and family. The prayer closes by recalling the ministry of Jesus to the sick.

458 *Dear Lord, for All in Pain*

This is one of the few hymns about a universal affliction, pain. There are three parts to the prayer: first, that God will remove the cause of our pain; second, that those with medical skill can give relief; third, that if pain must be endured we may have a peaceful end. The simple tune can be learned readily by any group, and the hymn is particularly useful for healing services.

459 *The Serenity Prayer*

This brief and well-known prayer requests three things: that we may accept realistically what we cannot alter, that we may have the strength to change what we can, and that we may know one from the other. It is a most useful petition in times of turmoil and confusion. The prayer, usually attributed to Reinhold Niebuhr, is drawn from traditional sources.

460 *In Time of Illness*

This is a prayer for use by persons who are ill, not a prayer of intercession on behalf of the sick. It is very appropriate for services of healing, as well as for use in hospitals and homes where illness prevails. It is characterized by honesty and asks not for miracles of extraordinary healing but for confidence and grace to accept whatever must be endured. The author, Georgia Harkness, was one of the leading U.S.A. Methodist theologians and educators in the middle of the twentieth century.

461 *For Those Who Mourn*

Perhaps the greatest gift to those who mourn is an insight into the heart of God who weeps. Jesus' tears at the tomb of Lazarus give us permission not to hide our anguish but to express it, knowing that God accepts and understands human sorrow, and strengthens those who mourn. The prayer is based on Jn. 11:35 and Mt. 5:4. It may be used at funerals or other services of worship where prayer is needed for those who mourn, or in private devotion when we remember persons who mourn.

462 *'Tis So Sweet to Trust in Jesus*

Louisa M. R. Stead, a missionary in Africa, wrote this text soon after her husband's death. It states that trusting in Jesus is necessary for the Christian who wishes to have a close relationship with Christ. This trust makes Jesus a personal Savior and a Friend who stays with us to the end.

463 *Lord, Speak to Me*

Frances Havergal based this hymn on Rom. 14:7, "None of us lives to himself and none of us dies to himself." It first appeared in 1874 under the title "A Worker's Prayer." God speaks to the believer who in turn may speak and minister to others. Each stanza begins with a prayer: "speak to me"; "O strengthen me"; "O teach me"; "O fill me"; and, "O use me." This hymn is appropriate at any time of commitment.

464 *I Will Trust in the Lord*

"I Will Trust" is one of those spiritual oddities that points an accusing finger at the congregation and seeks to exact testimony concerning the immediate intentions of the accused. Correctly sung, those questioned should always respond by singing stanza 1, ("I will trust . . ."), while the questions are found in all the other stanzas. The tune resembles that of the shape note melody PISGAH and was likely adapted from it, since the camp meetings of frontier U.S.A. allowed interracial attendance, resulting in many shared, borrowed, and adapted tunes and texts. This spiritual of conviction traditionally is sung moderately slowly with heavy rhythmic accents, producing a dignified swaying body motion.

465 *Holy Spirit, Truth Divine*

Samuel Longfellow, brother of Henry Wadsworth Longfellow, was a Unitarian pastor and poet. His text names qualities of the Holy Spirit (Truth, Love, Power, and Right) and prays that each of these may act in the life of the Christian. Each stanza centers around one of these qualities. The final line of the text is an interesting example of paradox: "Be my Lord, and I shall be firmly bound, forever free." The hymn may be used as a prayer at Pentecost or whenever the emphasis is upon the Holy Spirit. Have women sing stanza 2 and men sing stanza 3, or all sing stanza 3 a cappella.

466 *An Invitation to Christ*

This Russian prayer from the seventeenth century addresses Jesus Christ with a richness of biblical titles (Light, Life, Physician, King) and also hints at the work of the Holy Spirit (Flame). Each title is followed by a petition related to the title. While the prayer may be used on any occasion, individually or corporately, it is especially suitable just before or after the singing of the hymn "Spirit of God,

161

Descend upon My Heart" (500). Note the phrases in the hymn related to portions of the prayer:
"Take the dimness of my soul away."
"Hast thou not bid me love thee, God and King?"
"The kindling of the heaven-descended Dove,
My heart an altar, and thy love the flame."

467 Trust and Obey

During a revival meeting where Dwight L. Moody was preaching, a young man came forward and said, "I am not quite sure, but I am going to trust and I am going to obey." The song leader at the revival, Daniel Towner, conveyed the story to John Sammis, a Presbyterian minister, and suggested that he write a text on the topic "Trust and Obey." This is the result.

468 Dear Jesus, in Whose Life I See

In this text, John Hunter, an English Congregational pastor, looks to Jesus as both the ideal whom we seek to be like and the one who can help us grow toward that ideal. Our lives fall short of our dreams; but we are inspired by Jesus, "whose deeds and dreams were one." This hymn is suitable for general use or during Lent. It also makes an excellent prayer of confession. Sung as a solo or as a congregational prayer, its plaintive quality may be enhanced by singing the second stanza a cappella.

469 Jesus Is All the World to Me

Will Thompson became famous for his many gospel songs, as well as for secular and patriotic songs. The evangelist Dwight L. Moody greatly admired his work. This text and tune express a personal relationship to God as it calls God "friend,"—a metaphor with great appeal and meaning.

470 *My God, I Love Thee*

In singing this hymn we examine the motives we have for loving God, contemplating what God has done in Christ for our salvation. We love God because God first loved us. Do not omit any stanza but rather build with voices and instrumental support to the final declaration in stanza 5.

471 *Move Me*

Richard Alan Henderson's text is a paraphrase on Mt. 6:10, "Thy will be done." Intended as a response, it is most effective when sung softly and slowly in precise rhythm. A soloist may sing simple echoes of the prior measure or provide some other appropriate embellishment. Take care to give the eighth notes their full value so that they do not resemble sixteenth notes.

472 *Near to the Heart of God*

Presbyterian pastor Cleveland B. McAfee's text and tune were written after the death of his nephew in 1901. The soothing, reassuring music has a healing quality that enables the singer to experience "quiet rest," "comfort sweet," and "full release." It may be used in worship before a time of prayer. This hymn is especially well-loved among United Methodists from the Evangelical United Brethren tradition. Often used in camp and retreat settings, it sings well with piano, piano and organ, or without accompaniment.

473 *Lead Me, Lord*

This call to scripture is based on portions of Ps. 5:8 and Ps. 4:8. Samuel Sebastian Wesley, the grandson of Charles Wesley and one of England's greatest church musicians, wrote this music as part of a longer anthem. It may be sung by the congregation, the choir, or both together.

474 Precious Lord, Take My Hand

Many experts have called Thomas A. Dorsey the father of black gospel music. The poem "Precious Lord" is inspiring and original, and the tune, PRECIOUS LORD, has a kinship to the hymn tune MAITLAND ("Must Jesus Bear the Cross Alone"). The words express sentiments about the last days of life's journey. Written during a family crisis by which he was deeply affected, Dorsey's song is a petition to God for strength in time of need. It traditionally is sung with rhythmic freedom and intense emotional expression.

475 Come Down, O Love Divine

This devotional text is a translation of a poem by the fifteenth-century monk Bianco of Siena. The tune DOWN AMPNEY has been called by Erik Routley "the most beautiful hymn-tune composed since OLD 100TH." Its composer, Ralph Vaughan Williams, one of England's greatest composers, contributed much to English church music through choral works, hymn-tunes, and the introduction of folk hymns into hymnals. The contemplative text and its expressive tune make this an excellent hymn for meditative times in worship. A steady half note pulse should be maintained with full support. Highlight the melody with an instrument and the choir when first teaching this tune to the congregation.

476 Lonely the Boat

This text by Helen Kim, one of the most distinguished Korean scholars and lay leaders, is a vivid description of the fear and helplessness felt by Christians sailing on a cruel sea. The author reminds us to seek the protection and guidance of our Master who alone can overcome all peril and bring peace. The tune utilizes Korean folk rhythm in 6/8 time and is a favorite among Koreans. The somewhat solemn mood of the melody matches the feeling of the text quite well. For variety, men may sing stanza 2, women stanza 3, and a soloist stanza 4, while others hum in parts without accompaniment. Then all may sing stanza 5.

477　For Illumination

This prayer is from the pen of the nineteenth-century British poet Christina Rossetti, who wrote many hymns and poems for use by children. It may be used as the prayer for illumination at any service or in a variety of other ways. Because of its request for openness to divine love, it may appropriately be used in conjunction with singing the hymn "Open My Eyes, That I May See" (454).

478　*Jaya Ho* (Victory Hymn)

"*Jaya ho*" are Hindi words for praising God and are the refrain of this hymn, which became known after an Indian choir toured the U.S.A. in the mid-1950s. Many Indian lyrics are devotional in character. To "bow in quiet reverence" is a typical posture of humility as is paying homage to the great and Holy God; praying for forgiveness and protection from harm and evil are primary concerns of the faithful. It is suitable as an opening hymn. Musical ornamentation is essential to Indian songs. Except for the solo sections, some members of the congregation or choir may continuously sing the tonic (low B♭) with the optional fifth above as a reiterated drone.

479　*Jesus, Lover of My Soul*

A Charles Wesley text of sober lament and supplication, this was originally entitled "In Temptation." The basic situation is that of the psalmist, crying out for help amidst the troubled waters of life (Ps. 17:8; 27:5). The address of Jesus as the "lover of souls" (Wisdom of Solomon 11:26) rests finally in the remembrance of his promise to give the water of eternal life (Jn. 4:14). The expansive minor Welsh tune ABERYSTWYTH faithfully evokes the plaintive yet hopeful spirit of this text.

480 *O Love That Wilt Not Let Me Go*

George Matheson, a Scottish pastor, wrote this comforting text during a time of "mental suffering." He reflects, "I had the impression rather of having it dictated to me by some inward voice than of working it out myself." Each stanza characterizes the gifts from God that sustain us: "Love" that will let go, "Light" that follows all my way, "Joy" that seeks me through pain, and the "Cross" that lifts up my head.

481 *Prayer of Saint Francis*

This set of petitions, attributed to Francis of Assisi, is one of the most beloved prayers in the Christian tradition. Its power lies both in its content and in the balanced phrases of this English translation. It may be used either corporately or by individuals at prayer.

482 *Lord, Have Mercy*

Traditionally, the Kyrie Eleison often has been expanded to the threefold form: *Kyrie eleison. Christe eleison. Kyrie eleison* ("Lord, have mercy. Christ, have mercy. Lord, have mercy"). In this form, as in the shorter form, it is a fitting response to the opening prayer(s), wonderfully combining proclamation, praise, and supplication. It is written to be sung in either English or Greek, first by a cantor (soloist) and then repeated by the congregation. Because of its call and response pattern the congregation may sing without music.

483 *Kyrie Eleison*

For comment on the text *Kyrie Eleison* see 484. Here it is set in the unaccompanied style of the Eastern Orthodox liturgy. Although originally set to be sung by men only, it can be sung by a congregation or choir of women but preferably by women and men each singing three parts to provide a rich six-part sound.

484 *Kyrie Eleison*

The Greek *Kyrie eleison* ("Lord, have mercy") is one of the oldest liturgical texts and is appropriate as a response to the opening prayer(s). Contrary to common impression, it is not a prayer of confession but combines proclamation, praise, and supplication. Teach the congregation the melody first, and let the choir add the harmony. The simple chant from Taizé could be sung three times: melody, harmony, harmony plus descant.

485 *Let Us Pray to the Lord*

This response may precede or follow the prayer of confession or other opening prayer. In a time of intercessory prayer, after each petition the leader may sing "Let us pray to the Lord," and the congregation may respond with a single "Lord, have mercy."

486 *Alleluia*

"Alleluia" comes from the Hebrew words for "praise" and "God" (Hallelu - Yah) and makes use of the short Hebrew name for God, "Yahweh." Alleluias have been sung in Christian churches from early times, generally before the reading of the Gospel for the day.

487 *This Is Our Prayer*

The congregation may sing this response after each petition or as a response to any prayer. If the petition or prayer has been prayed by an individual, it is the congregation's way of making it their prayer and sharing one person's prayer.

488 *Jesus, Remember Me*

This simple refrain, based on Lk. 23:42, is typical of congregational song created in the religious community of Taizé, France. The easy melody and the limited harmony make the song easy to learn. In time no music will be needed by the congregation. Use it as a response to prayer, especially prayers of confession, as the response to each petition of intercessory prayer, or during Holy Communion.

489   *For God's Gifts*

This poem was written by a distinguished black American, the late Dr. Howard Thurman, dean of the chapel at Boston University. It is appropriate for use by individuals or groups on almost any occasion. The attributes of God (holy, loving, of peace, generous) that open each section are related closely to the successive petitions, giving the prayer a richness and depth that should not be overlooked by a casual reading.

490   *Hear Us, O God*

This anonymous prayer response is for use as a congregational response during intercessory prayers. Teach the congregation either "Hear us, O God" or "Lord, hear our prayer" and ask them to sing this response after each prayer petition.

491   *Remember Me*

The tune CLEVELAND is named for the late J. Jefferson Cleveland, co-editor of the hymnal *Songs of Zion*. The refrain is a part of an almost forgotten slave song, based on the words spoken by the penitent thief on the cross (Lk. 23:42). "Remember Me" traditionally is sung softly and slowly and is well sustained. This short refrain is effective as an introit or a response after prayer, especially a prayer of confession.

492 *Prayer Is the Soul's Sincere Desire*

James Montgomery's poem states that prayer is more than public prayers heard or spoken in church. It is, rather, "the soul's sincere desire, unuttered or expressed," a sigh, a tear that no one but God can hear; a form of speech available to the youngest simple child; the voice of the contrite sinner. It is the vital breath of the Christian who asks, "Lord, teach us how to pray!" Alternate stanzas between right and left or choir and congregation in order to get the full meaning of this important text. Be sure not to rush.

493 *Three Things We Pray*

One of the oldest and most often quoted prayers from the Church of England is this by Richard, Bishop of Chichester in the thirteenth century. Its durability is evident from an adaptation included in the popular musical *Godspell*. All too often, however, only the closing words are known, and these need to be seen in the context of the opening of the prayer: Our petitions are the fruit of our thanksgiving for the Christ's sacrifice, even as the answers to our requests are the fruit of his victory over death. While the prayer may be used on almost any occasion, it is appropriate when the theme is Jesus' passion and death.

494 *Kum Ba Yah* (Come By Here)

"Kum ba yah" originated in the South Carolina low country, U.S.A., and the title phrase is from the Gullah language used there. In many coastal regions of the South, words and idiomatic expressions that appear to be of African origin are used. The simple utterance "Come by here, my Lord," is universally appealing and has found popularity wherever Christians gather for worship. The tune, DESMOND, is named after Desmond Tutu, Anglican Archbishop of Capetown and anti-apartheid activist in South Africa.

495 The Sufficiency of God

A leading thinker and writer of the fifteenth century was Juliana (or Lady Julian) of Norwich, England. In this prayer she affirms that nothing less than the presence of God is sufficient to satisfy our deepest longings and need. To suggest that in order to be worthy of God we must ask for the very presence of God is a bold and startling assertion; it runs counter to the popular (but nonbiblical) notion that we must make ourselves worthy of God by doing the right things. We cannot make ourselves worthy, and what we are to do is simply to ask for divine goodness as a gift.

496 Sweet Hour of Prayer

This text by William Walford stresses personal devotion and closeness to God. It speaks of the importance of setting time aside for prayer; the joys prayer brings and the burdens it lifts. It is appropriate for Morning and Evening Praise and Prayer or as a call to prayer.

497 Send Me, Lord

The first stanza of this hymn is based on Isaiah's response to God's call—"Here am I! Send me" (Is. 6:8). Stanza 2 suggests Ps. 31:3b: "For thy name's sake lead me and guide me." Stanza 3 paraphrases Ps. 23:5b: "Thou anointest my head with oil, my cup overflows." The tune THUMA MINA is a traditional call and response pattern. The leader might be a prepared solo voice or a small group. This serene hymn traditionally is sung slowly and is well sustained.

498 My Prayer Rises to Heaven

The hymn is an earnest prayer for God's mercy to defend us from harm. It expresses our desire to dwell in the house of the Lord and concludes with a statement of our trust in God's love, justice, and truth. This hymn from Vietnam begins with a long refrain based on Ps. 141:2, followed by short stanzas. Its repetitive style makes it easy and effective for responsorial singing, either between choir and congregation or between a divided congregation. The last refrain, however, should be sung by all. This hymn is suitable for Morning Praise and Prayer.

499 Serenity

Two stanzas from "Dear Lord and Father of Mankind" (358) from the Quaker John Greenleaf Whittier's poem "The Brewing of Soma" are uniquely set by the brilliant and eccentric U.S.A. composer Charles Ives. The setting is a mystical treatment of "the silence of eternity interpreted by love" and is not intended for congregational singing. Instead, use a soprano or the treble section of the choir with light and sustained accompaniment. Use as a call to prayer.

500 Spirit of God, Descend upon My Heart

George Croly based this hymn text on Gal. 5:25: "If we live by the Spirit, let us also walk by the Spirit." The second stanza speaks directly when it says "I ask no dream, no prophet ecstasies . . . But take the dimness of my soul away." The text emphasizes the role of the Holy Spirit in teaching the believer the discipline of the Christian life. The symbolism of the dove and the flame for the Holy Spirit is used in the final line with these words: "The kindling of the heaven-descended Dove, my heart an altar, and thy love the flame." Accentuate the beautiful harmonies by singing a stanza a cappella.

501 O Thou, Who Camest from Above

This Charles Wesley text, first published in *Short Hymns on Select Passages of Holy Scripture* (1762), is based on Lev. 6:13, "The fire shall ever be burning upon the altar; it shall never go out" (KJV). Among the hymns "For Believers Working" in John Wesley's 1780 *Collection*, the Levitical symbol of Israel's continual consecration before God now becomes the standard of Christian worship and dedication in every sphere of life, including daily labor. The tune, by the grandson of Charles Wesley, should be sung at a moderate tempo that does not rush the eighth notes and dotted rhythm.

502 *Thy Holy Wings, O Savior*

The Swedish poet Caroline Sandell-Berg, also the author of "Children of the Heavenly Father," asks in this simple prayer of faith and trust for cleansing from sin, a willing spirit, and a clean and good heart. She draws upon the rich imagery of the psalms (91:4; 73:26; 119:114; and 51:10) and of 1 Pet. 3:18-22. Although the closing suggests an evening hymn, it is equally useful as a prayer hymn. The charming Swedish folk melody BRED DINA VIDA VINGAR will become a favorite after a few times of singing. This simple tune could be sung using a children's choir on the first stanza with the congregation joining on the second stanza.

503 *Let It Breathe on Me*

The writer draws from Jn. 20:22 to express and celebrate Christ's initial resurrection visit with the disciples. Christ breathes on his disciples and says to them, "Receive the Holy Spirit." These words assure us that we, too, can turn over the control of our lives to the will of the Holy Spirit. This religious waltzlike hymn is appropriate as a prayer response. If sung twice, a soloist may sing the words while the congregation hums.

504 *The Old Rugged Cross*

George Bennard was the son of a coal miner, converted during a Salvation Army meeting, who later became a Methodist evangelist in the Midwest and Canada. He wrote the words and music based on 1 Cor. 1:22-25 after an inspiring evangelistic meeting. This hymn on the meaning of the cross has become a favorite of many Christians.

505 *When Our Confidence Is Shaken*

Fred Pratt Green addresses a variety of situations in this text of searching faith—shaken faith, questions of faith and science, difficulty in prayer life, "drudgery of caring"—and reminds us that God's answer to our "why?" is love and redemption through Jesus Christ. It would be appropriate to read this text aloud before singing it. The text may also be used for meditation in difficult spiritual times. This is a sturdy tune that can be taught by allowing the congregation to listen to the tune while they silently read the text.

506 *Wellspring of Wisdom*

This hymn uses fresh images to describe God's meaning for our life: wellspring of wisdom, dawn of a new day, garden of grace, call to compassion. Seeking God in the midst of dry spiritual lives and nuclear threat we pray for wisdom as "faith-filled sons and daughters" and come to praise God's name. Written by Miriam Therese Winter, a Medical Mission Sister, this hymn is an excellent prayer hymn or spoken litany. Congregational rehearsal will facilitate the singing of this tune. Be sure to rehearse the off-beat entrances in measures three and four and the unusual ending.

507 *Through It All*

"Through It All" is a modern gospel song of trust and assurance with a central theme of deliverance through Christian experience. It traditionally is sung with hand clapping on beats two and four. This chorus may be sung one or more times while adding voices and instruments.

Based on Heb. 11, beginning "Now faith is the assurance of things hoped for," this text by Anders Frostenson speaks of our anticipation of fruit when we see the tree in blossom, and of the sunrise before we see the dawn. He also mentions the faith of Noah (Heb. 11:7; Gen. 6–8), Abraham (Heb. 11:8-10; Gen. 12:1-8), and the Hebrews crossing the Red Sea (Heb. 11:29; Ex. 14:21-31). Faith leads us to accept God's call by responding, "I am willing, Lord, send me." Copes's tune FOR THE BREAD, provides an uplifting setting that moves the congregation easily through the five stanzas.

509 *Jesus, Savior, Pilot Me*

Edward Hopper, a minister at a mission for sailors in New York City, composed this text for the spiritual needs of seamen. Based on Mk. 4:35-41, where Jesus calms the tempest, the text uses numerous sailing metaphors to describe God's care and guidance. Life is a "tempestuous sea"; "chart and compass," the scriptures; "rock and treacherous shoal," sin and temptation. Also using feminine imagery, the poet makes reference to Jesus not only as a pilot but also a mother. The concluding stanza, "When at last I near the shore," refers to the time of death, at which Jesus the pilot guides the soul to its heavenly rest.

510 *Come, Ye Disconsolate*

Thomas Moore, an early nineteenth-century Irish poet, was best known for his popular songs "Believe Me, If All Those Endearing Young Charms" and "The Last Rose of Summer." This text appeared in 1816 under the title "Relief in Prayer" and expresses the consolation from the depths of despair that we may experience in prayer. The hymn tune CONSOLATOR by Samuel Webbe was composed originally as a solo song. It is appropriate for use at funerals and memorial services or at any service where a hymn of comfort is desired.

511 *Am I a Soldier of the Cross*

Isaac Watts, called "the father of English hymnody," often wrote hymns to go with sermons, communion services, or other worship times. This text was written to conclude a sermon on "Holy Fortitude, or Remedies against Fear," based on 1 Cor. 16:13: "Be watchful, stand firm in your faith, be courageous, be strong." It is an effective hymn of commitment.

512 *Stand By Me*

Charles A. Tindley relates the story of Jesus' calming the storm (Mt. 8:23-27; Mk. 4:35-41; Lk. 8:22-25) to the deliverance Jesus brings us in the storms of life. "Tribulation," "faults and failures," "persecution," and "growing old and feeble" cause the Christian to look to Jesus and pray, "Stand by me!" Tindley also recalls how Jesus saved Paul and Silas (Acts 16:19-40), and he speaks of death as crossing the River Jordan (which is pronounced "Jerden") and claims the promise, "I will be with you" (Is. 43:2). At the end he addresses Jesus as his beloved "Lily of the Valley" (S. of S. 2:1). The combination of dotted eighth and sixteenth notes in this tune traditionally is sung as a combination of quarter and eighth notes in triplet figure, bringing about a serene slow rolling motion, rather than an interrupted jerking movement as the notation suggests (♪. ♪ = ♩ ♪).

513 *Soldiers of Christ, Arise*

Based on Eph. 6:13-18: "Therefore take the whole armor of God," this Charles Wesley text was originally part of a much longer poem entitled "The Whole Armour of God; Ephesians 6." In his 1780 *Collection*, John Wesley printed a three-part version among the hymns "For Believers Fighting," where, in keeping with the biblical background, the military imagery described the ongoing struggle of the Christian who is supported in daily conflict with evil by God's sanctifying grace. With its stirring tune DIADEMATA, this hymn is appropriate for times that emphasize social conscience, commitment, struggle, and affirmation.

175

514 *Stand Up, Stand Up for Jesus*

At a noonday prayer meeting in Philadelphia during the great revival of 1858, preacher Dudley A. Tyng's cry to the five thousand men present was "Stand up for Jesus." Three days later he was killed in a tragic accident. These words of Tyng's inspired George Duffield, a Presbyterian pastor in the same city, to write this poem, with which he concluded his sermon on Eph. 6:14 the next Sunday. Since Tyng had been persecuted for his strong stand against slavery, this text may have been written with the struggle against slavery in mind. Ever since its publication, this has been one of the most widely used hymns depicting the Church as an army fighting the foes of evil.

515 *Out of the Depths I Cry to You*

This is the famous penitential hymn of Martin Luther, written in 1523 as an extended paraphrase of Ps. 130. The hymn appeared in many early Lutheran hymnals and was sung at Luther's funeral in 1546. Stanza 1 summarizes the psalmist's distress in a time of sinful affliction. Beginning in the third line of stanza 2, Luther is no longer praying to God but describing the hope that the repentant sinner has for sustenance in God's Word, Spirit, redemption, and mercy. It is appropriate during Lent, at funerals and memorial services, or in healing services, as well as for general use. (*See also* "Canticle of Redemption," 516.) A moderately slow tempo will enhance the harmonies of this rich German chorale.

516 *Canticle of Redemption* **(De Profundis)**

Ps. 130 is the cry of a sincerely penitent person. For persons mired in the depths of anguish caused by sin, God's grace and forgiveness give strength and assurance to rise from despair. The psalm declares that forgiveness is a reality because God is with us and ends with a testimony to God's unfailing mercy. It is appropriate at funerals and memorial services, in healing services, or for general use.

517 *By Gracious Powers*

This hymn was written by the great German theologian and martyr Dietrich Bonhoeffer in a Nazi prison as he awaited his fate, not knowing when he might be executed. In spite of heavy burdens and evil foes, the believer is willing to accept gladly the cup as Christ did at Gethsemane and is grateful for each new day of life. Bonhoeffer wrote that daily singing of great hymns gave him faith and strength. Firm accompaniment is needed to support this striking tune. Taper the phrases as written allowing for breaths but without dragging the tune.

518 *O Thou, in Whose Presence*

Swain's text speaks of the good things Christ bestows on the believer—comfort, hope, and salvation; alluding to Ps. 23 with references to the "dear Shepherd," and "the valley of death." The poet expresses a sense of awe that God would care for wandering sheep. The American folk tune DAVIS, a jewel that complements the text, may be sung in C minor throughout; or stanza 3 may be sung in C minor by the choir with C major for the concluding stanzas sung by all.

519 *Lift Every Voice and Sing*

Most Afro-Americans have come to regard "Lift Every Voice" as their "national anthem." Florida-born brothers James Weldon Johnson and J. Rosamond Johnson wrote and composed this stirring hymn early in the twentieth century. Weldon was associated with the Harlem Renaissance movement, which did much to preserve, encourage, and instill the finest examples of Afro-American artistic efforts in the minds of the American people. Although "Lift Every Voice" bears special meaning for Afro-Americans, it profoundly evokes images of hope and faith with which all who love freedom readily can identify.

Believing they are correcting slave grammar, some editors print the first line, "Nobody Knows The Trouble I've Seen." This change leads the reader mistakenly to believe that the spiritual is addressing the *past* suffering of slaves when, in fact, it is addressing their immediate *future*. The stanzas focus attention on "up," "down," and "ground" which suggest "standing," "stooping," and "bending." These physical movements of the body are work symbols suggesting that it may have originated in the fields. It is highly probable that slaves used this communication song as a caution signal, alerting work gangs to cease inappropriate activities in view of approaching "trouble"—an overseer or some other authority. This spiritual traditionally is sung free of rigid rhythm with much expression.

521   *I Want Jesus to Walk with Me*

Afro-American slaves converted to Christianity sought comfort in a real and personal Savior who would be available to them as they made their pilgrimage out of bondage to the promised land. In this text, slave-poets petition Jesus to walk with them. The tune SOJOURNER is named for Sojourner Truth, the courageous freed slave woman who took to the dangerous byways of antebellum America preaching the abolition of slavery and equality for "all o' Gawd's chillun's." Sojourner Truth is identified with the singing of this spiritual, and it is quite possible that the stanzas refer to the dangers she encountered on her many treks. The pleading nature of the spiritual is shown by the style in which it traditionally is sung—like an intense, emotional "moan."

522   *Leave It There*

Most texts by Charles Albert Tindley were drawn from sermons he delivered to the great congregation at Philadelphia's Methodist Episcopal Tindley Temple. In this hymn is found Tindley's message of the social gospel as he preached the promise of hope found in the salvation of our Lord, Jesus Christ. The entire hymn bears out God's promise never to leave us alone. The theme of the poem puts to use sentiments of slave-poets who declared, "Mah lawd done jes' whut he say'd." The hymn should be approached in a relaxed and simple manner.

523 Saranam, Saranam (Refuge)

Saranam means "refuge" or "I take refuge." It is suggested by Ps. 61: "Thou art my refuge." Unlike the psalm, however, this hymn refers to Jesus as our refuge. The key word saranam is repeated many times, almost like a mantra, to reinforce the central idea. The Punjabi melody is in a contemporary popular style which has spread all over the Indian subcontinent, and many versions may be found. Use small handbells on the root and/or fifth of the chord on the strong beat of each measure.

524 Beams of Heaven as I Go

Charles Albert Tindley served America's largest black Methodist church, Tindley Temple in Philadelphia, for more than three decades. He is called the father of black gospel music. His poetic style, and to a lesser extent his musical style, is a continuation of the traditional Afro-American spiritual. Tindley's urban black hymns still speak directly to us today. This hymn, often entitled "Some Day," traditionally is sung slowly and inwardly to one's own self, sustaining and savoring each tone and syllable.

525 We'll Understand It Better By and By

In this text Charles A. Tindley explores the meaning of life. Drawing from 1 Cor. 13:12: "Now I know in part; then I shall understand fully," he develops the theme that life is filled with "howling tempests," "want of food and shelter," "trails dark on every hand," "temptations," and "hidden snarls." A thread of hope, however, lies in the promise of God's rapture. In God's own time, when the saints are gathered home, we will be permitted to understand fully those things that now must remain a mystery. This black gospel hymn from the turn of the century traditionally is sung in a rhythmic style of the cake-walk dance, which was in vogue at the time the hymn was written.

526 What a Friend We Have in Jesus

When all fails and life presses in with grief, despair, and burden, Jesus and our communion with him are our greatest solace. Joseph Scriven wrote this poem of comfort for his mother during a time of grief. Christians who have experienced pain and grief have found comfort in this text as they are able to share their burden with a great Friend.

527 Do, Lord, Remember Me

This Afro-American Lenten spiritual is drawn from the words of the penitent thief on the cross: "Lord, remember me when thou comest into thy kingdom" (Lk. 23:42, KJV). Jesus' response, "Today shalt thou be with me in paradise," was profoundly significant to the slave. It reaffirms the Christian belief that God is for us, even when all others are against us. Appealing for children and youth, it could be led in worship by either group accompanied by tambourine and hand clapping.

528 Nearer, My God, to Thee

This text by English poet and actress Sarah F. Adams describes the wandering soul seeking direction so as to be closer to God. It is based on Gen. 28:10-22, Jacob's dream at Bethel, his sinfulness and God's steadfast mercy and presence. An important text for congregational or personal devotion.

529 *How Firm a Foundation*

This anonymous text is a skillful paraphrase of portions of Is. 43:1-3, plus other biblical phrases, including "firm foundation" from 2 Tim. 2:19 and "I will never forsake you" from Heb. 13:5. This text, set to the strong American folk tune FOUNDATION, provides a message of hope and courage. Try singing the last stanza as a round.

530 *Are Ye Able*

Earl Marlatt's text is based on the words of Mk. 10:35-40: "'Are you able to drink the cup that I drink, or to be baptized with the baptism with which I am baptized?' And they said to him, 'We are able.'" It may be sung responsively, with the choir or soloist singing the stanzas containing the questions, and the congregation the affirmative refrain.

531 *For Overcoming Adversity*

In a time when many assume that God offers us easy and superficial comfort, this prayer for overcoming adversity (rather than evading it) is a needed antidote. It is especially useful on occasions when individuals or congregations face difficult times. The affinity of this prayer to the hymn "We Shall Overcome" (533) exists not merely in that both share the word "overcome" but in the origin and use of the two texts. The feisty Savonarola was in the fifteenth century much like Martin Luther King, Jr., in the twentieth—a very controversial public figure, much loved by his people but feared by the political order and martyred because of his bold call for the reform of society.

532 *Jesus, Priceless Treasure*

Johann Franck's hymn texts represent a move toward a more subjective, personal style. At first, such hymns were thought to be inappropriate for worship and were allowed only for personal devotion. *Jesu, meine Freude* (literally, "Jesus, my joy")—the opening words in the original German text as well as the name of the tune—was modeled after a well-known love song of Franck's day—*"Flora, meine Freude."* Its similarity to a love song is apparent, with its longing for Jesus and joy in his presence. Its popularity is due to the tune's extensive use in motets, cantatas, and organ works. Introduce the tune using a string instrument such as violin or cello or a similar organ stop to enhance the beauty of the sustained line and rich harmonies.

533 *We Shall Overcome*

This present-day song of human struggle is derived from several sources. It bears textual resemblance to Charles Albert Tindley's "I'll Overcome Someday," and melodic resemblance to the Afro-American spiritual "No More Auction Block for Me." The title is a paraphrase of Jn. 16:33—"Be of good cheer, I have overcome the world." It was sung popularly during the civil rights movement under the leadership of Martin Luther King, Jr., and is presently sung around the world wherever the oppressed gather in a common cause. It traditionally is sung by groups with hands clasped together, held high and swaying to the rocking motion of this soaring song.

534 *Be Still, My Soul*

Katharina von Schlegel was the leader of the eighteenth-century German Pietistic movement, a movement similar to the Wesleyan movement. This text, reflecting on Ps. 46:10, is a prayer for trust and submission to God's will in times of grief and pain. The tune FINLANDIA is from a portion of Sibelius's well-known orchestral tone poem *Finlandia*. The hymn is appropriate for funeral and memorial services, for general use.

535 *A Refuge amid Distraction*

This prayer from India, with its memorable image of a distraught ant, speaks to the frantic confusion of our age. Primarily a personal prayer, it also could be used in worship as a congregational prayer of confession.

536 *Precious Name*

There are many names in the scriptures given to Jesus, each one revealing a different facet of the nature of Christ. The name of Jesus brings us joy, just as does thinking of someone we love. New York Baptist poet Lydia Baxter asserts that living under Jesus' name brings comfort and joy and shields us from temptation. In the life to come the Christian will bow at the name of Jesus. The central message of the hymn is found in the refrain: "Precious name, O how sweet! Hope of earth and joy of heaven."

537 *Filled with the Spirit's Power*

From the hymnic explosion in England in the 1960s this hymn by Anglican priest John R. Peacey is one of the most popular and lasting products. Based on Acts 2 and suitable for Pentecost, the text emphasizes the power and fellowship of the Holy Spirit as well as the gifts of fellowship and unity. It is also a strong appeal for Christians to move like wind and fire through the world, demonstrating that we belong to Christ. Strong support from the choir and accompaniment is necessary when introducing this to the congregation. Let them hum the first stanza as the choir sings, then all join on stanzas 2 and 3.

538 *Wind Who Makes All Winds That Blow*

This Pentecost hymn focuses on images of the Holy Spirit coming out of creation and experienced as wind and fire. We feel the strength of powerful winds and fiery suns that reach into our own minds and souls, bringing the power and truth of the Holy Spirit at

Pentecost. The hymn is a prayer for the movement of the Holy Spirit within us. The striking quality of both the text and tune might be introduced by the congregation meditating on the powerful words and the vivid picture painted by the expressive tune.

539   O Spirit of the Living God

Henry Tweedy, a Congregational pastor and professor at Yale Divinity School, wrote this Pentecost hymn based on the events described in Acts 2. Each stanza deals with an element of the story of the coming of the Holy Spirit upon the Church—the element of fire to fill the Church with love, joy, power, righteousness, and peace; the element of wind to blow away "mists of error, clouds of doubt"; tongues whose speaking allowed all to understand the message at Pentecost. The hymn ends with the affirmation that today's Church can feel the same power as did the early Church. This is a moving prayer for utterance of "love which speaks loud and clear."

540   I Love Thy Kingdom, Lord

Timothy Dwight, a president of Yale, was an important scholar, hymn writer, and Congregational pastor in the early years of the United States. This expression of love and dedication to the Church, suggested by Ps. 137:5-6, is among the earliest texts written in America that are still in general use. Dwight writes of love for the Church, whose "walls before Thee stand," the Communion, the vows, and the hymns. But the Church he speaks of is only *represented* by these tangible elements. The Church itself consists of the redeemed, saved with Christ's own precious blood.

541   See How Great a Flame Aspires

Invoking biblical images of fire and rain, the unifying theme is the general spread of the gospel as a result of the outpouring of the

Holy Spirit (Acts 1:8; 2:3, 17; Jl. 2:28). Each stanza recalls an additional scriptural image—"I came to cast fire upon the earth; and would that it were already kindled" (Lk. 12:49); God's "word runs swiftly" (Ps. 147:15); God "calls into existence the things that do not exist" (Rom. 4:17); and Elijah's victory over the prophets of Baal (1 Kg. 18:36-46). The text is heightened by the fine Welsh melody ARFON (MAJOR). Most appropriate to celebrations for Pentecost, this hymn also would strengthen a special emphasis on mission.

542 *Day of Pentecost*

This prayer, while useful on many occasions, is intended particularly for the Day of Pentecost, being based on Luke's account in Acts 2. Luke mentions the presence in the Upper Room in Jerusalem not only of the apostles but of the women followers of Jesus, and of Mary his mother and his brothers (Acts 1:13-14). The words "kindle flaming hearts" also remind us of Wesley's "heart strangely warmed" and the flame that is a part of the official symbol of The United Methodist Church.

543 *O Breath of Life*

This hymn of invocation calls on the Holy Spirit—as Breath of Life, Wind of God, and Breath of Love—to come sweeping through us to renew and revive the Church. The tune, commissioned for this hymnal, is by Houston composer David Ashley White. Since this prayer hymn is based on the events of Easter (Jn. 20:22) as well as Pentecost (Acts 2), it is suitable throughout the season from Easter through Pentecost or for general use.

544 *Like the Murmur of the Dove's Song*

With rich use of imagery, this text calls the Holy Spirit (dove, wind, and flame) to the assembled Church (members of Christ's body, branches of the vine) to heal division, give voice to prayer, empower love and witness, and bring peace. It was written by Episcopal priest Carl P. Daw, Jr., then a seminary student, for the beautiful tune BRIDEGROOM by British composer Peter Cutts. Appropriate for Pentecost and generally as an opening prayer or prayer for illumination, it may be sung antiphonally—with one side singing lines 1–2, the other singing lines 3–4, and all singing line 5.

545 *The Church's One Foundation*

Samuel Stone's text makes important historic and theological statements about the Church in every stanza. Christ is the foundation of the church; is diverse yet unified in Christ; it experiences strife, turmoil, heresy, schisms in its struggle to carry out God's will on earth. The last stanza is a message of hope as the earthly Church is joined under the Trinity, with the saints who have gone on to their eternal rest. The tune is by Samuel Sebastian Wesley, the grandson of Charles, the hymn writer.

546 *The Church's One Foundation*

This adaptation of Samuel Stone's well-known text may be sung as an alternate to the traditional text found at 545. Here, Stookey, professor of worship at Wesley Theological Seminary, has provided a text that speaks about the Church in the first person ("our") rather than in the third person ("her"). This adaptation may be more acceptable to many congregations who wish to use this text of great meaning. It may be sung to the familiar tune AURELIA.

547 *O Church of God, United*

Based on Acts 2:5-11, this text by Frederick Morley exhorts the scattered Church to join together to "proclaim to all one message" of the gospel of Jesus. From every nation on the earth we should come forward to praise "one living Lord" and place our faith in God's Word. Though we speak different languages, we can be one people telling of the redemption we know in Jesus Christ. The final stanza reminds us of Jesus' prayer (Jn. 17) in which he asked the Father that we may be one. Set to the rousing tune ELLACOMBE, it is excellent as a processional or recessional hymn.

548 *In Christ There Is No East or West*

John Oxenham, an English Congregational Church layperson, based this hymn of Christian unity on Gal. 3:28: "There is neither Jew nor Greek, there is neither slave nor free, there is neither male nor female; for you are all one in Christ Jesus." The hymn speaks of the barriers of geography, race, slavery, and gender that prevent unity and peace. He points out that without the belief that Christ is the force that makes unity possible, the Church will not be able to carry the gospel to others. The tune MCKEE, from the Afro-American tradition, is becoming a favorite for many. The text also may be sung to the alternate tune ST. PETER.

549 *Where Charity and Love Prevail*

This antiphon from the ninth century tells us that we should love each other as Christ has loved us. It is used in many traditions on Holy Thursday when the washing of feet precedes Holy Communion. It may be sung as a communion hymn, and stanza 3 may be used as a response after a prayer of confession.

550 *Christ, from Whom All Blessings Flow*

Recalling 1 Cor. 12:4-31 and Gal. 3:27-28, this text reflects on the promise of unity in the body of Christ—a unity that celebrates the diversity of members' gifts yet "renders void" all distinction of social rank or class. Originally titled "The Communion of the Saints," the hymn serves well in ecumenical prayer services.

551 *Awake, O Sleeper*

Basing his text on Rom. 13:11-14 and Eph. 4:4-6, the author, F. Bland Tucker, exhorts unbelievers to learn Christ's love in all its dimensions. Christ brings release from sin and fear and gives peace. Eight times in stanza 3 the author mentions oneness in Christ's love, then admonishes believers to "walk in love" in words reminiscent of the Lord's Prayer's "forgive us our debts, as we forgive our debtors." The hymn concludes by exhorting the new believer to "go forth in faith" with the promise of Christ's life. The tune MARSH CHAPEL was composed by Max Miller, organist of Boston University's Marsh Chapel for this text. Use a male voice to introduce this tune, choir on stanza 2, and all on the remaining stanzas.

552 *Here, O Lord, Your Servants Gather*

This hymn, written for the fourteenth World Council of Christian Education Convention in Japan in 1958, employs the theme "Jesus Christ, the Way, the Truth, and the Life." The poet, Tokuo Yamaguchi, in response to the dawn of the new space age and to arms races when human beings increasingly are facing the threat of war and destruction, stresses that the ultimate answer to peace and to the chaotic world is Jesus Christ. This hymn was composed after a *Gagaku* mode (Japanese court music of ancient Chinese origin) and may be sung in unison unaccompanied or with a flute accompaniment.

553 *And Are We Yet Alive*

Charles Wesley's text first appeared in *Hymns and Sacred Poems*, 1749, in the section on "Hymns for Christian Friends." The opening lines recall the story of Jacob's joyful reunion with Joseph in Egypt (Gen. 46:30), applying this to the joy and hope that Christians share, even in the face of their own fears and struggles. Through "mighty conflicts past," and in the hope of salvation "to the uttermost," the hymn celebrates the ever-present grace and love of Jesus Christ. The practice of singing this as the opening hymn for sessions of Annual Conference began with John Wesley, who also placed it first in the section "For the Society Meeting" in his 1780 *Collection*. In keeping with this background, the hymn lends itself to begin other services of reunion, homecoming, and annual Charge Conference. You may wish to close these services with "Blest Be the Tie That Binds" using the same tune.

554 *All Praise to Our Redeeming Lord*

This text by Charles Wesley was first published in *Hymns for Those That Seek, and Those That Have, Redemption in the Blood of Jesus Christ*, 1747, entitled "At Meeting of Friends." The central point of praise has to do precisely with the joy of Christian fellowship, which is both a means of Christ's grace and a foretaste of "our high calling's glorious hope." As a celebration of the goal and process of Christian community (what John Wesley called "social religion"), it may be used in services commemorating the role of spiritual gifts in the body of Christ (1 Cor. 12; Eph. 4), or in the recognition and dedication of small group ministries.

555 *Forward Through the Ages*

Written for an installation service in the First Unitarian Church, Berkeley, California, where the author, Frederick Hosmer, was pastor, this text reminds us of our Christian heritage. With different gifts and oneness of heart, the "faithful spirits" move in an unbroken line. Remembering the prophets, martyrs, poets, and heroes, we are "bound by God's far purpose" as we move toward the "shining goal." Sullivan's tune, ST. GERTRUDE, written for "Onward, Christian Soldiers," is an excellent match for the text.

556 *Litany for Christian Unity*

That a United Methodist hymnal should contain a prayer by Pope John Paul II is a sign of the times, for both of our churches are far more open than previously to God's call for unity among all Christian people. This litany focuses upon faithfulness, trust, and mutual stewardship of God's gifts. We seek an understanding of the faith deeper than that which has caused us discord and division. While written by the world leader of one branch of Christ's Church, this prayer can be prayed with integrity by all Christian people of good will.

557 *Blest Be the Tie That Binds*

John Fawcett, a Baptist minister working at a parish at Wainsgate for a meager salary, received a call to join a larger parish in London. As he and his wife loaded the wagon with their possessions for the move they were surrounded by their beloved parishioners who came to bid farewell. Moved by their love and concern, Fawcett ordered the wagon unpacked and stayed for a total of fifty years. The text, written as a result of this experience, was entitled "Brotherly Love." It has become one of the most universally popular hymns on Christian love and is appropriate for any service that emphasizes Christian love, concern, and fellowship.

558 *We Are the Church*

This song by Avery and Marsh has been widely used in United Methodist church school curriculum since 1973 and is the most requested hymn for children in our denomination. It reminds us in strong, positive language that the Church is people—all kinds, all colors, all ages, "from all times and places." Not a building or a steeple, the Church is people! Sometimes the Church marches victoriously with purpose or is on fire for a cause or crusade, yet at times the marching stops and the Church rides in comfort and complacency. At times it hides in a cowardly manner. But all these experiences help the Church to grow. This is a good hymn to help make your worship intergenerational. Ask the children to lead the congregation in this affirmation of who we are.

559 *Christ Is Made the Sure Foundation*

This seventh-century anonymous Latin text is found in some of the earliest hymnals of the Christian Church. Based on Eph. 2:20-22 and 1 Pet. 2:4-7, it is widely used for the dedication of churches. The hymn came into the English-speaking church in 1851 in John Mason Neale's translation. The tune WESTMINSTER ABBEY is adapted from an anthem of the famous seventeenth-century English composer Henry Purcell. The hymn is perfect for building dedication services and for singing when either of the above scriptures is used. Since its use at the wedding of Princess Margaret and Antony Armstrong-Jones in Westminster Abbey, this hymn has had growing use at weddings. Often used as a processional, the tempo should not be hurried and the sound should be full. Use a trumpet or trumpet stop to bring out the melody.

560 *Help Us Accept Each Other*

The community of faith is bound together by loving acceptance of each other. Fred Kaan speaks eloquently of that acceptance and inclusion and prays for God's guidance in helping us to grow in love. Suitable for any occasion where we need reminding of God's call to us for active loving and caring, it is a hymn to grow into and grow with on our journey as Christians. Use variation in instrumentation or registration on each stanza to help keep this tune fresh and interesting. The tune by John Ness Beck was written for Kaan's text and published in 1977.

561 *Jesus, United by Thy Grace*

Accentuating the communal character of grace, this text by Charles Wesley was originally titled "Prayer for Persons Joined in Fellowship." To care for each other (stanza 2, Gal. 6:2) and be joined in Jesus' "spotless charity" (stanza 6, Col. 3:14) is not just a result of Christ's grace; it is its essence. The image of stanza 4 is

191

particularly striking; Jesus' love is like a magnet (lodestone) that draws people closer to one another as it draws them closer to Christ. The serene resolve of the tune ST. AGNES complements the text. This hymn is a natural prayer for small group ministries and ecumenical occasions, as well as for general use.

562 Jesus, Lord, We Look to Thee

Originally titled "For a Family," this Charles Wesley text assumes the difficulties and "stumbling" of real life. The secret is, with the help of the Prince of Peace, to "bear one another's burdens" (Gal. 6:2). A healing word for those who have suffered tension or division, the hymn might also serve in ecumenical services. The tune SAVANNAH probably came into John Wesley's Foundery Collection (1742) as a result of his earlier contacts with the Moravians.

563 Father, We Thank You

An anonymous text, adapted from the second-century Didache (Teaching of the Twelve Apostles), expresses gratitude to God for salvation through Jesus Christ, in whose love God has made provision for us all our days. It offers a plea for the Church, that God will save it, guard it, perfect it, and unite it, and that the Church will be gathered together by Jesus Christ. This text is set to contrasting tunes: ALBRIGHT, by American composer William Albright and RENDEZ À DIEU, a French psalm tune from John Calvin's Genevan Psalter, 1542 (see 565). With either tune a steady tempo is necessary so that meter changes are more easily sung.

564 For the Unity of Christ's Body

The familiar words from scripture and the service of Holy Communion, "This is my body, broken for you," are here given a striking twist. Recalling that Paul refers to the Church as the body of Christ, we pray that we will not be rebuked by Jesus for having caused disunity within the Church. We ask for magnanimity, that we may be gracious to fellow Christians from whom we may be alienated, and for restraint, that we may not boast about our own beliefs or belittle the faith of others whom Christ has made one with us through baptism. With great brevity this prayer from China carries an impact that is particularly suitable to ecumenical services and days of prayer for Church unity. We should also not overlook its possibilities within a single congregation that suffers from internal strife or contention.

565 *Father, We Thank You*

See **563.**

566 *Blest Be the Dear Uniting Love*

Originally titled "At Parting," this Charles Wesley text was a model for early Methodist leave-taking. Physical parting evokes the promise of unity in Christ, a goal that already can be celebrated because of Christ's "uniting love," that "appoints" a place for each, and that neither "life, nor death can part" (Rom. 8:38-39). The hymn commends itself as a blessing or benediction for the closing of regular gatherings, as well as for other special occasions of parting, leave-taking, sending out, or commissioning. If the choir sings a stanza a cappella, exchange the tenor and alto parts or have men sing the melody with women singing the tenor part up an octave.

567 *Heralds of Christ*

A challenging hymn on missions, this text was written by Laura Copenhaver, a Lutheran missionary in the southern Appalachian Mountains. She uses the striking image of "immortal tidings in your mortal hands" and alludes to Is. 40:3. "Make straight the highway of the king." The concluding stanza is a prayer for faith and peace. An excellent text for missions emphasis it has become popular in part because of the familiar tune, NATIONAL HYMN.

568 Christ for the World We Sing

In 1869 Samuel Wolcott attended a meeting of the Young Men's Christian Association of Ohio. Over the pulpit in the church hung the motto "Christ for the World, and the World for Christ." Inspired by the motto, he wrote this text after the meeting. The hymn is ideal for services with a mission emphasis.

569 We've a Story to Tell to the Nations

This missionary hymn by Ernest Nichol enumerates in each stanza the things we have to share with the world: a "story of peace and light," a "song that shall conquer evil," the message that God is love, the Savior who suffered that the world "might come to the truth of God." The refrain begins with darkness, moves to dawn and then to noonday brightness as Christ's kingdom comes on earth and the tune rises to accentuate its meaning. It is useful whenever there is a mission emphasis.

570 Prayer of Ignatius of Loyola

Both individuals and congregations may use this classic prayer for unselfish service from the pen of Ignatius of Loyola, sixteenth-century founder of the Jesuits. The parallel construction of its petitions commends it both for oral use and for memorization; and its contents drive home the gospel teaching concerning sacrifice and self-giving without thought of reward.

571 Go, Make of All Disciples

Based on Mt. 28:19-20—"the great commission"—this text by Leon M. Adkins, then pastor of the University Methodist Church at Syracuse, was written for use at Christian Education Week in 1955. The text follows the outline of the scripture with the commands "go," "make disciples," "baptize," and "teach." The final stanza centers on the promise: "Lo, I am with you alway, even unto the end of the world." (KJV). The hymn is suitable for services on mission and for ordinations, consecrations, and commissionings. It is also a fine closing hymn for general use.

572 *Pass It On*

Experiencing God's love as the warmth of a fire that begins with a simple spark is the theme of this hymn by Kurt Kaiser, popular among youth and young adults. When you have known God's love, it is only natural that you want to share that love with others—"you want to pass it on." The contagious spirit of a new or renewed believer sings forth in these stanzas. Pass it on!

573 *O Zion, Haste*

Mary Ann Thompson wrote the stanzas of this great hymn on missions in 1868; but, not satisfied with any refrain she could write, she left the hymn unfinished. Three years later she wrote the refrain. Although she intended the text to be sung to another tune, it has been sung to James Walch's tune TIDINGS ever since its first appearance in a hymnal—the 1894 hymnal of the Episcopal Church.

574 *For Renewal of the Church*

This anonymous prayer was included in *Cry Justice*, a collection of prayers, meditations, and readings from South Africa edited by John de Gruchy, a native South African who is professor of Christian studies at the University of Cape Town and an ordained minister in the United Congregational Church of Southern Africa. It can be used in congregational worship either as a prayer of confession or as a prayer of intercession.

575 Onward, Christian Soldiers

This text by Church of England priest Sabine Baring-Gould was written as a processional to be sung by children as they marched from one village to another for a religious festival. "The cross of Jesus going on before" referred to the processional cross, while "see his banners go" referred to the banners carried by the children. Stanza 2 makes it clear that the battle is a spiritual struggle against Satan. Mt. 16:18 is the basis for the phrase in stanza 4: "gates of hell can never 'gainst that Church prevail." The marching tune ST. GERTRUDE by the operetta composer Arthur S. Sullivan adds to the hymn's appeal. Its suggested omission by the Hymnal Revision Committee prompted the writing of eleven thousand messages of protest, which won its final inclusion.

576 Rise Up, O Men of God

This text was written by William Merrill, a Presbyterian pastor, for the Presbyterian Brotherhood Movement. The hymn is a charge for service in the kingdom of God—promoting brotherhood, righting wrongs, and serving the Church. The last stanza indicates that this may be done if we "tread where his feet have trod." The reference to brotherhood comes again in the phrase "As brothers of the Son of Man." This hymn has become a theme song for United Methodist Men.

577 God of Grace and God of Glory

This text by Harry Emerson Fosdick was written in 1930 for the dedication of the Riverside Church, New York City, where he was pastor. Fosdick was considered by many to be the finest preacher of his generation, and the funding of the building of Riverside Church by the Rockefeller family was in recognition of his fame. This text on the mission of the Church deals with issues of that day which are still with us: evil, doubts, war, and selfishness. Set to the sturdy Welsh tune CWM RHONDDA (despised by Fosdick!), the hymn has become a standard hymn on the Church.

578 *God of Love and God of Power*

While a pastor at Calvary Methodist Church in San Jose, California, during the years 1936-40, Gerald Kennedy wrote this text as a call to contemporary discipleship—asking God for grace, daring hearts, free spirits, courage, and loyalty. It is particularly effective when sung antiphonally, alternating phrases between two groups (left and right, or choir and congregation), with all singing the refrain. The resounding tune UNSER HERRSCHER adds vitality to this meaningful text.

579 *Lord God, Your Love Has Called Us Here*

Brian Wren wrote this text as an attempt to restate the ideas of Charles Wesley's magnificent text "And Can It Be that I Should Gain" (363). Wren writes in *Faith Looking Forward:* "The hymn sees God's gracious love in the context of sin built into socio-economic structures, but also of Christian hope." The tune can be taught by presenting the hymn as a choir anthem, with the congregation joining at stanza 5.

580 *Lead On, O King Eternal*

Ernest Shurtleff, a member of the class of 1887 at Andover Theological Seminary, was asked to write a hymn for the class commencement. Graduation is "the day of march"; the "days of preparation" are the years of study; the "fields of conquest" are the areas of ministry to come and "Thy tents" refers to the willingness of the pastor to follow where God leads. The reward given to the faithful servant is the crown.

581 *Lord, Whose Love Through Humble Service*

Albert F. Bayly's text was written in 1961 at the request of the Hymn Society of America as it searched for new hymns on social welfare. The hymn reflects concerns of the early sixties, yet its themes still present challenges to the Church in the closing years of the twentieth century including issues of the homeless, hungry, sorrowful, the sick, and the aged. Jesus' ministry is the model for ministry to both the physical and spiritual needs of people. The U.S.A. shape note melody BEACH SPRING complements this poignant text.

582   Whom Shall I Send?

The call to mission, here phrased in the words of Is. 6:8, often brings out our feelings of inadequacy and hesitation. Yet this text by Fred Pratt Green leads beyond our doubt to stand on faith and "dare to answer: Lord, send me." As the final stanza reminds us, it is God who will purify and strengthen us to do the task. With its strong eighteenth-century French tune DEUS TUORUM MILITUM, it is a fitting hymn of Christian calling and mission.

583   Sois la Semilla (You are the Seed)

A mission hymn from Spain by Cesareo Gabaraín, this colorful text widens our image of evangelization to include ongoing growth in the faith. Concepts of the kingdom of God, forgiveness, hope, and discipleship are interwoven in this call to spread the Good News. Sing the stanzas lyrically as an announcement for all Christians, then proceed into the marching cadence on the refrain, our commission to echo the message of Christ to all the world. A magnificent hymn for commissioning and ordination services, it may also be used for evangelistic purposes in local congregations. Use piano or guitar to accompany this bright melody.

584   Lord, You Give the Great Commission

The author, Jeffrey Rowthorn, a former professor and now a bishop of the Episcopal Church, provides us with an excellent new text on the commands of Christ to heal the sick, preach the word, baptize, teach, and forgive (Lk. 9:2; Mt. 28:19-20; Lk. 23:34). While

198

the message is that all of us are involved in the work of ministry, stanza 3 may be used for Holy Communion, and stanza 5 may be used as a benediction response. The very singable and popular tune ABBOT'S LEIGH, by Anglican priest Cyril V. Taylor, supports the message well. When introducing this hymn it could be read as a litany with the congregation responding with the refrain. The sweeping melody should be felt in an easy one beat per measure with a steady tempo throughout.

585   *This Little Light of Mine*

This Afro-American spiritual is here given in the slower of two existing settings. "Little Light" celebrates the slave's response to the birth of Jesus Christ. The words refer to 2 Cor. 4:6: "Let light shine out of darkness," they also reflect Mt. 5:14-16. Just as the Savior was promised and delivered to the people, slaves longed for their time of deliverance. Taking possession of the Good News, slaves responded in the affirmative to the circuit rider's query, "Sisters and Brothers, have you seen the light?" The tune LATTIMER is named for Louis Lattimer, a black inventor, who, along with others, worked on the electric light bulb with Thomas Edison. This spiritual is especially effective with a candlelight procession.

586   *Let My People Seek Their Freedom*

This text by T. Herbert O'Driscoll is based on the tribulations of the people of Israel in bondage in Egypt and later in the wilderness. Just as God called the people of Israel out of Egypt, where they had been for over four hundred years, so God calls us out of our familiar ways into new paths of service in the world. As the people of Israel murmured in their new freedom and longed for the bondage with which they were familiar, God continued to lead them forward; and God does the same when we hesitate today. In international relations, space travel, generational conflicts, hunger, and health problems, God challenges us to discover new ways. This text is powerfully conveyed by the sturdy Welsh tune EBENEZER.

587 *Bless Thou the Gifts*

Stewardship is the theme of this text by Samuel Longfellow, one of America's most famous Unitarian hymn writers. He acknowledges that what we give is our response to God, who will accept and use our offerings. The hymn is an effective offertory response.

588 *All Things Come of Thee*

This hymn is appropriate for the time of the offering. It is based on 1 Chr. 29:14b, which is part of David's last prayer of thanksgiving and petition uttered shortly before his death. David thanks God for the people's generous gifts for the building of the Temple and concludes by asking God to give his son Solomon "a perfect heart to keep thy commandments."

589 *The Church of Christ, in Every Age*

Fred Pratt Green, a British Methodist pastor now retired, outlines the task of Christ's caring Church: "We have no mission but to serve." The church, described here as essential to both history and to the world, is given Christ's task and led by the Spirit. This hymn for general use reminds us that we who are the Church are called to God's mission. A steady, bright accompaniment is needed for this easy tune with a slight ritard at the end of the final stanza.

590 *Christ Loves the Church*

Written for a church anniversary, this text by Brian Wren celebrates the relationship between Christ and the Church: Christ loves the Church, bears it through worse and better days, feeds the Church and needs the Church to "live and tell his story." Jane Marshall's tune HIGH STREET is named for the church that commissioned the text—High Street United Methodist Church in Muncie, Indiana. The hymn is appropriate for a variety of occasions: church anniversary, baptismal reaffirmation, ordination, mission, and dedication. Sing it with a slow feeling of two strong beats to the measure to preserve the dignity of both text and tune.

591   Rescue the Perishing

Fanny Crosby was inspired to write this text after she had visited a service in a New York City mission where she had been impressed by the great physical and spiritual needs of the men who were present. In her effort to express the urgency of rescuing these people whom God loves, she wrote a series of urgent commands: rescue, care, snatch, weep, lift up, and tell. She reminds us that though these people may reject God, they can still be moved to repentance; for "Jesus is merciful, Jesus will save." Crisp rhythm keeps this gospel favorite moving. As in the gospel style designate stanzas to alternating groups with all joining at the refrain.

592   When the Church of Jesus

Written in 1968 for a stewardship renewal campaign, the text pierces our layers of self-protection and religiosity as it reminds us that worship and prayer go hand-in-hand with giving and living in God's world. With the moving tune KING'S WESTON, by Ralph Vaughan Williams, this hymn is a fervent prayer: "Teach us, dying Savior, how true Christians live." This scalewise tune will be easy to sing after hearing it played once through while all listen or hum along.

593   Here I Am, Lord

God's mission and purpose is stated clearly in this hymn by Dan Schutte, a Jesuit. Each stanza tells of the needs of God's people and the care God will provide but ends with the question from Is. 6:8, "Whom shall I send?" The refrain begins with the confident response: "Here I am, Lord." A hymn for commitment and sending forth of Christ's disciples, it may be sung by a soloist, choir, or male or female voices with all singing the response to the call, "Here I am, Lord."

594 Come, Divine Interpreter

Either the first stanza or the entire poem may be used as a prayer for illumination at any service, or for personal devotional use. This Charles Wesley poem first appeared introducing the section on "The Book of the Church" in *Short Hymns on Select Passages of Holy Scripture* (1762). It is a meditation on Rev. 1:3: "Blessed is he that readeth, and they that hear the words of this prophecy, and keep those things which are written therein." (KJV). Try using the tune DIX (92) with this text.

595 Whether the Word Be Preached or Read

Originally published in *Short Hymns on Select Passages of Holy Scripture* (1762), this Charles Wesley poem builds upon 2 Cor. 3:6: "The letter killeth, but the spirit giveth life" (KJV). The poem, ending in the mode of prayer, takes us beyond worshiping the Bible to a personal encounter with the living Christ.

596 Blessed Jesus, at Thy Word

Swedish pastor Tobias Clausnitzer's text was written to be sung before the sermon. Set to LIEBSTER JESU, the hymn achieves a remarkable wedding of text and tune. The hymn may be used before the sermon, as a prayer for illumination, or at the opening of worship. Its structure lends the hymn to antiphonal singing. The first phrase may be sung by one group, the second phrase by another. Both groups should join together on the last phrase.

597 For the Spirit of Truth

From Kenya, Africa, comes a concise and perceptive prayer about our failure to seek truth in its fullness. This personal prayer of confession is suitable to private meditation as well as corporate use. It commends itself to memorization and quotation.

598   O Word of God Incarnate

William How, a priest and later a bishop of the Church of England, based this text about the scriptures on Ps. 119:105: "Thy word is a lamp unto my feet and a light unto my path" (KJV), adding to it Pr. 6:23: "For the commandment is a lamp; and the law is light; and reproofs of instruction are the way of life" (KJV). While this text is about the Bible and uses many metaphors in referring to it, note that it is *Christ* who is addressed as the living "Word of God incarnate" (Jn. 1:1-14). The last stanza is a prayer to make the Church a "lamp of purest gold." It is most effective as a sung prayer for illumination.

599   Break Thou the Bread of Life

This text and tune were born in 1877 at the Chautauqua Institution in New York, where Mary A. Lathbury was asked to write a hymn text to be sung at meetings of the Chautauqua Literary and Scientific Circle and for Bible study groups. The tune BREAD OF LIFE was composed for this text by William F. Sherwin, music director at Chautauqua. It is a long-standing Chautauqua tradition to sing this hymn at Sunday vesper services. Based on the story of the feeding of the five thousand beside the Sea of Galilee, this hymn is suitable for use in Sunday Schools or as a prayer for illumination in worship.

600   Wonderful Words of Life

The Sunday School movement of the nineteenth century produced a type of song that became important to America's churches. These simple words and music were written to be sung by children. The purpose of this song is to promote in the child a love and appreciation of the scriptures. It speaks to and for the child in all of us and is an effective hymn in intergenerational worship. Either the first stanza or the whole hymn makes an appropriate sung prayer for illumination.

601 Thy Word Is a Lamp

Singer Amy Grant adapted the words of Ps. 119:105 (KJV), and they were set to the tune THY WORD by Michael W. Smith. The combination of its message of God's word as a guiding light with this easy melody makes the song popular especially with children and youth. In worship, it may be used as a sung prayer for illumination.

602 Concerning the Scriptures

This prayer makes a particularly effective prayer for illumination in any worship service, Sunday School class, or Bible study group. Written during the Reformation in England, it draws from the language of Rom. 15:4 and teaches us how best to use the Scriptures. Thus nourished by God's Word, we may more adequately lead Christian lives and trust our future with God.

603 Come, Holy Ghost, Our Souls Inspire

Originally titled "Before Reading the Scripture," this Charles Wesley text appeared in John Wesley's 1780 Collection, where it served as a prayer for illumination, especially for those responding in faith for the first time. The emphasis throughout is upon the Spirit: as inspirer, revealer, and interpreter of the Word of God (1 Cor. 2:11). Either the second stanza or the whole hymn may be a sung prayer for illumination. It is also especially fitting with and for children receiving Bibles.

604 Praise and Thanksgiving Be to God

This fine new text on baptism, based on Lk. 3:21-22, was suggested by the Canadian hymnologist Stanley Osborne to Frank Whiteley, whose outline was put in poetic form by a third Canadian, Harold Yardley. Written in the ancient classic Sapphic mode (11 11 11.5.), it is sung easily to the tune CHRISTE SANCTORUM, familiar to many United Methodists.

605 *Wash, O God, Our Sons and Daughters*

"Water-washed and Spirit-born" are among the powerful images found in this lovely baptismal text which was commissioned for this hymnal. It is set to a gentle, uplifting early American tune, BEACH SPRING. Ruth Duck's text begins with a petition on behalf of the children that they be washed, accepted, blessed, encompassed with love, and anointed by the Spirit. Nurture and guidance are asked for the parents and congregation. The final stanza of praise asks for re-creation and transformation. This is a powerful reaffirmation of the whole congregation's covenant with God through Baptism. The tune may be sung in unison or as a canon with the second voice entering at "sons." For contrast, male voices can repeat the words "Cleansing waters" on the keynote F in the rhythm of the first four notes or on the open fifth, F and C.

606 *Come, Let Us Use the Grace Divine*

Closing the section "For the Society, Praying" in John Wesley's 1780 *Collection*, this Charles Wesley text undergirds the communal and ongoing character of Christian discipleship. The key image is that of covenant in Jer. 50:5: "Come, and let us join ourselves to the Lord in a perpetual covenant that shall not be forgotten" (KJV). Used by the Wesleys in their "Service of Covenant Renewal," it can also serve in services where the Baptismal Covenant is reaffirmed today. The flowing and deeply bracing character of the new setting, to the traditional English tune KINGSFOLD, will enhance the use of this hymn.

607 *A Covenant Prayer in the Wesleyan Tradition*

One of the heritages of the Wesleyan tradition is the Covenant Renewal Service. This is the central prayer from that service. We offer ourselves to God as a living sacrifice (Rom. 12:1), putting our desires and comforts secondary to God's will and desire. This prayer is suitable for both individual recommitment and congregational services of covenant reaffirmation.

608 *This Is the Spirit's Entry Now*

Written for the Baptism of the author's first child in 1965, Thomas E. Herbranson uses water as the central image. Water is seen as the sacred sign of our death to sin and rising to follow in the Way. Water is also the symbol for cleansing power, a sign of God's grace and forgiveness. Paired with the tune AZMON, it is sure to be a hymn United Methodists will learn quickly.

609 *You Have Put On Christ*

Taken from the Roman Catholic "Rite of Baptism for Children," this short response is designed to be sung by the congregation as an affirmation of baptism. The opening phrase may be sung by a leader or children's choir, followed by the congregation singing "Alleluia"; or, the entire response may be taught to the congregation. Use flute and bells to provide additional accompaniment.

610 *We Know That Christ Is Raised*

Here is a baptismal text by John B. Geyer, based on Rom. 6:3-11. The death and resurrection of Christ turns our despair to joy. In baptism we share in Christ's death and resurrection. We the Church are a new creation, Christ's new body. The joyous text is enhanced by Charles V. Stanford's tune ENGELBERG and is especially appropriate for Baptism at Easter. This tune should be sung in unison with no ritard at the "Alleluia" until the final ending.

611 *Child of Blessing, Child of Promise*

This lovely and joyous baptismal text was written by Ronald S. Cole-Turner for the Baptism of his child. It celebrates the love and joy surrounding the new life of the child, while acknowledging that this child comes from God, is given back to God in Baptism, and is indeed God's child. Contrast the stanzas by having the choir (adult or children) sing the third stanza a cappella.

612 *Deck Thyself, My Soul, with Gladness*

This seventeenth-century text by Johann Franck—a lawyer, mayor, and public servant—has been called the greatest German communion text ever written. The theme of joy in the Holy Communion is seen in the first line with the image of the soul clothing itself with gladness. The second stanza uses the image of light to express joy; and the third stanza addresses Jesus, the Bread of Life (Jn. 6:35-58). The hymn is ideal for use at Holy Communion. Clear articulation in the accompaniment is necessary to effect the dancelike syncopation which adds rhythmic interest to this chorale tune.

613 *O Thou Who This Mysterious Bread*

First published in *Hymns on the Lord's Supper* (1745), this Charles Wesley text recalls the events of Jesus' resurrection appearance on the road and at Emmaus (Lk. 24:13-35). Remembering how Jesus revealed himself in scripture and in the breaking of bread, believers still seek the risen Christ in the Service of Word and Table. The pastoral tune LAND OF REST provides a natural setting. This hymn is fitting particularly at Holy Communion or during the Easter season.

614 *For the Bread Which You Have Broken*

Louis Benson, a Presbyterian pastor and a great American hymnologist of his era, wrote this text to be sung following Communion. With a final stanza that sends the Church into the world to serve, it is ideal to close a communion service. The words reflect the accounts of the institution of the Lord's Supper in Mt. 26:26-29; Mk. 14:22-25; Lk. 22:15-20; and 1 Cor. 11:23-25. The final phrase echoes the Lord's Prayer. The tune FOR THE BREAD, by V. Earle Copes, was written in 1959 for this text, to be used at the National Convocation of Methodist Youth in 1960.

615 *For the Bread Which You Have Broken*

The tune BENG-LI was composed originally for a Passion play to be sung during the scene depicting the Last Supper. It was later paired with

Louis Benson's text (*see* 614), which is similar in content. This hymn is intended to be sung at the close of the communion service, after the bread and cup have been served. It will be effective if a stanza(s) is sung in unison without accompaniment.

616 *Come, Sinners, to the Gospel Feast*

Based on Jesus' parable in Lk. 14:15-24: "A certain man made a great supper, and bade many" (KJV), this Charles Wesley text proclaims the Wesleyan conviction that salvation is offered to all. The invitation to the great supper is here applied specifically to the Lord's Supper: "O taste the goodness of our God, and eat his flesh and drink his blood" (Ps. 34:8 and Jn. 6:48-58). With the calm reflective tune HURSLEY, this hymn is suitable for singing during the serving of the bread and cup. Hymn 339, taken from the same Charles Wesley poem, is an invitation to Christian discipleship.

617 *I Come with Joy*

This text by contemporary British pastor and hymn writer Brian Wren gathers in all the elements of the Lord's Supper—joy, forgiveness, remembrance, community, love, praise, thanksgiving, and dedication. Persons gather ("I come"), become one in Christ, and then disperse into the world ("we'll go"). With the joyful early American folk tune DOVE OF PEACE, this is a fine hymn for any communion celebration. The entire hymn may be sung during the serving of the bread and cup, or stanzas 1–3 (or 1–2) may be sung as an invitation to the table and stanzas 4–5 (or 3–5) after receiving the bread and cup.

618 *Let Us Break Bread Together*

"Let Us Break Bread" is a testimony to slaves' affirmation of the Lord's Supper. It is appealing and instructive, and might have been conceived out of a need to help guide "invisible" slave congregations through the ritual of Holy Communion.* It is

---

*"The invisible church," a phrase coined by James Cone, refers to the slave church's secret meetings at night.

universally known and sung by Christians of all denominations and is treasured for its easily sung melody and built-in petition of pardon. Here, an effort has been made to restore the spiritual to a traditional performance practice uniting voices with keyboard. This restoration has been dressed in "black harmonies," including the traditional musical variant for the fourth stanza. This uplifting music should be sung in full voice with profound conviction. The 2/2 meter indicates that the spiritual should be sung throughout in a rocking manner, without interruption between stanzas.

619   *Now the Silence*

The fourteen lines of this text identify many facets of the experience of Holy Communion—silence, peace, uplifted hands, kneeling, our pleading words, the Father's welcoming arms, our hearing, our feeling of power, the cup ready for pouring, the body, the blood, the celebration, the wedding, the songs, the forgiven heart, the visit of the Holy Spirit, the Son's appearance, and the Father's blessing. Both past and future are gathered into the immediate experience of the "now." Both the beginning and the ending point toward the ultimate mystery of our communion with God. A hymn that may be introduced by men and women alternating phrases and joining for the last six measures. Let the last three measures become softer and softer.

620   *One Bread, One Body*

Drawing upon 1 Cor. 10:16-17, Gal. 3:28, and 1 Cor. 12, John B. Foley, a Roman Catholic Jesuit priest, pictures in this communion text our oneness in Christ. Ecumenical in its appeal, the text celebrates the diversity of believers who are "one body in this one Lord." Foley's tune ONE BREAD, ONE BODY adds to the beauty of the text with its gentle melody which may be accompanied with piano, organ, guitar, or auto harp and adding an instrument to highlight the melody.

621 *Be Present at Our Table, Lord*

John Cennick, a follower of the Wesleys who later became a Moravian, wrote this simple grace. Some advocate changing the word "creatures" to "mercies" and "paradise" to "fellowship," but the original wording is retained because it preserves insights that would otherwise be lost. The word "creatures" means "anything created" and is a reminder that both we and the food and drink on our table are God's creatures. The word "paradise" reminds us that not only Holy Communion but all eating and drinking together should be for Christians a foretaste of the heavenly "supper of the Lamb" (Rev. 19:9). Sung to the well-known tune OLD 100TH, this stanza may be used as a grace before the meal in the home or at church meetings or fellowship dinners. It is also appropriate at communion services.

622 *There Is a Fountain Filled with Blood*

William Cowper used an Old Testament reference from Zech. 13:1: "In that day there shall be a fountain opened to the house of David" (KJV) to suggest the first line. Connecting the blood of Jesus with this fountain as a fulfillment of the prophecy, the poet compares himself to the dying thief who rejoiced to see the fountain and then addresses the dying lamb, whose blood will never lose its power. The text closes with an affirmation of God's redeeming love here on earth and in the life to come.

623 *Here, O My Lord, I See Thee*

Horatius Bonar, a nineteenth-century Scottish preacher and writer, beautifully tells what happens when we meet Christ in Holy Communion. The first three stanzas anticipate the experience and may be sung *before* the bread and cup are served. The fourth and fifth stanzas assume that Communion has been given and received and may be sung *after* the bread and cup have been served. The feast is over, but the risen Christ remains. Having had a foretaste, we look forward to "the Lamb's great bridal feast" (Rev. 19:6-9). The stateliness of the tune is felt with two strong beats per measure. Stanzas 1–3 may be sung before Communion or by the choir during Communion with all singing stanzas 4–5 following Communion; or, the entire hymn may be sung in preparation or as a response to receiving Communion.

624 Bread of the World

Reginald Heber was an important hymn writer of the Church of England. This text, based on Jn. 6:35-58, remains one of our most often sung communion hymns. The tune EUCHARISTIC HYMN was composed for this text by an American organist John Hodges. A simple devotional hymn, the stanzas may be sung quietly, unhurriedly, and in unison.

625 Come, Let Us Eat

Billema Kwillia, according to the *Companion to the Lutheran Book of Worship* (1981), is a contemporary Liberian who while working as a literacy teacher for a number of years became a Christian and an evangelist. He sang this hymn, which he had written and composed, for a meeting, and it was recorded on tape. It was translated by Margaret Miller, and a fourth stanza was added by Gilbert Doan. This text is based on 1 Cor. 5:7-8: "Christ our passover is sacrificed for us: Therefore let us keep the feast" (KJV). This hymn is a teaching tool; the uninitiated are instructed and the faithful are reminded of the proper actions when celebrating Holy Communion. Like most music from the west coast of Africa, the tune is based on a five-note (pentatonic) scale. This hymn, set in the ancient call-and-response pattern, should be sung peacefully, moderately slow, and with precise rhythm throughout. Using the rhythm of the first measure, a hand drum might prove effective when singing this hymn.

626 Let All Mortal Flesh Keep Silence

The roots of this text are found in the ancient Liturgy of St. James of the Syrian Orthodox Church, at the point where the bread and wine are brought to the altar. The text refers to the image of Jesus as "heavenly food" in Jn. 6:35-58 and to the visions in Is. 6:1-4 and Rev. 4. The traditional French tune PICARDY adds to the sense of awe and wonder in the presence of God.

627 O the Depth of Love Divine

First published in *Hymns on the Lord's Supper* (1745) in the section entitled "A Sign and a Means of Grace," this Charles Wesley text declines to debate the *how* of sacramental causality, in order to concentrate on the *Who* of sacramental presence, identity, and power (Jn. 6:35-59). Its flowing folk-style tune STOOKEY was written for this text by Carlton R. Young. This is an important hymn for teaching the meaning of the Lord's Supper in the Wesleyan tradition.

628 Eat This Bread

In the religious community of Taizé, France, a simple form of congregational song has been developed. The community sings a simple refrain to a well-crafted melody, while a soloist sings appropriate scriptural words for the stanzas. This song is for Holy Communion and may be sung by the congregation (led by the choir) while the bread and cup are being served. It is based on Jn. 6:35. Easily memorized, this has become a favorite all over the world.

629 You Satisfy the Hungry Heart

This hymn, written to be sung during the distribution of Communion, was a joint effort by Cincinnati Roman Catholic hymn writer and editor Omer Westendorf and a Denver composer Robert E. Kreutz. The words reflect Jn. 6:34 and 10:1-5 and 1 Cor. 10:16-17. The melody of the congregational refrain has a natural flow, enhanced by the changing meters. The choir or soloist(s) sings the various stanzas, always followed by the refrain. This is one of the most popular hymns written in recent years.

630   Become to Us the Living Bread

This beautifully crafted Holy Communion text was written in 1970 by Miriam Drury, a retired Presbyterian church musician. She begins with the image of Jesus as the "living bread" upon which we are to feed (Jn. 6:35-58) and continues with the image of Jesus as "never-failing wine, the spring of joy." She ends with a call for Christian unity at the Lord's table. The tune is presented in three contrasting themes, with an exuberant threefold Alleluia. Clear instrumental articulation is necessary to sing the syncopation with ease.

631   O Food to Pilgrims Given

This Latin communion text, based on Jn. 6:35-58 and translated by J. A. L. Riley, prays for nourishment, for "food to pilgrims given." The cup is "the stream of love" and the "purest fountain" that revives us. The final stanza addresses Jesus, who invites us to this holy meal, expressing the hope that, while he is hidden here in the bread and wine, we shall see in heaven his "countenance divine." The tune, first published in 1539, was used by J. S. Bach in both the *St. Matthew* and the *St. John Passions* and in Cantatas 13, 44, and 97. The meditative quality of the tune should be reflected in the tempo.

632   Draw Us in the Spirit's Tether

This communion text by Percy Dearmer, prominent hymn writer and editor, begins with the prayerful request that we might be drawn in the tether (rope, chain, or halter) of the Holy Spirit, recalling Jesus' promise that "where two or three are gathered in my name, there am I in the midst of them" (Mt. 18:20) and the experience of those who touched the hem of Jesus' garment and were healed (Mt. 9:20-22; 14:35-36, KJV). To introduce this to the congregation it may be sung as a litany with the choir singing the first four phrases and the congregation responding with the section beginning "Alleluia."

633 *The Bread of Life for All Is Broken*

This elegant text was written in the early 1930s in semiclassical Chinese by a leading and important hymn writer, Timothy Tingfang Lew. He uses specific terms and images from traditional Buddhism with which traditional Chinese can easily identify. The text asserts that believers are gathering humbly to witness and remember the sufferings of Christ, to pray for his presence that we may unite with him, and to share the heavenly joy. Do not rush the tempo but rather follow the rhythm of the text. The melody may be introduced using a flute or recorder instrument.

634 *Now Let Us from This Table Rise*

What is our response to the wondrous gift of communion with Christ? Fred Kaan, pastor of a congregation in England in the mid-1960s, sensed a need for a congregational response to this important act, a response that would give voice to renewed dedication in following Christ and doing Christ's work. As his response to the need for a vital postcommunion hymn, this is appropriately sung after the bread and cup have been served. The eighteenth-century French church melody DEUS TUORUM MILITUM gives joyous and strong movement to the text.

635 *Because Thou Hast Said*

The opening lines of this Charles Wesley text recall Jesus' words instituting the Lord's Supper: "This do in remembrance of me" (Lk. 22:19, KJV). In keeping with the fullness of the Wesleys' sacramental theology, the hymn recognizes both the "memorial" and "mystical" aspects of Holy Communion and also celebrates the sacrament as a means of grace, renewing the community in the image of God's love. This text is pertinent particularly to the celebration of the Lord's Supper on Holy Thursday.

636 *Christian People, Raise Your Song*

This joyful communion text was written by Colin P. Thompson, a British pastor in the United Reformed Church who is the son of a Jewish refugee from Vienna and an English Congregationalist pastor. Christ "has pioneered the way of the new creation" (*see* 1 Cor. 15:22) and "comes to restore us." Thompson likens our greeting the risen Christ in Holy Communion to our greeting the spring as it rises out of winter. What a great reason for singing!

637 *Una Espiga* (Sheaves of Summer)

This beautiful communion hymn from Spain, by Cesareo Gabaraín, is a favorite in Latin America and in Hispanic churches in the United States. Moreover, it has been translated into over forty languages and sung around the world and has special meaning in ecumenical communion celebrations. Sing it while the bread and cup are being served, keeping the pace moderate, light and dancelike. Try it with guitar accompaniment, flute, and rhythm instruments.

638 *This Is the Feast of Victory*

This festival canticle has become immensely popular because of its fine tune by Richard Hillert. To be sung at the celebration of the Holy Communion, it is most effective when done antiphonally—the congregation singing the refrain and the choir singing the stanzas. It could also be used as an Easter processional.

639 *Bread and Justice*

This is a prayer to be studied with care and prayed with deliberation. Images such as coffee, an open door, and shouts of children in the first half of the prayer contrast sharply with images such as lack of bread, closed doors, and sad children in the second half. The prayer is intended particularly for private or group use at a service of Holy Communion; we ask that the sacramental signs of God's goodness may make us more aware of the world around us, with both its gifts and its pain.

640 Take Our Bread

Appropriate for singing at Holy Communion, especially while the bread and cup are being served, both text and tune are by Joe Wise, a Roman Catholic from Louisville, Kentucky. The hymn begins with the refrain as we offer our bread, our hearts, and our lives to God. This commitment continues as we stand at the Lord's Table and eat the bread, acknowledging that we are redeemed and filled with the Spirit but needing further nourishment. It may be sung with guitar accompaniment.

641 Fill My Cup, Lord

Richard E. Blanchard was born in 1925 of missionary parents in China, studied in Georgia, and has served for many years as a United Methodist pastor in the Florida Conference. In 1958, while pastor of Wesley Church in Coral Gables, Florida, he wrote "Fill My Cup, Lord" while waiting for a couple who were very late for their premarital counseling appointment after having been late for their previous appointment. Blanchard says that he "was not in a mood to be used by God, but God was in a mood to use" him. The text reflects the words of Jesus in Jn. 6:35: "I am the bread of life; he who comes to me shall not hunger, and he who believes in me shall never thirst." This chorus lends itself for use in Holy Communion as a prayerful request for spiritual nourishment. Since the complete song has three stanzas as well as this chorus, a soloist or choir may sing the stanzas, with the congregation joining in the chorus.

642 As Man and Woman We Were Made

Here is a delightfully joyful wedding text by contemporary British pastor and hymn writer Brian Wren, set to the traditional English carol SUSSEX CAROL. The text anchors nuptial joy securely in the source of love—the God who created us and has revealed love through Jesus Christ. This same Jesus, who has lived and died for us, celebrates with us on the wedding day and promises to be with us in the unknown future. A light, buoyant rhythm should be maintained when singing this joyful hymn. Chimes or other instruments may be added.

643 *When Love Is Found*

This reflective wedding text by British pastor and hymn writer Brian Wren considers the breadth of love as lived out in marriage as a covenant under God. In several aspects it is different from other wedding texts because Wren asks us to reach out with love beyond our own homes, and as he reflects on the trying times of marriage, calling us to love and growth. This text, set to an English folk tune, GIFT OF LOVE, is a hymn to come back to when love is tried or torn for reassurance and strength. Highlight the simple melody by varying the registration or instrumentation on different stanzas according to the text.

644 *Jesus, Joy of Our Desiring*

This text, of uncertain origin, addresses Jesus as the object of our desires. Jesus Christ is the Incarnate Word of God, involved in our creation, giving us life and a quest for truth. We are reminded that confidence brings peace and recall the promise of Christ that "whoever drinks of the water that I shall give . . . will never thirst" (Jn. 4:14). It concludes with the assurance that they who follow Christ know beauty and wisdom and joys unknown. Because the love of husband and wife is grounded in the love of Christ, this hymn is often sung at services of Christian marriage. A graceful 3/4 tempo will best reflect the beauty of both text and tune.

645 *O Perfect Love*

This text by Dorothy Gurney shows great insight into the nature of the Christian marriage. It addresses God as the "perfect Love" who joins together the couple in love, and as the "perfect Life" who assures the quality of their life together. Contemplating the mystery of love that joins two into one, the text names assurance, tender charity, faith, hope, and quiet, brave endurance as necessary traits for Christian marriage. It prays that the couple in their life together may know joy, peace, and eternal life. Joseph

Barnby's graceful tune PERFECT LOVE was originally an anthem composed for the wedding of Princess Louise of Wales and the Duke of Fife in 1889. This is an often sung wedding hymn.

646 Canticle of Love

This rhythmical prose text summarizes the biblical understanding of love. A scripture song adapted by S. T. Kimbrough, a consultant to the Hymnal Revision Committee, it stresses the continuity of the biblical ideas of love that culminate in the love of Christ, which binds each heart and every relationship. God's love in Christ alone is the foundation of enduring relationships. While appropriate for marriages, the canticle emphasizes the inclusiveness of God's love for all persons in all relationships and, therefore, has multiple worship and devotional uses.

647 Your Love, O God, Has Called Us Here

This fresh new hymn for Christian marriage by Russell Schultz-Widmar, rather than focusing on the bride and groom, focuses on the worship of God and asks God's blessing for the wedding couple and for the witnessing congregation. A soloist may sing the first stanza, a choir, the second, and the congregation sing the third as a community affirmation and prayer.

648 God the Spirit, Guide and Guardian

This text, written for the ordination of Jeffery Rowthorn, appears for the first time in any hymnal. The text reverses the usual order of trinitarian hymns by addressing first the Holy Spirit, then Christ as Savior, and finally God the Creator. The last half of each stanza is directed to the body of the Church and its ministry. In addition to its use at ordinations and consecrations, it is suitable on other occasions where the theme is Christian ministry.

649 *How Shall They Hear the Word*

Contemporary British author Michael Perry includes this strong call for witness, based on Paul's similar questions in Rom. 10:14-15, among forty-one new texts written for *Hymns for Today's Church.* The first two stanzas present the problems generally, while stanza 3 brings the call down to our personal commitment. If we are negligent, who will speak for Christ? This is a fine new hymn for mission, commitment, and dedication, as well as for ordinations and consecrations.

650 *Give Me the Faith Which Can Remove*

This is one of Charles Wesley's "Hymns for a Preacher of the Gospel." The original opening lines expressed the desire for renewed zeal: "O that I was as heretofore." As in John Wesley's 1780 *Collection,* our version begins with the original stanza 3, the pleas for "faith to move mountains" (Mk. 11:20-25), and applies this to the common calling of all believers to "publish the sinner's Friend" (Mt. 11:19). It is set here to the buoyant tune CAREY'S (SURREY) by Henry Carey and is particularly fitting at ordinations and consecrations since it also emphasizes the evangelical mission of the Church at large.

651 *Come, Holy Ghost, Our Souls Inspire*

This ninth-century Latin hymn, attributed to Rhabanus Maurus—a Benedictine monk, abbot, and archbishop, has been in constant use in the Church for more than a thousand years. The tune VENI CREATOR is a metrical adaptation of the historic chant and is one of the most singable plainsong melodies. It may be sung with two or three bells ringing the tonic and dominant tones or unaccompanied to recreate the plainsong style. The hymn was intended originally for Morning Prayer on the Day of Pentecost and is suited particularly for use on that day, as well as at ordinations and consecrations.

652 *Canticle of Remembrance*

These wise words from the Apocrypha (Wisdom of Solomon 3:1-9) are attributed to King Solomon and are a hymn in praise of those who live for God and are judged to be righteous. They are wise and not ungodly. For the righteous, death is no punishment but the fulfillment of hope. The canticle affirms what the Bible says from beginning to end: "Those who trust in God will understand truth, and the faithful will abide in love," because God's grace and mercy reign over the faithful. It is appropriate for funerals and memorial services, All Saints' Day (Sunday), or general use.

653 *Christ the Victorious*

Carl P. Daw, Jr., a contributor to *The Hymnal 1982* of the Episcopal Church, wrote this text to be sung to the famous and stirring RUSSIAN HYMN of imperial Russia, popular with congregations. With its theme of death and resurrection, it is appropriate for All Saints' Day (Sunday) and for Services of Death and Resurrection (funerals and memorial services). The theme of victory over death gives the hymn a triumphant, positive quality in contrast to the sorrow and grief most often associated with death.

654 *How Blest Are They Who Trust in Christ*

British Methodist pastor Fred Pratt Green, now retired, has centered this funeral/memorial hymn on the power of Christ and the strength that faith in Christ can give us in time of death. Without discounting our loss, he reminds us that the dead remain in our hearts and have eternal life in Christ. Finally, our Christian reaction to grief and sorrow bears witness to "the strength and splendor of belief."

655 *Fix Me, Jesus*

Some Afro-American slaves viewed their lot as being similar to that of slain martyrs. They found biblical expression for their views in

Rev. 6:11 and 7:9-14 and in many spirituals celebrated a desire to be included in "that number." Here, slave-poets long for elevation to saintly status replete with "white" tribulation robes that have been "washed in the blood of the lamb." When effectively sung in worship, this spiritual becomes a petition for Christian perfection. Rehearse the "glides" with the congregation so that they can experience the moaning quality of the plea "Oh, fix me."

656 *If Death My Friend and Me Divide*

This eloquent expression by Charles Wesley of faith in the midst of grief is based on 1 Th. 4:13: "But we would not have you ignorant, brethren, concerning those who are asleep, that you may not grieve as others do who have no hope." Without denying the way of grief, the mournful soul is borne up by the hope that friendship is a blessing restored in eternity. This poem may be read effectively at Christian funerals and memorial services, and also on All Saints' Day (Sunday).

657 *This Is the Day*

Ps. 118:24 is set to a traditional tune of unknown origin in a call-and-response pattern. Congregations can join in easily by repeating each phrase after the leader; or, they can sing it antiphonally—left/right, front/back, or men/women. This chorus is most effective at the opening of worship. Children and youth find it especially appealing.

658 *This Is the Day the Lord Hath Made*

This call to worship, which may be sung by the choir or the entire congregation, is a paraphrase by Isaac Watts of Ps. 118:24. The text acknowledges that God has made everything, including the day and all its hours. This recognition that everything belongs to God is an excellent place to begin the worship of God. The final phrase invites heaven and earth to rejoice and surround God's throne with praise.

This hymn, believed to be the earliest Christian hymn in the Cheyenne oral tradition, was inspired by the gospel song "What a Friend We Have in Jesus." Sung in the early 1900s by both Cheyenne and Arapaho nations, whose territories extended from Canada to Texas, its origin remains obscure. According to *Cheyenne Spiritual Songs*, a collection of hymns and songs sung by Cheyenne Christians, one story centers around Ova'hehe or Mrs. Bear Bow. As Mrs. Bear Bow, one of the first Cheyenne Christians at Old Colony, heard the church bells ring at the nearby Reformed church she was inspired to make this song. Another story relates that Watan, an Arapaho leader, sang a song which used the same melody and related the same message as the Cheyenne song. Still another story tells of Ho'evoo'otse (Buffalo Meat), who made the hymn as a "gathering song" for his people at Kingfisher, Oklahoma. Children may be taught this hymn using a wooden flute and sticks to provide percussion throughout or at the spoken notes.

660 *God Is Here*

This text was commissioned in 1978 of Fred Pratt Green, a retired British Methodist pastor and renowned contemporary hymn writer, to be sung to the glorious and exuberant tune ABBOT'S LEIGH, written in 1941 by Cyril V. Taylor. This hymn celebrates music, the other arts, and the breadth of our worship life, as we dedicate ourselves to be Christ's Church. The first and last stanzas are excellent as introit and benediction response respectively. Accompaniment should be strong and full throughout, supporting the majestic tune with a waltzlike tempo.

661 *Jesus, We Want to Meet*

This hymn was written by Nigerian A. T. Olajida Olude, who promoted the use of native Yuroba music in the worship of Nigerian churches. It came to be used in the U.S.A. through Biodun Adebesin, who translated it and, while serving at the United Nations, introduced it to Austin Lovelace and Carlton

Young. Ideal for the opening of worship, the hymn is in the form of a litany between a leader and the congregation. A drum part is provided in keeping with the African character of the music. The "leader" may be a soloist, a small group, or two small groups alternating the leader's part from front to back or left to right. This joyful tune may be accompanied with finger cymbals and tambourine.

662 *Stand Up and Bless the Lord*

This text is by Moravian James Montgomery, a champion of the abolition of slavery, who had a long association with Methodists. It is based on Neh. 9:5: "Stand up and bless the Lord your God from everlasting to everlasting." Stanza 2 echoes Is. 6:6-7 as it speaks of a flame brought from God's altar to "touch our lips." Stanza 4 echoes Ps. 118:14 in calling God "our strength and song" and our salvation. With the tune ST. MICHAEL, adapted from the *Genevan Psalter*, this hymn has become a favorite in many United Methodist congregations.

663 *Savior, Again to Thy Dear Name*

Written a century ago for the close of a choral society festival, this remains one of the best hymns for the close of worship. The hymn is a prayer that opens with words of praise, then asks for peace on the way home, through life, and into the eternal life. It may be sung by the choir or congregation as a response to the benediction.

664 *Sent Forth by God's Blessing*

This text draws together the themes of the enabling power of worship and our being sent out into the world to carry Christ's name and share our faith. From its opening line, "Sent forth by God's blessing," it is an effective congregational benediction response. With its singable Welsh folk tune THE ASH GROVE, it will find its way easily into the hearts of a congregation. Written by Omer Westendorf, a prominent Roman Catholic musician, it appeared in the first English-language Roman Catholic hymn and service book in 1964.

665 *Go Now in Peace*

Natalie Sleeth, a well-known United Methodist composer of choral music, wrote this simple benediction response after attending an Orff instruments workshop. It reminds us that as we leave worship God's peace and love go with us everywhere. It may be used as a response or as the benediction itself, and may be sung in unison or as a round with piano, Orff instruments, and/or handbells.

666 *Shalom to You*

These words by United Methodist Elise S. Eslinger are easy to memorize and sing as a benediction. The Hebrew word *Shalom* means both greeting and farewell. It also expresses a deeper desire for a world of harmonious relationships, justice, and peace. The tune from Mexico should be sung slowly, softly, and reverently, repeated several times if desired.

667 *Shalom*

This is the familiar Israeli melody widely known and sung in youth groups. The Hebrew word *Shalom* is now widely used in English to refer to "peace" that includes justice and comprehensive well-being. The text is given in Hebrew and English and may be sung as a closing response to a service. It may also be sung as a two-part or four-part round.

668 *Let Us Now Depart in Thy Peace*

Beginning with a phrase from Lk. 2:29 (the Canticle of Simeon, or *Nunc Dimittis*, 225), the text calls on Jesus to bless us as we leave worship for faithful service in the world. This New Mexican folk song is learned easily and may be sung as a round between women and men, the second part beginning after one measure. It makes a nice benediction response for choir and congregation.

669 *The Apostolic Blessing*

This act of blessing is suitable for use by a leader of worship at the close of any service. It also may be used whenever blessing is appropriate, as when dismissing from their place in front of the congregation those who have just been baptized or confirmed, or those who have just been installed in office. It is called the Apostolic Blessing because it closes the Second Letter of the Apostle Paul to the Church of Corinth (2 Cor. 13:14).

670 *Go Forth for God*

This text by J. R. Peacey calls for our response to God's summons, with each stanza elaborating on a particular quality of life—peace, love, strength, joy—which we are to carry into the world. It is a powerful text calling the Church to action and makes a fine closing hymn. The strong familiar tune GENEVA 124 is the setting for Ps. 124 in the *Genevan Psalter*. The last four measures make a beautiful congregational response, emphasizing "peace, love, strength, and joy."

671 *Lord, Dismiss Us with Thy Blessing*

John Fawcett's text for the closing of worship focuses not on the *security* but rather on the *faithfulness* of the worshiper. It is a prayer for joy, peace, grace, and faith of the believer. Fawcett was acquainted with George Whitefield and joined the Methodists for a time, but then became a Baptist pastor. His text is set to the singable tune SICILIAN MARINERS.

672, 673 *God Be with You till We Meet Again*

This "Christian farewell" came into wide use in the late nineteenth century as a closing song at revivals and camp meetings, and it remains one of the most popular benediction hymns today. The text is a prayer for God's care and safekeeping through the troubles of life. It is set to two very different tunes, making it usable to a wide variety of congregations. The tune GOD BE WITH YOU, by William G. Tomer, is in the nineteenth-century gospel style with a repetitive refrain. The tune

RANDOLPH, by Ralph Vaughan Williams, provides an attractive alternative which combines unison and part singing.

674 *See the Morning Sun Ascending*

This text is based on Rev. 5:11-14 and 7:11-12, which tell of the hosts of heaven surrounding the throne and singing praises to the Lamb. It connects us with those hosts above, with the words: "So may we, in lowly station, join the choristers above." The rising of the sun reminds us daily of the steadfast love of God, to whom we sing praise. Perfect for the opening of morning worship, it is set to the tune UNSER HERRSCHER, by Joachim Neander.

675 *As the Sun Doth Daily Rise*

Based on a Latin office hymn, this text likens each day's rising sun to our daily gratitude for God's goodness. Not only food for physical needs but spiritual nourishment comes from God. The author also petitions God to be guard and guide and prays for wisdom from God's Word. The text, set to the tune INNOCENTS, concludes with a Doxology praising the Trinity. An excellent hymn for children to learn and introduce to the congregation; stanza 3 may be sung by the choir in harmony, all singing stanza 4 a cappella, and stanza 5 with full accompaniment.

676 *For a New Day*

From the Eastern Orthodox Church comes this simple prayer for the beginning of the day. Easily memorized, it may be used in personal devotions upon arising, or as a breakfast table grace, or at an early morning service of worship. Of particular note is the insight that serving God, far from being bondage, is perfect freedom.

677 *Listen, Lord (A Prayer)*

This prayer is intended specifically for the opening of congregational morning worship, particularly on occasions when the previous week has been filled with stress and sorrow. It is an extract from the collection of poetic sermons in the black idiom entitled *God's*

Trombones, by James Weldon Johnson, who also wrote the text of the hymn "Lift Every Voice and Sing" (519).

678   *Rise to Greet the Sun*

This is a prayer for the beginning of a new day—an expression of thanks for revived life in nature and a petition for God's guidance and molding of Christian character. It concludes with a statement of desire to live a content and simple life, knowing that God is the provider of all needs. Author Chao Tzu-ch'en tries to relate Christian faith to the daily experiences of the people. The first appearance for this hymn in a hymnal in the U.S.A. was in *The Methodist Hymnal* (1966). This is an excellent hymn for Morning Praise and Prayer and may be sung as a round with voices one measure apart.

679   *O Splendor of God's Glory Bright*

Ambrose of Milan is considered to be the father of Latin hymnody. This text probably was designed for use at lauds (the daily morning praise and prayer service) and speaks of dispelling the darkness of night. The image of light and God's splendor pervades every phrase of the text. The final stanza is a prayer for guidance, love, and grace. This hymn is appropriate for Morning Praise and Prayer and at Epiphany, emphasizing the light coming to the world.

680   *Father, We Praise Thee*

Pope Gregory the Great is often given credit for this text, but there is no conclusive evidence that he wrote this or any other hymn. Gregory's great contribution to worship came by way of his interest in the liturgy and music of the early Medieval Church and his representation of it in sixth-century Roman liturgy. He set the course of church music for a thousand years. The phrase "active and watchful, stand we all before Thee" in the second line gives the ideal attitude for those gathering to worship God.

681 *For Help for the Forthcoming Day*

This prayer is intended for individual or corporate use at the beginning of a new day. We give thanks for God's protection during the previous night and ask that during this day we may live according to God's righteous will. The petition is an expansion upon the sentence in the Lord's Prayer, "Lead us not into temptation, but deliver us from evil." This prayer is an adaptation of the traditional Collect for Grace, a Latin prayer used in England since the sixteenth century.

682 *All Praise to Thee, My God, This Night*

Thomas Ken's *Manual of Prayers for the Use of the Scholars of Winchester College* (1674) included three hymns for the boys to sing every morning, noon, and night. This is the night hymn from that collection and is one of the most loved evening hymns. The text begins with praise and in the following stanzas asks for forgiveness, for help in living righteously, and for restful sleep. The last stanza is the well-known "Doxology," praise of Father, Son, and Holy Ghost (*see* 94 and 95). The tune TALLIS' CANON was composed by one of England's greatest sixteenth-century composers, Thomas Tallis. The hymn may be sung easily and effectively by a congregation in unison or as a round.

683 *The Day Is Past and Over*

This evening hymn comes from the early Greek church and may have been sung while candles were lighted for worship. In this text, darkness is compared to sin, while light symbolizes Christ, who defeats sin. This is very useful for Evening Praise and Prayer. A soloist or small group may lead the singing of this quiet hymn.

684 *Christ, Mighty Savior*

This tenth-century Spanish hymn was written to be sung at evening worship. Filled with words about light, changing from radiant day to star-filled night, it praises God for creation, while asking forgiveness, seeking rest, and trusting in the peace of Christ. This plaintive tune by David Hurd promises to become a favorite. The congregation will quickly learn this new tune after hearing a few of the stanzas. Diminishing the accompaniment at stanza 5 will be effective, letting the choir support the congregation.

685 Now, on Land and Sea Descending

Samuel Longfellow wrote this hymn for evening worship at the Second Unitarian Church of Brooklyn in 1859. Based on Psalm 19—"The heavens are telling the glory of God"—it emphasizes the qualities of the sky and its telling forth of God's love. The "Jubilate" refrain on the third line conveys a joyful mood not often seen in evening hymns. It is excellent for Evening Praise and Prayer. Add bells or chimes at the refrain.

686 O Gladsome Light

This ancient Greek hymn, also known as the *Phos Hilaron*, is an important link to the early Church as it is associated with an ancient tradition dating to the fourth century. Sung in Greek Orthodox Church worship at the close of the day when lamps were lighted, the believing community ends the day by praising the Light of all lights, Jesus Christ. It is appropriate for Evening Praise and Prayer or any other evening worship occasion when it may be sung or read.

687 Day Is Dying in the West

After the founding of the Chautauqua Institution in 1874, its co-founder (later a bishop) John H. Vincent asked Mary A. Lathbury to write the first two stanzas of this text in 1877 for Sunday evening services on the assembly grounds. She added stanzas 3 and 4 in 1890. Chautauqua's music director,

William F. Sherwin, wrote the tune CHAUTAUQUA for this text in 1877. This hymn is still sung every Sunday during the nine-week summer season, both at the 5:00 vesper service and at the evening sacred song service in the amphitheater. Lathbury uses the ancient image of the heavens (universe, firmament) as a dome from which the stars are hung each evening like lanterns (lamps). The refrain is a metrical version of the *Sanctus* (Holy, holy, holy Lord), based on Is. 6:3 and Rev. 4:8 and since ancient times part of the Great Thanksgiving at Holy Communion. The phrase "Heaven and earth are full of thy glory" inspired the writer to dwell on the beauty of nature seen in the evening.

688   *God, That Madest Earth and Heaven*

Reginald Heber was the first to write texts for specific times, days, and seasons in the Christian year. He wrote this text as a one-stanza evening benediction, to which Frederick Hosmer later added a second stanza. The two stanzas are well balanced, as the first asks for rest and safekeeping through the night while the second prays for strength and will to rise to a new day of service. The beautiful Welsh melody AR HYD Y NOS ("All Through the Night") supports the mood of the text.

689   *At the Close of Day*

This prayer may be used by groups meeting at the close of the day—in retreat settings, for example—or by individuals at bedtime. It incorporates thanksgiving and confession concerning the day past, with trust and petition for the night ahead. It is from the pen of the German Christian theologian Dietrich Bonhoeffer, who was martyred by the Nazis just before the close of World War II.

690   *The Day Thou Gavest, Lord, Is Ended*

As the Church in one part of the world rests at night, prayers and hymns are taken up in another part of the world as earth and sun continue their courses. That is the sentiment expressed in this text by John Ellerton, based on Ps. 113:2-3: "From the rising of the sun to its setting the name of the Lord is to be praised!" With its beautifully flowing tune ST. CLEMENT, by Clement Scholefield, it is one of our most beautiful evening hymns.

691 *For Protection at Night*

This sentence prayer from India is for use at the close of day. It may be a part of a Service of Evening Praise and Prayer or an act of private devotion before retiring. The language is reminiscent of Jesus' description of himself as a mother hen in Mt. 23:37 and Lk. 13:34.

692 *Creator of the Stars of Night*

This anonymous ninth-century Latin hymn is a grand statement of the nature of Christ. Beginning with the creation of the heavens, the text continues with the image of Christ as the everlasting light. The concluding Doxology, reflecting Phil. 2:10-11, is one of the earliest statements of this Christian formula of praise, which is often seen in hymns of later centuries. With the elegant Sarum Plainsong melody CONDITOR ALME, the hymn inspires a mood of reverence and awe.

693 *For a Peaceful Night*

This traditional African prayer for the close of the day, most likely for use just before bedtime, is a word both of petition for safety through the night and of confidence in the God who is awake while we sleep.

694 *Come, Ye Thankful People, Come*

Based on the parable of the wheat and the weeds (Mt. 13:24-43) and the parable of the seed growing secretly (Mk. 4:26-29), this eschatalogical text focuses on judgment in the last days—joy and sorrow grow together only to be separated on judgment day. With George J. Elvey's much-loved tune ST. GEORGE'S WINDSOR, this has become a popular harvest hymn for Thanksgiving services.

695 O Lord, May Church and Home Combine

This text was published in 1961 by the Hymn Society of America in a collection entitled *Thirteen New Marriage and Family Life Hymns*. Its theme is timely for today's Church—combining the power of church and home to nurture people toward Christian maturity. Gentleness, love, grace, fellowship, faith, prayer, joy, and peace provide the atmosphere for this growth. With its beautiful U.S.A. folk tune LAND OF REST, the hymn is appropriate for weddings and services on the home and family.

696 America the Beautiful

A view from Pike's Peak with plains spread below was the inspiration for the opening of this poetic national hymn. Katharine Lee Bates in the second stanza expands the poem to pay tribute to the heroes who fought for the United States' liberty. "Alabaster cities" in the third stanza refers to the buildings of the 1893 Columbian Exposition in Chicago, which Bates had seen on her way west. The strength of this text lies in its vision of a better nation. It is appropriate for national celebrations such as Independence Day (Sunday).

697 America (My Country, 'Tis of Thee)

Samuel Smith, a theology student at Andover Seminary in 1831, was inspired to write a patriotic hymn that could be sung to the English tune "God Save the King." The resulting hymn about freedom and liberty is also a declaration of love for the natural beauty of the United States of America. This national hymn is appropriate for national celebrations such as Independence Day (Sunday).

698 *God of the Ages*

Written for the centennial of the United States, July 4, 1876, Daniel C. Roberts's text, originally with the first line "God of our fathers," has become one of the most loved national hymns. It is a prayer for safekeeping and righteousness with the beginning and ending notably acknowledging God as leader. Roberts was a private in the 84th Ohio Volunteers during the Civil War and then became an Episcopal priest. This hymn is appropriate for national celebrations such as Independence Day (Sunday). The tune NATIONAL HYMN may be enhanced through the use of trumpets or a solo trumpet stop on the organ for the fanfares.

699 *Come, and Let Us Sweetly Join*

Composed from a longer hymn originally entitled "The Love-feast," this hymn recalls early Methodist and Moravian love feasts, inspired by the "agape feast" of the early Church (Jude 12). Similar yet distinct from the Lord's Supper, the love feast was an occasion for Christian testimony, anticipating the "joys above" (st. 2) and celebrating the presence of "our common Lord" (st. 1) through mutual care and sharing. This hymn is useful at Holy Communion, love feasts, and ecumenical services. The first and last stanzas combined also make an excellent table blessing.

700 *Abide with Me*

The words from Lk. 24:29, "Abide with us: for it is toward evening and the day is far spent" (KJV), inspired Henry Lyte to write this text a few months before his death. The text provides a confident view of death. The hymn originally was used at evening services, but its theme makes it appropriate for funerals and memorial services.

701 *When We All Get to Heaven*

Author Eliza E. Hewitt and composer Emily D. Wilson attended Methodist camp meetings at Ocean Grove, New Jersey, where they collaborated on this hymn, which first appeared in 1898. Perhaps their campmeeting experiences were a foretaste of the glory of heaven, when we "shall be caught up . . . to meet the Lord" (1 Th. 4:17) "in the mansions bright and blessed [where] he'll prepare for us a place" (based on Jn. 14:2, KJV). The hymn celebrates Christ's love and promises of eternal life, the joyous hope of the community of believers. Use piano or piano and organ to accompany, filling in long notes with chords or arpeggios. Alternate stanzas with all singing the refrain.

702 *Sing with All the Saints in Glory*

This Easter text, inspired by 1 Cor. 15:20, celebrates in beautiful poetic language the meaning of the eternal life won for us in Christ's resurrection. The text is cosmic in its expression, looking beyond individual deaths to the consummation of all things, when "amidst earth's closing thunders," "the storms of time shall cease." With the tune HYMN TO JOY, from Beethoven's Ninth Symphony, this is an exultant hymn for the Easter season.

703 *Swing Low, Sweet Chariot*

"Swing Low" bears a "mask" and sends two distinct messages. On the surface, "Swing Low" focuses attention on Elijah's chariot, recorded in 2 Kg. 2:11, where the performer longs for a ride to a heavenly home in paradise. Beneath the surface, however, slave-poets have concealed an expressed desire for earthly deliverance. In this case, "home" and "band of angels" represent a present physical reality; and "heavenly bound," a geographic point of reference. "Swing Low" traditionally is sung slowly and expressively. Execute the combination of dotted eighth and sixteenth notes as written and mark them well with accents on the first syllable of the combination so that they sound like a vocal spasm.

704 *Steal Away to Jesus*

"Steal Away" was widely known and sung by American slaves. It has come down to us almost "pure" (free of geographic variation) and was most likely inspired by 1 Cor. 15:51-52: "For the trumpet will sound, and the dead will be raised." The words "steal away" mask a double meaning. Underground railroad "conductor" Harriet Tubman sang this spiritual to prospective "passengers." Natalie Curtis-Burlin (*Songs and Tales of the Dark Continent*, 1920) suggests that this "signal song" outlined a planned route of escape along the eastern seaboard of the United States. "Stealing" one's freedom was, no doubt, an idea constantly played out in the mind of many slaves. In recent times, "Steal Away" has become identified with funeral and memorial services. In these settings, it is sung serenely and very slowly with intense emotional expression.

705 *For Direction*

This prayer, asking for divine help in everything we do, is suitable on a multitude of occasions. The use of plural pronouns (we, us, our) in this and other prayers should not prevent us from using them in personal devotion, even as we do not hesitate to pray "Our Father, who art in heaven" when we are alone. For always we are joined to the company of all praying Christians, even when no other human being is physically near.

706 *Soon and Very Soon*

"Behold, he is coming with the clouds, and every eye will see him" (Rev. 1:7). This prophecy inspired stanza 1 of this song. Stanzas 2 and 3 are drawn directly from Rev. 21:4: "He will wipe away every tear from their eyes, and death shall be no more, neither shall there be mourning nor crying." Here, John's comforting prediction has been set in highly spirited music with accented syncopations. It is customarily used in procession and should sound and look like a "snappy" religious march. Try left-to-right upper body swaying on beats one and three throughout the song. The natural rhythm of the song should not be interrupted by stops after each stanza.

707 Hymn of Promise

There is a wonderful sense of mystery and miracle in this hymn by United Methodist composer Natalie Sleeth. Upon its completion, her husband, Ronald, the well-known United Methodist professor of preaching, asked that it be sung at the time of his funeral. In somewhat the manner of 1 Cor. 15:35-58, the author compares the mystery of new life in nature to the mystery of our death and resurrection. For adults and children alike, the hymn holds a sense of wonder and joy in recognition of the greatness of God in all creation, God's design for this world, and the promise for each of us. This is a fitting hymn for funerals and memorial services. Children can introduce the hymn to the congregation with choir or congregation singing stanza 2 and all singing stanza 3. A fitting intergenerational hymn, you may combine children and older adult choirs in introducing it to the congregation.

708 Rejoice in God's Saints

There are few good hymns about "saints," but retired British Methodist pastor Fred Pratt Green has provided the Church with a classic. It deals with who saints are, what they do, their importance to us today, and how their examples can guide us. Since HANOVER is a fairly familiar tune, the hymn can be included easily in services for All Saints' Day (Sunday) or other times of commemoration and celebration—especially church anniversaries.

709 Come, Let Us Join Our Friends Above

Originally published in *Funeral Hymns* (1759), this Charles Wesley hymn celebrates the "communion of the Saints," the unity of the church militant and the church triumphant. At the same time, the biblical image of "crossing" over Jordan (Jos. 1:2) conveys the early

Methodist concern with "dying well." The traditional English melody FOREST GREEN provides an appropriate setting for use on All Saints' Day (Sunday) and reinforces a note of hope and celebration appropriate to Christian funeral and memorial services.

710 Faith of Our Fathers

Nineteenth-century hymn writer Frederick Faber, having converted from the Church of England to the Roman Catholic Church, wrote this hymn, loosely based on Heb. 12:1, to call the Church of England to return to Roman Catholicism. The original third stanza, with its reference to "Mary's prayers," makes this intention clear and is usually omitted from Protestant hymnals. Protestants use the remaining stanzas in recalling the great martyrs of the Church and to see in their faithfulness an example that calls us from our easy religion. While the words "our fathers" have been criticized as excluding women of the faith, these words in the title line have proved difficult to change. A footnote suggests that "the martyrs" may be substituted. The hymn is appropriate for All Saints' Day (Sunday), Heritage Sunday, church anniversaries and commemorations, and other services on Christian heritage.

711 For All the Saints

This 1864 text by William How is described in the 1970 *Companion to the Hymnal*: "Majestic in language and emotionally powerful, the hymn gloriously unites the church militant and church triumphant in a paean of endless praise." The tune SINE NOMINE, by Ralph Vaughan Williams, is considered to be one of the finest hymn tunes of the twentieth century, supporting the meaning of the text and causing it to soar. This hymn, ideal for All Saints' Day (Sunday), is also used at church anniversaries and commemorations and at funerals and memorial services.

712 *I Sing a Song of the Saints of God*

Here is a text written by a devoted mother for children to help them understand who saints are. Saints are defined as persons who "toiled and fought and lived and died for the Lord they loved and knew." She mentions several individuals, such as a doctor, a queen, a shepherdess, a soldier, and a priest, who were saints. The final stanza reminds us that we live among saints today and points out that each of us can be a saint, too. The text is set to the folklike tune GRAND ISLE, by John Henry Hopkins, Jr. This simple tune will appeal to all ages, and children may introduce it using Orff and other rhythm instruments.

713 *All Saints*

This prayer is suggested for congregational worship on All Saints' Day (November 1) or the Sunday following, when the communion of all God's people is the theme of the day. It affirms that God has joined into one body all Christian people. As a part of this communion of saints, we ask that we may follow the example of all holy people who have preceded us, and that we may at last join them in the heavenly realms. Thus, past, present, and future are linked.

714 *I Know Whom I Have Believed*

While the stanzas acknowledge the limitations of human knowledge and the mysteries of God's redemption and grace, the refrain, taken directly from 2 Tim. 1:12 (KJV), is a strong statement of faith and belief: "I know whom I have believed, and am persuaded that he is able to keep that which I have committed unto him against that day." The hymn is suitable for use whenever the theme is the return and reign of Christ or for general use.

715, 716 *Rejoice, the Lord Is King*

Originally titled "Rejoice Evermore," the refrain of this Charles Wesley text echoes the bidding of Phil. 4:4—"Rejoice in the Lord alway: and again I say, Rejoice" (KJV). First published in *Hymns for Our Lord's Resurrection* (1746), the text celebrates Jesus' lordship over all history as the basis for Christian joy and courage. This text set to DARWALL'S 148TH is well known to United Methodists. Handel's tune GOPSAL, though relatively unfamiliar to American ears, was especially composed for this text. An excellent hymn for the season after Pentecost (Kingdomtide) and Christ the King Sunday, the exuberant and joyful meter was known in early American hymnody as Hallelujah Meter.

717   The Battle Hymn of the Republic

When Julia Ward Howe visited a Union Army Camp in December 1861, she heard the soldiers singing the song "John Brown's Body." She was impressed with the camp meeting tune to which they sang it and determined to write her own words to that tune. She did so, and the resulting "Battle Hymn of the Republic" became one of America's greatest national hymns. While the hymn was written in response to the slavery issue of the time, it is sung today not only in the U.S.A. but in churches elsewhere in the world as a hymn of confidence in Christ's final victory over all evil. The final stanza, added later to the hymn, makes this wider meaning clearer. This hymn is suited for national celebrations, for Emancipation Day, for Martin Luther King, Jr., Day, and (perhaps omitting stanzas 2 and 4) for Christ the King and other Sundays when Christ's coming victory over evil is being celebrated. When a vote of the Hymnal Revision Committee recommended omitting this hymn and "Onward, Christian Soldiers" from the proposed hymnal, 11,000 letters protesting that action poured in and quickly persuaded the committee to include both hymns.

718   Lo, He Comes with Clouds Descending

Originally published in *Hymns of Intercession for All Mankind* (1758) under the title, "Thy Kingdom Come," the grandeur of this Charles Wesley hymn springs from the vision of Rev. 1:7: "Behold, he cometh with clouds; and every eye shall see him" (KJV). Anticipating the coming of Christ as King, this would be especially appropriate for Christ the King Sunday (the Sunday before Advent) and for the Sunday or two immediately preceding it and also for the first Sundays of Advent and other occasions when the theme is the coming again of Christ. The spirited tune HELMSLEY supports the theme with all due boldness and vigor.

719 My Lord, What a Morning

The brothers James Weldon and J. Rosamond Johnson, in *The Book of American Negro Spirituals* (1925), used the dialectic spelling "morning," and advised the reader that the title of this song had at times been erroneously printed "My Lord, What a Mourning." A survey of early sources reveal that "morning"—as in the dawn of a new day—is used far more often than "mourning"—as in sorrow. The confusion stems mainly from conflicting spellings used by Theo. F. Seward in 1882 and T. P. Fenner in 1874. In Rev. 6:17, the word "day" appears; vss. 12-13 of the same chapter (as well as Mt. 24:29 and Mk. 13:24-25) describe an extraordinary event in which the sun and moon are darkened and the stars fall. Slave-poets concluded that this would happen in the morning. This is consistent with the time factor in other spirituals about "last things." Slave-poets viewed judgment as a happy event for the survivors—the righteous. The call to "hear the trumpet sound" reflects 1 Cor. 15:51-52. The tune is named for Harry T. Burleigh, who adopted Seward's spelling for his arrangement of this text.

720 Wake, Awake, for Night Is Flying

Both the text and the tune WACHET AUF, "the king of chorales," were written by Philipp Nicolai about 1599 during a time when his city in Westphalia, Germany was in the throes of a plague. The story of the bridegroom (Mt. 25:1-13) is the basis for the text. The reference to the watchmen crying from the walls comes from Is. 52:8. Being prepared for the coming of Jesus is the message of the text; those who are prepared will rejoice in Christ's coming. This hymn is suited especially to the last Sundays before Advent, as well as Sundays during Advent. If it is unfamiliar to the congregation, have the choir sing the first stanza a cappella then add accompaniment and congregation on stanza 2, concluding with tenors and sopranos trading lines on stanza 3.

721 Christ the King

The prayer alludes to the biblical linkage between royalty and priesthood, both monarchs and priests having been anointed as a sign of divine election and authority. The mention of "the glorious and gentle rule" of Christ sets divine rule in contrast to the often unseemly and heavy-handed authority of earthly rulers. This prayer is suitable for congregational or personal use on the Sunday of Christ the King (the Sunday before Advent) or on any occasion that celebrates the reign of Christ.

722 I Want to Be Ready

Rev. 21:10-27 inspired this widely sung spiritual. In a vision John "saw the holy city, new Jerusalem, coming down out of heaven from God." Slaves envisioned themselves as residents of this new city and thought it to be their promised land. In many songs, they celebrated their longing for such a city and expressed a desire to enter through one of its "twelve gates." Here, the slave-poets draw on the theme "get yo' house in order" to point out an obligation and need for special preparation to gain entrance into such gates. Lovell (*Black Song: The Forge and the Flame*, 1971) and others have categorized this rollicking song of rejoicing as a "jubilee" spiritual. It is traditionally sung in a lively "foot-pattin'" manner with a leader singing the stanzas and the congregation responding to the questions. The refrain is taken up by all.

723 Shall We Gather at the River

Robert Lowry, a Baptist preacher from Philadelphia, wrote both text and tune. The text is based on Rev. 22:1-5, "a pure river of the water of life . . . proceeding out of the throne of God and of the Lamb" (KJV). The tree of life by the river bears fruit and its leaves are for the "healing of the nations." This is the river where "angel feet have trod," where the saints gather, and where we shall worship God forever. The final stanza assures us of the joy we shall know when our pilgrimage is over, and "we reach the shining river." This hymn requires articulation and precise rhythm from the accompaniment. If using organ or piano and organ provide a fuller sound at the refrain.

724 On Jordan's Stormy Banks I Stand

Because of the hardship and uncertainty of the harsh frontier life, many hymns popular in the nineteenth-century American frontier and rural areas dealt with the subject of the heavenly reward. Samuel Stennett, an English Baptist preacher, used the story of the children of Israel crossing into Canaan as a metaphor for the joys of heaven. Just as Canaan was a land flowing with milk and honey, our heavenly home is a place of pleasantness, health, and joy. Crossing the river Jordan (pronounced Jerden) is symbolic of death that takes the believer to heaven. All will be able to sing the joyful refrain, which requires articulation between the dotted eighths and sixteenths. Clapping is certainly appropriate.

725 Arise, Shine Out, Your Light Has Come

Brian Wren, United Reformed Church pastor in England, is one of today's most successful hymn writers. His prophetic text begins with Is. 60:1 and tells of the time when God's will shall be done on earth. Wren's text is inclusive, contemporary, and trinitarian as it provides a fresh view of an ancient theme. The tune DUNEDIN is skillful and lyrical and is not difficult to learn with repeated use. It is well suited to the season after Pentecost (Kingdomtide).

726 O Holy City, Seen of John

Walter Russell Bowie's text expresses the conviction that the Kingdom of God is not a far-off possibility but something that can be realized in part here on earth. Its basis is John's vision of the Holy City in Rev. 21:1–22:5. It is appropriate for the season after Pentecost (Kingdomtide) or whenever the emphasis is on social justice.

727 O What Their Joy and Their Glory Must Be

Depicting the fulfillment of God's promises as the New Jerusalem, this text juxtaposes the "meanwhile" as our life in exile (st. 4). Written by the famous medieval French theologian and philosopher Peter Abelard, it was used at his theological school, House of the Paraclete, where Heloise served as Abbess. Sung to the tune O QUANTA QUALIA, it is appropriate for services focusing on the completion of creation or for funeral and memorial services.

728 Come Sunday

During the latter years of his life, Edward Kennedy "Duke" Ellington created unique music for his sacred concerts. "Come Sunday," a hymn of rejuvenation and praise, is one of the gems from that effort. Duke Ellington was aware that many black Christians fiercely guard the first day of the week as a day of renewed resurrection. As in Mt. 28:7, "He has risen from the dead," Sunday is a time when the faithful are transported from a world where death is all too present to a land of new delights. In essence, every Sunday becomes Easter! Introduce as written, first rehearsing the congregation on the refrain.

729 O Day of Peace That Dimly Shines

This stirring text by Carl P. Daw, Jr., is a prayer for peace in our world—a peace that includes "justice, truth, and love." The first stanza refers to Is. 2:4 and to the song of the heavenly host at Jesus' birth (Lk. 2:14). The second stanza is based on Is. 11:6-7. It was written at the request of the Standing Commission on Church Music of the Episcopal Church to go with Charles H. H. Parry's tune JERUSALEM. This hymn is appropriate for the season after Pentecost (Kingdomtide) or whenever the theme is peace with justice.

730 *O Day of God Draw Nigh*

The reign of the Kingdom of God is the subject of this text by Robert B. Y. Scott, a twentieth-century Canadian Old Testament scholar. The first and last stanzas are prayers for God's return to earth in judgment. The central stanzas enumerate the good things this reign will bring: calm to our troubled minds, justice, and peace. This return of justice is compared to the creation of light at the beginning of time. It is appropriate for the season after Pentecost (Kingdomtide) or services that deal with peace and justice.

731 *Glorious Things of Thee Are Spoken*

John Newton, best known as the author of "Amazing Grace," had been a slave trader, was greatly influenced by George Whitefield and the Wesleys, was converted and became a pastor and leader in the evangelical movement in the Church of England and in the anti-slavery movement. This great text on the Church and the city of God is based on Ps. 87:3 and Is. 33:20-21 and includes a wealth of other scriptural images. The tune AUSTRIAN HYMN was adapted to be sung as the national anthem for Austria by Haydn. He later used it in his *Emperor Quartet.* It was almost immediately used as a hymn tune and has been a favorite ever since.

732 *Come, We That Love the Lord*
733 *Marching to Zion*

Isaac Watts first published this in 1707 as a ten-stanza text entitled "Heavenly Joy on Earth." In 1737, John Wesley altered the "we" to "ye," and it has appeared that way in English and American Methodist hymnals with the exception of the 1935 *Methodist Hymnal*. Robert Lowry composed the rousing tune MARCHING TO ZION in 1867 and added the campmeeting refrain. The hymn unifies us as we move "to fairer worlds on high." This is a popular communion hymn in many black United Methodist congregations. The familiar tune ST. THOMAS is used in 732.

734 *Canticle of Hope*

This composite biblical song is based on the description of the new Jerusalem in Rev. 21 and 22. It expresses hope in God's new creation of life, where earthly fear of darkness vanishes before God's perpetual light. It also emphasizes the eternal hope of the faithful in three affirmations of God: "God's dwelling is with mortals"; "I make all things new"; and, "I am coming soon." This canticle is particularly appropriate for services of death and resurrection, memorials, renewal, watch night, and the new year.

EXPLANATION OF INFORMATION TO BE FOUND ON EACH HYMN PAGE

(1) CHRIST'S GRACIOUS LIFE

(2) **276**　　(3) **The First One Ever**

(4) *Unison*　(5) Em　　　　D　　　　Em　　D　　Em

(6)

(7)

1. The　first　one　ev - er,　oh,　ev - er　to　know　of　the
2. The　first　one　ev - er,　oh,　ev - er　to　know　of　Mes -
3. The　first　ones　ev - er,　oh,　ev - er　to　know　of　the

(8) WORDS: Linda Wilberger Egan, 1980, alt. (Lk. 1:26-38, 45; Jn. 4:7-26; Lk. 24:1-11)　　(11) BALLAD
(9) MUSIC:　Linda Wilberger Egan, 1980　　　　　　　　　　　　　　　　　　　　(12)　Irr.
(10) © 1980, 1983 Linda Wilberger Egan　　　　　　　　　　　　　　　　　　　　(13)

(1) Hymn classification. For detailed explanation see Appendix 2.
(2) Hymn number.
(3) Hymn title, usually the first line of the hymn.
(4) Only melody should be sung.
(5) Chord designation. For use with guitar or other instruments.
(6) Key signature. Tells in what key the hymn is to be played and sung.
(7) Time signature. The top number refers to the number of beats to a measure, and the bottom number tells what kind of note counts as one beat. (4 = quarter note, 2 = half, 8 = eighth, etc.)
(8) Author, translator, adapter, and/or arranger.
(9) Composer/arranger information.
(10) Copyright information. Owners of texts and/or tunes are cited here. Material without copyright information cited is usually in the public domain. For further information on copyright owners and use of materials belonging to The United Methodist Publishing House see copyright page and pages 906-13 in *The United Methodist Hymnal*.
(11) Name of the hymn tune. Helpful for use with metrical index.
(12) Meter. Refer to metrical index or Appendix 5 for information.
(13) Alternate tune.

ORGANIZATION OF THE HYMNS

The organization of the hymns, prayers, and canticles in *The United Methodist Hymnal* reflects two basic and interlocking patterns: doctrine and experience.

Explicitly, the organization reflects the pattern of the Apostles' Creed. The first three sections focus on the persons of the Trinity; the fourth, upon the doctrine of the Church; and the fifth, on "the last things." In hymns, however, the Creed is not a dry enumeration of doctrines but a living invocation of the Triune God, whose love touches every reach of human joy, suffering, struggle, and hope.

Implicitly, the hymnal also reflects a pattern of Christian experience. To use the old Wesleyan word—as in John Wesley's 1780 *Collection of Hymns for the Use of the People called Methodists*—it is "experimental," evoking what it means to be a community believing in God in this way. In the section on the Holy Spirit, for example, the pattern of the Wesleyan "way of salvation" becomes visible, touching the full range of prevenient, convincing, justifying, sanctifying, and perfecting grace. These "experiments" with *and* in grace are not, however, mere descriptions of felt emotion. Grounded in prayer, they reflect the larger doctrinal and creedal structure, depending at every turn on specifically biblical ways of understanding and addressing God.

Together, these patterns of doctrine and experience constitute the basic shape of Christian prayer and worship, both in Wesleyan traditions and in *The United Methodist Hymnal.*

I. The Glory of the Triune God
   A. Praise and Thanksgiving
   B. God's Nature
   C. Providence
   D. Creation

II. The Grace of Jesus Christ
   A. In Praise of Christ
   B. Christ's Gracious Life
      1. Promised Coming
      2. Birth and Baptism
      3. Life and Teaching
      4. Passion and Death
      5. Resurrection and Exaltation

III. The Power of the Holy Spirit
   A. In Praise of the Holy Spirit
   B. Prevenient Grace
      1. Invitation
      2. Repentance
   C. Justifying Grace
      1. Pardon
      2. Assurance
   D. Sanctifying and Perfecting Grace
      1. Rebirth of the New Creature
      2. Personal Holiness
      3. Social Holiness
      4. Prayer, Trust, and Hope
      5. Strength in Tribulation

IV. The Community of Faith
   A. The Nature of the Church
      1. Born of the Spirit
      2. United in Christ
      3. Called to God's Mission
   B. The Book of the Church: Holy Scripture
   C. The Sacraments and Rites of the Church
      1. Baptism, Confirmation, and Reaffirmation
      2. Eucharist (Holy Communion or the Lord's Supper)

BIBLIOGRAPHY OF
SOURCES IN HYMNODY

Allchin, A. M. *We Belong to One Another: Methodist, Anglican, and Orthodox Essays*. London: Epworth Press, 1965.

Allen, Ware and Garrison. *Slave Songs of the United States*. New York: A. Simpson and Peter Smith, Co., 1867.

Alves, Rubem. *I Believe in the Resurrection of the Body*. Translated from the Portuguese by the Ecumenical Center of Documentation and Information, Rio de Janeiro. Philadelphia: Fortress Press, 1986.

Anderson, Fred R. *Singing Psalms of Joy and Praise*. Philadelphia: Westminster Press, 1986.

Appleton, George, ed. *The Oxford Book of Prayer*. Oxford: Oxford University Press, 1986.

Bailey, Albert. *The Gospel in Hymns*. New York: Charles Scribner's Sons, 1950.

Baker, Frank. *Representative Verse of Charles Wesley*. London: Epworth Press, 1962.

Barrett, James E., ed. *The Hymnary: A Table for Service Planning*. Missoula, MT: The Hymnary Press, 1979.

Barz, Hermine. "The Development of the Poetry of the Negro in North America." Doctoral thesis, Mainz, Germany, 1951.

Bebey, Francis. *African Music*. Westport, NY: Lawrence Hill and Company, 1969.

Benson, Louis. *The English Hymn: Its Development and Use in Worship*. New York and Philadelphia: Hodder and Stoughton, 1915.

Bonner, Clint. *A Hymn Is Born*. Nashville: Broadman Press, 1959.

Bower, O. Richard, Betty L. Hart, Charlotte A. Meade, eds. *Prayer in the Black Tradition*. Nashville: The Upper Room, 1986.

Braun, H. Myron. *Companion to the Book of Hymns Supplement*. Nashville: Discipleship Resources, 1982.

Brawley, Benjamin. *The Negro in Literature and Art*. New York: Duffield & Company, 1930.

Burlin, Natalie Curtis. *Songs and Tales of the Dark Continent*. New York: G. Schirmer, 1920.

Chirgwin, A. M. "The Vogue of the Negro Spiritual." *The Edinburgh Review* 247 (January 1928).

Clark, Keith C. *A Selective Bibliography for the Study of Hymns*. Fort Worth, TX: Hymn Society of America, 1980.

Clark, Thorburn. *Hymns That Endure*. Nashville: Broadman Press, 1942.

Cleveland, J. Jefferson. "A Historical Account of the Negro Spiritual." In *Songs of Zion: Supplemental Worship Resources 12*. Nashville: Abingdon Press, 1981.

Colquhoun, Frank. *A Hymn Companion*. London: Hodder and Stoughton, 1985.

Courtlander, Harold. "Spirituals and Their Double Meanings." *Journal of American Folklore* (February, 1938).

Cutts, Peter, and Brian Wren. *Faith Looking Forward*. Carol Stream, IL: Hope Publishing Company, 1983.

Davie, Donald. *Purity of Diction in English Verse*. London: Chaltto and Winders, 1952.

De Grucy, John, ed. *Cry Justice!* Maryknoll, NY: Orbis Books, 1986.

Di Nola, Alfonso M., ed. *The Prayers of Man*. New York: Ivan Oblensky, 1961.

Doberstein, John W., ed. *Minister's Prayer Book*. Philadelphia: Fortress Press, n.d.

Doran, Carol and Thomas H. Troeger. *New Hymns for the Lectionary: To Glorify the Maker's Name*. New York: Oxford University Press, 1986.

Doughty, W. L., ed. *The Prayers of Susanna Wesley*. Grand Rapids, MI: Zondervan, A Clarion Book, 1984.

Dubois, W. E. B. *The Negro*. New York: Henry Holt Company, 1915.

Dudley-Smith, Timothy. *Lift Every Heart*. Carol Stream, IL: Hope Publishing Company, 1984.

Edwards, Charles L. *Bahama Songs and Stories*. Boston: Houghton Mifflin Company, 1895.

Ellinwood, Leonard, ed. *Dictionary of American Hymnology*. Fort Worth, TX: The Hymn Society of America. Not yet published.

Emurian, Ernest K. *Sing the Wondrous Story*. Natick, MA: W. A. Wilde, 1963.

Fleming, Daniel J., ed. *The World at One in Prayer*. New York: Harper & Brothers Publishers, 1942.

Fox, Selina Fitzherbert, ed. *A Chain of Prayer Across the Ages*. New York: E. P. Dutton and Co., 1916.

Frost, Francis. "Biblical Imagery and Religious Experiences in the Hymns of the Wesleys." *Proceedings of the Wesley Historical Society* 4, no. 6 (December 1980): 158-66.

Gallaway, Craig. "Patterns of Worship in Early Methodist Hymnody, and the Task of Hymnal Revision." *Quarterly Review* 7, no. 3 (Fall, 1987): 14-29.

Gallaway, Craig. "The Presence of Christ with the Worshipping Community: A Study in the Hymns of John and Charles Wesley." Ph.D. dissertation, Emory University, 1988.

Gealy, Fred R., Austin C. Lovelace, and Carlton R. Young. *Companion to the Book of Hymns*. Nashville: Abingdon Press, 1970.

Gonzales, Justo and Catherine. *In Accord: Let Us Worship*. New York: Friendship Press, 1981.

Green, Barbara and Victor Gollancz, eds. *God of a Hundred Names*. London: Victor Gollancz, Ltd., 1962.

Green, Fred Pratt. *Hymns and Ballads of Fred Pratt Green*. Carol Stream, IL: Hope Publishing Company; London: Stainer and Bell, 1982.

Hall, Frederick. "The Negro Spiritual," *The Midwest Journal* 1 (1949).

Hare, Maude Cuney. "Afro-American Folk-Song Contribution." *The Musical Observer* 15 (1917).

Harkness, Georgia. *The Glory of God: Poems and Prayers for Devotional Use*. New York and Nashville: Abingdon-Cokesbury Press, 1943.

Hatchett, Marion J. *Commentary on the American Prayerbook*. New York: Seabury Press, 1980.

Hawkins, Thomas R. *The Unsuspected Power of the Psalms*. Nashville: The Upper Room, 1985.

Herskovits, Melville J. *Patterns of Negro Music: A Social History of the Negro*. Springfield, IL: Illinois State Academy of Sciences, 1941.

Hubbard, W. L. *History of American Music*. Toledo, OH: Irving Squire, 1908.

Huck, Gabe, ed. *A Book of Family Prayer*. New York: Seabury Press, 1979.

Idle, Christopher. *Stories of Our Favorite Hymns*. Grand Rapids, MI: Eerdmans Publishing, 1980.

Japanese Sambika Committee. *Sambika Ryakkai 1* (1955) and 2 (1974). Tokyo: Nippon Kiristo Kyodan Publishing House.

Johnson, James Weldon. *God's Trombones*. New York: Viking Press, Penguin Books, 1980.

Julian, John, ed. *A Dictionary of Hymnology*. Vols. I and II. New York: Dover Publishing, Inc., 1957.

Kaan, Fred. *Pilgrim Praise*. London: Gallaird Ltd., 1972.

————. *The Hymn Texts of Fred Kaan*. Carol Stream, IL: Hope Publishing Company, 1985.

Kagawa, Toyohiko. *Meditations*. Translated by Jiro Takenaka. New York: Harper & Brothers, 1950.

Kepler, Thomas S. *The Fellowship of the Saints: An Anthology of Christian Devotional Literature*. New York and Nashville: Abingdon-Cokesbury Press, 1948.

Kimbrough, S. T., Jr. *Lost in Wonder: Charles Wesley, the Meaning of His Hymns Today*. Nashville: The Upper Room, 1987.

Klepper, Robert F. *Methodist Hymnal Concordance*. Metuchen, NJ: The Scarecrow Press, 1987.

Leaver, Robin A., and James H. Litton. *Duty and Delight: Routley Remembered*. Carol Stream, IL: Hope Publishing Company, 1985.

Loh, I-to. "Mini Companion to *Hymns from the Four Winds*." Typescript. Nashville: United Methodist Board of Discipleship, 1982.

Lovelace, Austin C. *The Anatomy of Hymnody*. Chicago: G.I.A. Publications, Inc., 1982.

————. *Hymn Festivals*. Fort Worth, TX: Hymn Society of America, 1978.

————. *Hymn Notes for Church Bulletins*. Fort Worth, TX: Hymn Society of America, 1986.

Lovelace, Austin C. and William C. Rice. *Music and Worship in the Church*. Rev. and enl. ed. Nashville: Abingdon Press, 1976.

Lovelace, Austin C. *The Organist and Hymn Playing*. Rev. ed. Carol Stream, IL: Hope Publishing Company, 1981.

Lovell, John. *Black Song: The Forge and the Flame*. New York: Macmillan, 1972.

Luther, Martin. *Luther's Works*. Vol. 53: *Liturgy & Hymns*. Edited by Ulriche S. Leupold and Helmut T. Lehmann. Philadelphia: Fortress, 1965.

Manning, Bernard L. *The Hymns of Wesley and Watts*. London: Epworth Press, 1942.

Mbiti, John S. *The Prayers of African Religion*. Maryknoll, NY: Orbis Books, 1975.

McCutchan, Robert Guy. *Hymns in the Lives of Men*. Nashville: Abingdon-Cokesbury Press, 1945.

McElroy, Paul Simpson, ed. *Prayers and Graces of Thanksgiving*. Mount Vernon, NY: Peter Pauper Press, 1966.

Merritt, Nancy Gertrude. "Negro Spirituals in American Collections: A Handbook for Students Studying Negro Spirituals." Doctoral thesis, Howard University, 1940.

News of Hymnody. No. 9. Bramcote: Grove Books, 1984.

Northcott, Cecil. *Hymns We Love*. Philadelphia: Westminster Press, 1954.

Nuelsen, J. L. *John Wesley and the German Hymn*. Translated by T. Parry,

S. H. Moore, and A. Holbrook. Yorkshire, England. A. S. Holbrook, 1972.

Osbeck, Kenneth W. *The Endless Song: Music and Worship in the Church.* Grand Rapids, MI: Kregel Publishing, 1987.

Outler, Albert. *Theology in the Wesleyan Spirit.* Nashville: Tidings, 1975.

Parampanthi, Swami. "Negro Spiritual in American Folksong and Folklore." *Folkmusic and Folklore 1* (1967).

Parker, Alice. *Creative Hymn Singing.* Chapel Hill, NC: Hinshaw Music, Inc. 1982.

Parrish, Lydia. *Slave Songs of the Georgia Sea Islands.* New York: Creative Age Press (Farrar, Straus, & Giroux), 1942.

Patton, Alan. *Instrument of Thy Peace.* New York: Seabury Press, 1968.

Porter, Dorothy, ed. *Early Negro Writing, 1760-1837.* Boston: Beacon Press, 1971.

Potts, J. Manning, ed. *Prayers of the Middle Ages.* Nashville: The Upper Room, 1954.

Rattenbury, J. Ernest. *The Eucharistic Hymns of John and Charles Wesley.* London: Epworth Press, 1948.

———. *The Evangelical Doctrines of Charles Wesley's Hymns.* London: Epworth Press, 1941.

Reynolds, William J. *Companion to the Baptist Hymnal.* Nashville: Broadman Press, 1976.

———. *Hymns of Our Faith.* Nashville: Broadman Press, 1964.

Richardson, Alan. *A Theological Word Book of the Bible.* New York: Macmillan and Company, 1950.

Rodenmayer, Robert N. *The Pastor's Prayerbook.* New York: Oxford University Press, 1960.

Routley, Erik. *Church Music and the Christian Faith.* Carol Stream, IL: Agape Press, 1978.

———. *An English-Speaking Hymnal Guide.* Collegeville, MN: The Liturgical Press, 1979.

———. *Exploring the Psalms.* Philadelphia: Westminster Press, 1975.

———. *Hymns and the Faith.* Grand Rapids, MI: Eerdmans Publishing Company, 1968.

———. *The Music of Christian Hymns.* Chicago: G.I.A. Publications, 1981.

———. *A Panorama of Christian Hymnody.* Collegeville, MN: The Liturgical Press, 1979.

Ruffin, Bernard. *Fanny Crosby.* United Church Press, 1976.

Runyon, Theodore, ed. *Sanctification and Liberation.* Nashville: Abingdon Press, 1981.

Schilling, S. Paul. *The Faith We Sing.* Philadelphia: Westminster Press, 1983.

Seton, Bernard E. *Our Heritage of Hymns: A Swift Survey*. Berrien Springs, MI: Andrews University Press, 1984.

Shorter, Aylward. *Prayer in the Religious Traditions of Africa*. New York and Nairobi: Oxford University Press, 1975.

Smith, M. G. "The African Heritage in the Caribbean." In *Caribbean Studies: A Symposium*, edited by Ruben Vera. Jamaica, B.W.I.: University College of the West Indies, 1957.

Smith, Timothy. "The Holy Spirit in the Hymns of the Wesleys." *Wesleyan Theological Journal* 16, no. 2 (Fall 1981): 20-48.

Snyder, Howard A. *The Radical Wesley*. Downers Grove, IL: Inter-Varsity Press, 1980.

Spencer, Donald A. *Hymn and Scripture Selection Guide*. Valley Forge, PA: Judson Press, 1977.

Stanislaw, J. "Some Remarks on the Development of Musical Creation among African People." In *The Preservation of Traditional Forms of the Learned and Popular Music of the Orient and the Occident*, edited by William K. Archer. Urbana: Institute of Communications Research, 1964.

Steltenkamp, Michael F. *The Sacred Vision: Native American Religion and Its Practice Today*. New York: Paulist Press, 1982.

Stulken, Marilyn Kay. *Hymnal Companion to the Lutheran Book of Worship*. Fortress Press, 1981.

Sydnor, James R. *Hymns: A Congregational Study*. Carol Stream, IL: Hope Publishing Company, 1983.

————. *Hymns and Their Uses*. Carol Stream, IL: Hope Publishing Company, 1982.

Telford, John. *The Life of the Rev. Charles Wesley, M.A.* London: Wesleyan Methodist Book Room, 1900.

Terry, Lindsay I. *Devotionals From Famous Hymn Stories*. Granada Hills, CA: Baker Press, 1974.

Thurman, Howard. *Meditations of the Heart*. New York: Harper & Row, 1953.

Vining, Elizabeth Gray. *The World in Tune*. New York: Harper & Brothers, 1954.

Wainwright, Geoffrey. *Eucharist and Eschatology*. New York: Oxford University Press, 1981.

Welch, Barbara A. "Charles Wesley and the Celebration of Evangelical Experience." Ph.D. diss., University of Michigan, Ann Arbor, 1971.

Wesley, Charles. *The Journal of the Rev. Charles Wesley. M.A.* Ed. John Telford. London: Robert Culley, 1909.

Wesley, Charles and John Wesley. *The Poetical Works of John and Charles Wesley*. Edited by George Osborne. 13 vols. London, 1868-72.

Wesley, John. *John Wesley's Prayers*. Edited by Frederick C. Gill. London: Epworth Press, 1951.

———. *The Works of John Wesley.* Edited by Thomas Jackson. 14 vols. 3rd ed. Peabody, MA: Hendrickson, 1984.

———. *The Works of John Wesley.* Editor in Chief, Frank Baker. Vols. I-IV: *Sermons,* ed. Albert Outler. Nashville: Abingdon Press, 1984-87; and Vol. VII: *A Collection of Hymns for the Use of the People called Methodists,* ed. Franz Hildebrandt and Oliver A. Beckerlegge with the assistance of James Dale. Oxford: Clarendon, 1983.

White, James. *Christian Worship in Transition.* Nashville: Abingdon Press, 1976.

———. *Introduction to Christian Worship.* Nashville: Abingdon Press, 1980.

Wojtyla, Karol. *Prayers of Pope John Paul II.* New York: Crossroad Publishing Company, 1982.

Wren, Brian. *Praising a Mystery.* Carol Stream, IL: Hope Publishing Company, 1986.

Wright, Jeremiah A. *The Treatment of Biblical Passages in Negro Spirituals.* Doctoral thesis, Howard University, 1967.

CONTRIBUTORS

Mary Brooke Casad
Mary Brooke Casad, a graduate of Southern Methodist University, is a free-lance writer who resides in Texas. She served as a member of the Hymnal Revision Committee. Mrs. Casad is the author of several children's books. Certified as a Christian communicator by United Methodist Communications, she is a frequent contributor to church publications and curriculum. Her husband is a United Methodist pastor.

Craig B. Gallaway
Craig Gallaway is a recent graduate of Emory University (Ph.D.), and now editor for Discipleship Resources, Nashville, Tennessee. His long-standing interests in music, worship, theology, and the arts found expression in his dissertation on the theology of the Wesley hymns, leading also to his work as a consultant to the Hymnal Revision Committee. An accomplished guitarist and songwriter, Dr. Gallaway is a member of the North Texas Conference and has been active in worship renewal both in The United Methodist Church and beyond.

Raymond F. Glover
Raymond F. Glover, general editor of *The Hymnal 1982* and *The Hymnal 1982 Companion,* has been involved with the revision of the hymnody of the Episcopal Church since his appointment in 1969 to the Standing Commission on Church Music. He was chair of the Hymn Committee that produced *Supplement II* to *The Hymnal 1940* and *Hymns III.* Mr. Glover, who holds degrees from the University of Toronto and Union Seminary School of Sacred Music, has been organist and choirmaster in several churches. In his role as an educator, he has held posts as an

instructor at Berkeley Divinity School and as head of the music department at St. Catherine's School in Richmond, Virginia.

Hoyt L. Hickman
Hoyt L. Hickman is director of resource development on the staff of the Section on Worship of the General Board of Discipleship. He is editor of *The Book of Services, The Worship Resources of The United Methodist Hymnal,* the Supplemental Worship Resources publications, and *Handbook of the Christian Year.* He is the author of *United Methodist Altars, A Primer for Church Worship, Holy Communion, The Acolyte's Book,* and numerous shorter resources and articles. He is a member of the North American Academy of Liturgy and the Consultation on Common Texts. He has served on the staff of the Hymnal Revision Committee.

S. T. Kimbrough, Jr.
S. T. Kimbrough, Jr. was educated at Birmingham Southern College, the Divinity School of Duke University, and earned a Ph.D. degree in Old Testament and Semitic Languages at Princeton Theological Seminary. Also educated as a musician, he performs and records internationally and lectures and writes in the areas of church music, literature, theology, Bible, and the arts. He is the author of *Israelite Religion in Sociological Perspective, Lost in Wonder,* and *Sweet Singer* (new arrangements of Charles Wesley hymns); editor of *The Unpublished Works of Charles Wesley,* Wesley's *Short Hymns on Select Passages of the Holy Scriptures (1762);* and he is one of the editors of *The United Methodist Liturgical Psalter* for the hymnal. He has served United Methodist churches in Alabama, North Carolina, and New Jersey, and is a member of the North Alabama Conference. He is currently a member of the Center of Theological Inquiry in Princeton, New Jersey.

Thomas A. Langford, III
Andy Langford is the assistant general secretary of the Section on Worship of the General Board of Discipleship. He serves on the Consultation on Common Texts, as chair of the task force on the Common Lectionary, and is a member of the North American Academy of Liturgy. He is the author of *Worship and Evangelism, Planning a Christian Funeral, The Worship Handbook,* and numerous shorter resources and articles. He has led workshops on worship throughout The United Methodist Church. He served as staff on the Psalter and Worship Resources Committee of the Hymnal Revision Committee.

George Lockwood
George Lockwood, a former music missionary in Costa Rica, has pastored

several Hispanic congregations in Arizona and California. He served on the editorial committee of the *Celebramos II* hymnal supplement and has translated a large number of new hymns from Spain and Latin America. Dr. Lockwood has traveled extensively in Latin America interviewing church musicians and collecting new hymns, and has conducted presentations and training workshops for national conferences and local Hispanic churches on the singing of new sacred music from the Spanish and Portuguese cultures.

I-to Loh
I-to Loh was a professor of church music at Tainan Theological College and was active in the Asian scene before coming to the University of California at Los Angeles for his Ph.D. in music. He is well known in the Asian community through his participation in the Christian Conference of Asia and through his editorship of *the New Songs of Asian Cities*, 1972. I-to Loh has published numerous articles, hymns, and anthems and has compiled and edited various music collections, including: *A Festival of Asian Christmas Music, Let the Hills Sing, African Songs of Worship, Asian Songs of Worship, Sing a New Song to the Lord,* and *Hymns from the Four Winds.* He continues to teach at Tainan Theological College and at the Asian Institute for Liturgy and Music, Manila, Philippines and is currently the editor of the *New CCA Hymnal 1990.*

Austin C. Lovelace
Austin C. Lovelace has served churches in Nebraska, New York, New Jersey, North Carolina, Illinois, Texas, and Colorado. He has taught at Union Theological Seminary in New York, Garrett Seminary in Evanston, Illinois, Queens and Davidson Colleges in North Carolina, Colorado Women's College in Denver, the University of Nebraska, and at Iliff School of Theology in Denver, Colorado. He is a well known author and composer and has served as editor for several hymnal resources. He also has served on the national boards of the Choristers Guild, the Hymn Society of America and the National Council of the American Guild of Organists, and is past president and honorary fellow of the Hymn Society of America.

Jane Marshall
Jane Marshall is a teacher and composer living in Dallas, Texas, where she serves on the continuing education faculty in church music at Perkins School of Theology. She served as chairperson of the task force that prepared the *Supplement to the Book of Hymns,* 1982, and served as a consultant to the Language/Theology Subcommittee of the Hymnal Revision Committee.

William J. Reynolds

William J. Reynolds is professor of church music, Southwestern Baptist Theological Seminary, Fort Worth, Texas. He has written several hymns and hymn tunes and is the author of two hymnal companions: *Hymns of Our Faith*, 1964, and *Companion to Baptist Hymnal*, 1976; he is co-author of a college textbook, *A Survey of Christian Hymnody*, 1987. He was general editor for *Baptist Hymnal*, 1975, and has served internationally as a consultant for a number of hymnals involving several denominations, as well as for the 1971 edition of *The Sacred Harp* (Denson Revision). An active member of the Hymn Society of America for many years, he served as its president, 1978-80.

Diana Sanchez

Diana Sanchez is the director of music resources for the Section on Worship of the General Board of Discipleship. She is a graduate of Perkins School of Theology, Master of Sacred Music, and the Meadows School of the Arts, Master of Music in Choral Conducting. She is the editor of *The Hymns of the United Methodist Hymnal* and author of many articles and other resources on music and worship. She has led workshops on worship, the creative use of hymns and other music resources throughout The United Methodist Church. Diana served as staff on the Hymns and Service Music Committees of the Hymnal Revision Committee.

Richard Shadinger

Richard Shadinger is professor of music at Belmont College in Nashville, Tennessee, where he teaches music history, church music, and piano and serves as chairman of the Department of Performance Studies in the School of Music. A native of Carrollton, Georgia, he is a graduate of Shorter College and earned the M.C.M. and D.M.A. degrees from Southern Baptist Theological Seminary School of Church Music in Louisville, Kentucky. He is organist and deacon at Immanuel Baptist Church of Nashville.

William Farley Smith

William Farley Smith is minister of music at Harlem's St. Mark's United Methodist Church in New York City. He is founder of the Harlem Multi-ethnic Choral Symposium. Dr. Smith, formerly a faculty member at Montclair State College in New Jersey, is a workshop lecturer on the Afro-American spiritual and served as a black consultant/editor/arranger for the Hymnal Revision Committee. His "restorations" and research of spirituals have been cited by the American Conference of Jewish Reformed Rabbis and Cantors and the National Association of Negro

Musicians. He was a contributor to *Songs of Zion* and a member of the advisory board of the *Liturgy of Zion*. Dr. Smith has earned four advanced music degrees and is a graduate of Manhattan School of Music and Columbia University.

Laurence Hull Stookey
Laurence Hull Stookey is Hugh Latimer Elderdice Professor of Preaching and Worship at Wesley Theological Seminary, Washington, D.C., where he has served on the faculty since 1973. He is a ministerial member of the Peninsula Annual Conference. As a member of the Hymnal Revision Committee, he chaired the committee on Worship Resources. He is on the board of directors of the Liturgical Conference, and has written several books on worship, including *Baptism: Christ's Act in the Church* and *Handbook on the Christian Year*, written with Hoyt L. Hickman, Don E. Saliers, and James F. White.

Marjorie Beadles Tuell
Marjorie Beadles Tuell lives in California, where she leads hymn sing programs and teaches in workshops. She holds certification as a director of music in The United Methodist Church. She has written articles for *Music Ministry* and *Response* magazines and edited *Tell the Blessed Tidings: Hymn Texts by Women*, in 1984. During the 1984-88 quadrennium, she was a member of the Hymnal Revision Committee, chairing the Texts Committee.

Robin Knowles Wallace
Robin Knowles Wallace has served over twenty years as organist and choir director in United Methodist churches in Ohio, Georgia, and Michigan. She holds degrees from the University of Cincinnati and Scarritt College in music and a Master of Theological Studies from Candler School of Theology, where her thesis was "The Language of Hymnody: The Hymn Texts of Fred Kaan." She is currently the music director/organist at Aldersgate UMC in Detroit and resource editor for *Newsnotes*, the journal of the Fellowship of United Methodists in Worship, Music, and Other Arts. She is married to a United Methodist pastor and has two children.

Terry W. York
Terry W. York is the hymnal project coordinator for the Church Music Department of the Baptist Sunday School Board of the Southern Baptist Convention. He holds the Bachelor of Arts degree from California Baptist College and the Master of Church Music and Doctor of Musical Arts degrees from New Orleans Baptist Theological Seminary. Dr. York stays

actively involved in conferences, workshops, and writing articles dealing with the general areas of music in worship and hymnology. A member of the American Society of Composers, Authors, and Publishers, York is the author of a number of anthem texts, hymns, poems, and musical dramas. His book *Great Hymns of Missions* was published in 1979.

Carlton R. Young

Carlton R. Young is editor of *The United Methodist Hymnal* and its precursor, *The Methodist Hymnal*, 1966 *(The Book of Hymns)*, and a teacher, composer, and conductor, presently on leave of absence from Candler School of Theology, Emory University, where he is professor of church music. He is past president of the Hymn Society of America.

USING THE METRICAL INDEX

The metrical index lists hymns by their metric designation. It begins with the first lines containing the fewest number of syllables and/or words and progresses to longer lines and ends with the IM (PM) meters or irregular (peculiar) meters. The index shows the variety of meters found in the hymnal and aids the worship planner by grouping hymns with the same meter together. Texts and tunes with the same metrical pattern may be interchanged.

The metrical pattern of a given hymn refers to the number of pulses in a poetic line. The most common metrical pattern, CM, is designated by the term *common meter* and has an 86.86 pattern.

In an 86.86 pattern, the first poetic line has eight pulses, the second poetic line has six, and then the entire pattern is repeated. "Amazing Grace" is a good example.

Amazing Grace! How sweet the sound	8 syllables
that saved a wretch like me!	6 syllables
I once was lost, but now am found;	8 syllables
Was blind, but now I see.	6 syllables

By using the metrical index, other tunes designed for the 86.86 pattern of the common meter can be used with these words. For example, the tune for "O For a Thousand Tongues to Sing," AZMON, is written in common meter and may be sung with the words of "Amazing Grace."

Another use for the index is exchanging unfamiliar tunes for familiar tunes. Perhaps you want to sing "In Christ There Is No East or West" for World Communion Sunday, but your congregation is unfamiliar with the tune. Since it is a common meter text, you would look in the metrical index to see what other tunes match the meter. Among your many choices are

AZMON, the tune to "O For a Thousand Tongues to Sing," ANTIOCH, the tune to "Joy to the World," and ST. ANNE, the tune to "O God Our Help in Ages Past."

Common meter (CM), short meter (SM), and long meter (LM) are all in the iambic pattern, that is, they begin with an unaccented syllable, followed by an accented syllable. Other metrical patterns may be either iambic or trochaic, which is an accented syllable followed by an unaccented syllable. It is important to know which of these patterns a tune follows. Tunes with the same meter will not work if they do not follow the same pattern of accented and unaccented syllables. The metrical index tells you if a tune is iambic or trochaic.

The metrical index is an excellent tool for enhancing music in worship. Use it to expand the congregation's repertory of hymns and to better coordinate the hymn texts with theme, scripture, and sermon.

TABLE OF METRICAL ABBREVIATIONS

SM—Short Meter. 66.86 pattern. Exemplified in BOYLSTON, the tune to which we sing "A Charge to Keep I Have."

SMD—Short Meter Double. 66.86.66.86 pattern. Exemplified in DIADEMA-TA, the tune to which we sing "Crown Him with Many Crowns."

CM—Common Meter. 86.86 pattern. Exemplified in AZMON, the tune to which we sing "O For a Thousand Tongues to Sing."

CDM—Common Meter Double. 86.86.86.86 pattern. Exemplified in MATERNA, the tune to which we sing "O Beautiful for Spacious Skies."

LM—Long Meter. 88.88 pattern. Exemplified in DUKE STREET, the tune to which we sing "From All That Dwell Below the Skies."

LMD—Long Meter Double. 88.88.88.88 pattern. Exemplified in SWEET HOUR, the tune to which we sing "Sweet Hour of Prayer."

IM—Irregular Meter. An irregular meter signifies that the meter does not follow a regular pattern and can rarely be substituted for another text with an irregular meter. Several examples of irregular meter are "Go Tell It on the Mountain," "Were You There," "God of Many Names," and "Stille Nacht."

THE LITURGICAL USE OF "AMEN"

Erik Routley has contributed a great deal to musicians and the Church through his study and insights on hymns and church music. In *Church Music and the Christian Faith* (pages 96-99), he gives a helpful and concise explanation of the history of the use of "amen," and its implications for the church today:

"There are two authentic uses of amen—the asservative and the responsive. The first is as it appears in solemn sayings of our Lord as recorded in the Gospels, beginning in English, 'Verily, verily . . .,' which is in Greek 'Amen, amen.' It is used to introduce, not conclude, a statement of special importance. The other use is as a response by people in whose name or to whom something has been said. This is the only liturgical use of the word, and it is of the greatest importance. It is here part of a conversation (as in 2 Cor. 1:18-22). In ancient times it was used this way in worship, where people responded to prayers, and especially to the great prayer at the eucharist, with a solemn and loud 'Amen,' meaning 'We are associated with that.' It is heard sometimes less formally but even more intensely where people in some congregations interject 'amen' when the preacher's words echo their own convictions. At any time when one voice says a prayer and all voices respond, the simplest and most ancient response is 'amen.'

"The use of this word at the end of a hymn which everybody has sung has therefore, at first sight, no justification whatever. But the custom has an origin which has deceived many people into considering it a modern necessity. The fact is that all the ancient Ambrosian hymns end with a trinitarian doxology followed by 'Amen.' It is believed that Ambrose himself composed songs for orthodox Christians to sing in reply to certain songs invented and sung in a belligerent spirit by the unorthodox Arians, who at this time (the later fourth century) were in open conflict with the orthodox. It may therefore have been the custom for some to sing the hymn, and all within earshot to sing a responsive 'Amen'—'That's what we all believe about the Trinity' (the point largely in dispute).

"Ambrosian hymnody, however, very soon developed in monastic settings rather than controversial ones, and here we are on firm ground—their plainsong tunes always included an amen after the doxology, which still always stood at the end. It is reasonably certain that liturgically these office hymns (as they came to be called—hymns of the 'office' or routine daily worship) were sung antiphonally. We should not by any means assume that the doxology was sung by all present, but we can more safely assume that the amen was.

"However, the whole nature of hymnody changed at the Reformation. There was no question of singing amen at the end of hymns in Luther's time (nor has there ever been such a tradition in the German-speaking churches). The *Gloria* did not appear in the Genevan Psalter, though it was included in the English and Scottish psalters presumably for optional use; but no amen is appended to that in the early editions.

"In fact, in the English and early American system of hymnody, amen is never sung after hymns until the mid-nineteenth century. Isaac Watts and Charles and John Wesley knew nothing of it. What brought it back was the revived interest in medieval hymnody aroused in England by the Oxford Movement from 1833 onward, generating a wave of translation from the Latin which eventually made the whole Sarum system of Latin hymnody available in English. The doxologies, with their amens, were included in the translations.

"So eager were the Tractarians to make it clear that the medieval culture alone was the pure religious culture, and medieval hymnody the proper norm for all other hymnody, that at a number of points in their hymnals they appended doxologies with amens to existing hymns. The most notorious instance was the adding of a spurious doxology to "When I survey the wondrous cross," but there were many others. Doxology or no, amen was added to every hymn, and since virtually every non-plainsong tune in that book ended with a perfect cadence the amens were set uniformly to a plagal cadence. This hymnal was the most famous of all hymnals, the 1861 edition of *Hymns Ancient and Modern*.

"The custom spread through Anglican hymnals and was imitated by the Congregationalists and Presbyterians, and to a limited extent by the Methodists and Baptists, for no reason but the obscure and irrational notion that the Church of England knew its work in matters of liturgy. Around 1920 the Anglicans recognized that adding amens had been an anachronism and an error, and began to abandon them. Obediently the

270

nonconformists followed them at about a twenty-year interval, and by about 1950 the amen on hymns had virtually disappeared in England, although it was retained for some time in Scotland.

"Now consider what a patchwork of misunderstanding and anachronism all this is. Singing amen after post-Reformation hymns was unknown before about 1850. There is no older precedent for it, it was in any case an error, and those who initiated it have long since repented of it. It is an excellent example of a custom which people still jealously guard in America, any criticism of which arouses great indignation, and any argument against which is disregarded. When by a series of accidents the minister and organist of one Presbyterian Church heard the arguments against it and expressed themselves in favor of acting on them, the church solemnly decreed by congregational meeting, in the year 1976, that it must be retained."

Musically, there is little reason for the use of "amens" after most hymns and often they detract from the melodic completion of a hymn. It is important, however, to consider the wishes of a particular congregation in any decision regarding the use of "amens." One possibility is to retain the "amen" after the closing hymn, giving a sense of finality to the singing for the day, and closing the worship service in the familiar pattern. Another possibility is to encourage the responsive use of "amen" at several points in the service, to reinforce its most important usage in the liturgical setting. The omission of "amens" from the end of most hymns can be an opportunity for teaching the congregation about the traditional uses of "amens" and how they might be used to enhance the entire experience of worship.

EXPANDED INDEX OF SCRIPTURE AND ALLUSIONS TO SCRIPTURE

Entries in boldface italics indicate allusions to Scripture; entries in roman type indicate direct scriptural references.

273

277

278

INDEX OF FIRST LINES AND COMMON TITLES OF HYMNS, CANTICLES AND ACTS OF WORSHIP